Incarcerated Mothers
Oppression and Resistance

Incarcerated Mothers
Oppression and Resistance

edited by

Gordana Eljdupovic
and
Rebecca Jaremko Bromwich

DEMETER PRESS, BRADFORD, ONTARIO

Published by:
Demeter Press
140 Holland Street West
P. O. Box 13022
Bradford, ON L3Z 2Y5
Tel: (905) 775-9089
Email: info@demeterpress.org
Website: www.demeterpress.org

Demeter Press logo based on Skulptur "Demeter" by Maria-Luise Bodirsky <www.keramik-atelier.bodirsky.edu>

Cover Artwork: Rebecca Jaremko Bromwich, "Incarcerated Mother," 2012, acrylic on canvas.

Printed and Bound in Canada

Library and Archives Canada Cataloguing in Publication

      Incarcerated mothers : oppression and resistance / Gordana Eljdupovic and Rebecca Jaremko Bromwich, editors.

Includes bibliographical references.
ISBN 978-1-927335-03-1

    1. Mothers—Canada. 2. Women prisoners—Canada.
3. Women prisoners—Family relationships—Canada.
4. Motherhood—Social aspects—Canada. 5. Mothers.
6. Women prisoners. 7. Women prisoners—Family relationships.
I. Eljdupovic, Gordana, 1960– II. Bromwich, Rebecca

HQ759.I54 2013   306.874'3086927   C2013-900727-X

To my mother Ljubinka, with love and gratitude.
—Gordana

With love to my mother, Beverley, for many reasons,
and most of all because you taught me that mothering is a political act.
—Rebecca

Unless otherwise indicated, all authors' views are theirs alone and do not reflect official statements of any, body, agency or group of any kind.

Table of Contents

CONTENTS

Photo: Patricia Block

I was 30 years old and three months pregnant when I received a sentence of two years. The program to keep incarcerated mothers and babies together had been suspended. My daughter's name is Amber Joy and she is almost three years old now. The day at the hospital when I had to kiss my baby goodbye was the most hopeless, miserable, and empty experience of my life. I often asked why was she being punished for something that I did?

—Patricia Block

Introduction

GORDANA ELJDUPOVIC AND REBECCA JAREMKO BROMWICH

IN THE WINTER OF 2012, headlines broke across the United States with stories of incarcerated women who had successfully sued U.S. prisons after having been forced to give birth alone, with no assistance. These situations gave rise to public shock.[1] It is surprising and uncomfortable for the general public to think about incarcerated people being women. It is even more discomfiting to consider that a large proportion of incarcerated women are mothers.

This book is about the lives, needs and rights of mothers who are, or have been, incarcerated. Mothering and incarceration are generally perceived as being contradictory. Mothering is distinctly or primarily a female phenomenon, while incarceration is primarily, statistically and stereotypically, male. Although there are men who engage in "mother-work," such work is often—if not invariably and cross-culturally—understood to fall within the women's domain. Similarly, it is consistent across countries that the number of incarcerated males, by far exceeds the number of women. As a result, incarcerated mothers are "doubly stigmatized" or "double odd." They are where most of the women are not or should not be. They are in jail, like men. At the same time, incarcerated mothers are *not* doing what social expectations dictate that "good" mothers should do; they are not providing daily care to their children. Rather, they are separated from their children, leaving them in the care of someone else, often a stranger.

In this introduction, we review considerations feminist scholars have raised about motherhood that particularly pertain to issues addressed in this collection of essays. We then discuss and review perspectives on female crime and incarceration with a specific focus on incarcerated mothers.

Finally, we present the essays in this collection and identify what this book does and does not address, in so doing we provide suggestions for future inquiries.

MOTHERHOOD AND MOTHERING

Motherhood has been a central and inseparable area of scholarly feminist inquiry over a number of decades. It would be difficult to find feminist analysis that does not in some way examine this domain of women's lives. Furthermore, some feminist scholars have developed and significantly advanced this particular area of inquiry providing specific theories of motherhood. The theoretical underpinnings for this book are primarily drawn from the work of motherhood theorists Sara Ruddick and Andrea O'Reilly. Ruddick, who died in March of 2011, was a leader in advancing the notion that motherhood carries with it a set of thought practices that can be of tremendous benefit in social activism and towards global peace making. O'Reilly, a Canadian academic, developed a mother's movement of scholarship and action that further expanded and brought into being Ruddick's vision.

Feminist scholars and activists have critiqued the traditional characterization of motherhood as a natural and ideal role for women. As is the case with feminist scholarship in general, initial and dominant discussions of issues pertaining to this area were based on patriarchal families in the western world. Feminists showed that the cluster of activities and biological functions that presumably define mothering is not inevitably female, although it is understood as a "natural" outcome of what until recently has represented the only legitimate family structure: the patriarchal nuclear family. This family structure is characterized by biological parents being married, with the mother assuming the role of a nurturer, and the father, the role of the provider.

By ascribing the public sphere to men and the private one to women, a power imbalance between genders has been created and legitimized, placing women in a disadvantaged position. As Ruddick reminds us, "the hand that rocks the cradle has certainly not ruled the world" (36). An extremely powerful mechanism of maintaining these social arrangements involves socializing women and men into gender specific roles. This mechanism leads women to want to mother, to want to have a family and nurture, and to strive for the roles as assigned to them (Polatnick). In other words, women "choose" to do the unpaid labour and take care of others. They remain disengaged from political and social domains, which renders them with minimal decision making power and economically dependent. Moreover and equally important is the fact that the role of a nurturer is characterized by significant emotional demands. As Adrienne Rich and many other scholars have shown based on explorations of their own mothering, demands for unconditional, on-going, selfless and endless love, care and affection for children are unattainable and exhausting for the mother. Further, it is socially unacceptable for the mother to acknowledge that she may feel tired, frustrated or yearn for something else. For those reasons, a mother may feel isolated, ashamed, incompetent and incapable of responding to her "calling."

Given the deeply ingrained social ascription of the mother role and women's relegation to the private sphere, it is not surprising that most single parent families are mother-headed. In these family structures, it is predominantly the mother who has custody of children and is responsible for providing care, food and shelter. However, by being assigned the "private" sphere, women have had fewer opportunities to develop their "public" competencies, gain knowledge and education. Thus, a considerably lower educational level, fewer employable skills and diminished access to resources compared to men tend to character-ize women who are sole care-providers for their children. This constellation of factors tends to "drag" women even further down the poverty lane and disadvantaged path. High rates of single parenthood among women and lone mother households are universally associated with the concept of "feminization of poverty," recognized by the United Nations, scholars, researchers and other agencies. This notion highlights the fact that lone mother households are at the highest risk of poverty for women due to lack of income and resources (Chant; Moghadam; Weitzman).

Thus, women's "choice" to remain primary care providers for their children considerably affects their socioeconomic position. Consequently it may nega-tively affect their own, as well as their children's well-being. Day to day living under economically challenging circumstances represents a source of tremendous psychological stress for mothers (Atwood and Genovese; Brown and Moran; Williams; Koch, Lewis and Quinones; Millar and Glendinning). They face everyday struggles to make ends meet, as well as demands and social expec-tations to be emotionally and physically available for their children 24-hours a day, all the while being selfless and loving. Moreover, they also have to deal with society's negative perceptions of poor and single mothers.

Often women perceive their poverty, distress, lack of education, and other difficulties, as their own fault rather than as a result of their social situatedness. Due to the process of socialization, they perceive and judge themselves through the eyes of the dominant discourse and its values. Feminists have challenged the notion of a "good" mother in patriarchal western ideology showing that "goodness" in this particular discourse carries the attributes of a white, middle class, married, and stay at home mother. As Cynthia Garcia Coll, Janet L. Surrey and Kathy Weingarten indicate, the notion of a "good" mother is closely tied to particular childcare arrangements that are associated with standards of the white middle-class.

Unable to attain these goals, many single mothers tend to develop low self-esteem and a sense of inadequacy (Ali and Avison; Brody and Flor; Brown and Moran; Kazdin Schnitzer; Ruddick). A woman may experience feelings of not being a good enough mother because she cannot provide for her children as much as she would like to and as much as she is expected to by society, both materially and/or emotionally (Atwood and Genovese; Kazdin Schnitzer; Parnel and Vanderkloot; Ruddick). As Lucia Valeska points out, "how well we do anything directly depends on the economic and social environment in which we do it" (71). Thus, those mothers who do not have access to the economic, social and community resources that are available to the dominant class are positioned on the margins. Un-captured or distorted by the lens of the dominant discourse, they often remain either invisible or marginalized.

The foregoing points about female-led, lone parent households reflect statistical generalities. As with any pattern, exceptions to the general trends exist and those exceptions are important. It is vital that mother-heading families not be pathologized and it must be recognized that such families are not necessarily always associated with poverty or with a mother's negative self-perception. Over time, generations of highly educated women with well-paying and prestigious jobs have emerged. Some of them are single mothers but they do not necessarily experience hardship and marginalization as described here. Furthermore, as the essays in this collection will show, being resource poor does not necessarily mean that the mother will develop a low self-esteem and a belief that she is mothering her children inappropriately.

Thus, feminist scholars have shown that motherhood, for centuries considered simple, idyllic, natural and normal for women, is in fact multilayered, complex and socially constructed, embedded in existing socio-economic and historical contexts, and a source of oppression for women. However, we would not do justice to feminist scholarship and the manifold realities of mothering, if we did not address equally important perspectives on motherhood which highlight its unique and enriching elements, and which have specific values in women's lives and society as a whole.

Enriching experiences intrinsic to motherhood in spite of the burdens related to it, have also become a focus of feminist thought (Rich; Ruddick; O'Reilly 2004; Young). For instance, specific situations, such as pregnancy, labour and breast-feeding, allow women to identify with a child and form a unity with him/her that is unique. These situations create specific bodily experiences associated with women's biological characteristics that are generally inaccessible to men. Further, regardless of motherhood's biological underpinnings, unique experiences and expertise stemming from nurturing and caring have been highlighted and discussed as a specific and distinct set of values in and of themselves. As Iris Marion Young points out, "as feminists we should affirm the value of nurturing; an ethic of caring does indeed hold promise for a more human justice..." (91). Thus, although questioning and criticizing family structures and the institution of mothering that are oppressive for women, feminist

4

thought also allowed and fostered alternative and empowering representations and practices of mothering, in which caring and nurturing are of high value and sources of mothers' resistance.

In *Maternal Thinking: Toward a Politics of Peace*, Sara Ruddick argued that, "*preservation, growth*, and *social acceptance*—are fundamental elements in maternal work; to be a mother is to be committed to meeting these demands by works of preservative love, nurturance, and training" (17).

At times, Ruddick has been misunderstood as an essentialist. However, at the heart of her argument is a notion that gender is performed and that mothering is a particular kind of caring labour. While women disproportionately perform this work and engage more often than men in "maternal" thinking, these are learned behaviours not innate to women biologically. Ruddick discusses mothering and birth-giving as two distinct activities. Mothering is, for Ruddick, "work, not an identity" (xi).

"A mother is a person who takes on responsibility for children's lives and for whom providing child care is a significant part of her or his working life. ... There is no reason to believe that one sex rather than the other is more capable of doing the maternal work." (40) The reason why Ruddick and other scholars refer to the mother as "she" and "her" is that for the most part, childcare has been historically associated with women's work and as such, considerably more women than men perform this task. It is not because they believe that mother-work is intrinsically a domain and duty of the female sex.

It is beyond the scope of this collection to determine whether women nurture and care because they were socialized to value it, or because they derive specific values from it "independently" of their gender socialization. It is also not the ambit of this collection to make blanket pronouncements about whether or not mothers should ever be incarcerated and whether some mothers and children are better off, for a myriad of mental health, social and other circumstances, apart. Rather, the present collection of essays explores the circumstances of incarcerated mothers based on the assumption that mothering is not just a source of oppression and imposed identity, but it is also a political identity whereby mothers hold certain values and develop resistance in actualizing them.

This collection of essays problematizes the reductive understanding of the mother role as produced entirely by oppressive forces. Even if a woman experiences hardship and difficulties related to taking care of children and develops apparently inadequate parenting practices, it does not mean that she does not want to mother, does not make significant social contributions through her mother work, and does not derive certain satisfaction, self-esteem and intellectual or spiritual sense of value from the fact that she is a mother. Indeed, when women from the margins do mother, they place value on themselves and on children that the society in which they live has deemed unworthy of investment. Mothers from the margins may "resist" imposed perceptions and negative stereotypical or ideological assessments of their mothering, and yet, maintain values stemming from mothering in high regard and of utmost importance. They may find ways to distinguish the experience of mothering from the oppressive, confining and isolating institutions of motherhood that negatively affect that experience (Garcia Coll, Surrey and Weingarten; Ruddick). They may develop resistance, resiliency and strategies to maintain their views of themselves as good mothers. "Welfare moms equate managing to put food on the table and a roof over their children's head with being a good mother" (Garcia Coll, Surrey and Weingarten 276). Essentially, while women from the margins may perceive themselves through the eyes of dominant discourse, and so perceive themselves as not measuring up to standards of good mothering, "*preservation, growth,* and *social acceptance*" the fundamental elements in maternal work according to Ruddick, may be values of utmost importance in and of themselves.

We will now turn to some general considerations regarding female criminalization and incarceration, prior to examining specific ways in which feminist approaches to mothering are reflected in the lives of incarcerated mothers and their children, as discussed in the present collection of essays.

CRIMINALIZATION AND INCARCERATION OF WOMEN

The proportion of incarcerated women in Canada's federal and provincial custody systems is quite small relative to that of men. As is discussed in several of the articles in this volume, other countries also consistently report significantly smaller proportions of incarcerated women, compared to men. Reports about the number of incarcerated women in Canada show that in 2005-2006, six percent of individuals in provincial/territorial custody and four percent of those in federal custody were women (CSC). Currently, it is estimated that there are about 500 incarcerated federally sentenced women, representing six percent of the entire Canadian federal offender population (CSC), and approximately the same percentage of women (six percent) are in the provincial systems (CAEFS of Ontario).

In Canada, there are different venues for incarceration depending upon the crime for which one is sentenced. Types of crimes that would result in federal sentencing are Schedule I offences such as violent crimes including first or second degree murder, and Schedule II offences, including serious drug offences or conspiracy to commit serious drug offences. Federally sentenced offenders are those who have been sentenced in relation to an indictable (or more serious) criminal offence for a period of over two years in custody. Provincial or territorial sentences generally result from summary conviction, or less serious, offences, that can extend up to two years in duration. Common summary conviction offences include thefts, fraud charges and other property crimes such as vandalism and mischief. Less serious offences to the person, such as minor assaults, can also be dealt with by means of summary conviction.

However, in recent years, across many countries including Canada, there has been a staggering increase in the numbers of incarcerated women. As many reports indicate, including the essays in this collection, recently the number of incarcerated women has doubled or tripled. The increase in the incarceration of women internationally has exceeded the pace of increase of male incarceration. For instance, in the last ten years, the number of women admitted to Canadian federal jurisdiction increased 35.5 percent, whereas during the same time period, there was an increase of 21.9 percent in the number of men (CSC).

It has been only fairly recently that woman "offenders" have come to be studied as a separate population with unique characteristics. Until the middle of the twentieth century, women were the subjects of little study. In the rare cases where women offenders were studied, it was assumed that what applied to men, also applied to women. This "logic" in itself is not unique to the study and understanding of women's criminalization. Until feminist scholarship began to be undertaken, researchers in practically all disciplines took a gender "neutral" approach. Feminist scholarship has demonstrated that this purported neutrality was an illusion: what was presented as the general norm was in fact a presentation of the male *as* the norm. Thus, the lens that was used precluded observers and researchers from seeing the gendered quality of the landscape as well as unique texture of female criminality and society's response to it. The fact that historically there has always been, and continues to be, a considerably greater proportion of men, rather than women who are involved in crime, likely contributed to this tendency. It represented a "justification" that it is indeed the men that are the norm when studying these issues, making "criminology, among the disciplines, almost quintessentially male," as Meda Chesney-Lind and Lisa Pasko pointed out (2).

Over a number of decades, feminist scholarship has guided social theorists, policy makers and researchers away from essentializing individuals and groups of people. It has been increasingly acknowledged that people should not and cannot be defined simply by their genitals, socio-economic status, race, ethnicity or other characteristics individuals obtained "by birth" or by their "throwness into this world" (*geworfenheit*) and which they neither choose nor to which they necessarily ascribe. Initially, feminist scholarship introduced to criminology and social science primarily the gender lens. As presented earlier, it highlighted the oppression of women and the male dominance. It showed how these historically ingrained processes created and maintained a power imbalance, rendering one gender—women—subjugated, weak, disempowered and voiceless, as a group and as reflected in a woman's personal experience of herself, her roles in life and position in society. As feminist scholarship evolved, a plethora of lenses were added, which allowed researchers to see and focus on many interlocking and interwoven imbalances and power issues, such as, those pertaining to class, race, ethnicity and sexual orientation, to name just a few.

There is no single, unified feminist perspective on female criminality (Boritch). What feminist perspectives do have in common is that they problematize and question traditionally accepted individualistic and gender "neutral" approaches to studying criminal behaviour that decontextualize phenomena and individuals' actions. As Chesney-Lind and Pasko argue, historical theorizing paid little attention to gender—the network of behaviours and identities associated with the terms masculinity and femininity—that is socially constructed from relations of dominance, power and inequality between men and women (2).

Once these domains were considered, many studies about women offenders revealed that these women occupied multiple disadvantaged social positions prior to getting into conflict with the law. Studies of incarcerated women have also shown that they hail overwhelmingly from marginal social positions. Most incarcerated women come from low socio-economic levels of society and are poorly educated (Chesney-Lind and Pasko; Comak; Maidment). Often, they are further marginalized within the crimes for which they are sentenced; typically they are accessories to crime or minor players in more serious crimes involving male leadership, influence or abuse. This reflects findings of feminist criminologists' analyses that there are "...strong links between the subordinate social and economic status of women and their involvement with the criminal justice system" (Boritch). For that reason, feminists' studies approach women's experiences and actions as embedded in their economic, social and cultural situations, and they point out the extent to which this milieu shapes individuals' characteristics, actions and/or private life.

There is considerable evidence that the prevalence of mental disorders is higher among women compared to men in general and across countries. Furthermore, there is an extremely high prevalence rate of mental disorders, and reported histories of sexual, physical and verbal abuse particularly among incarcerated women (Leschied), which considerably exceeds the one found among incarcerated men and non-incarcerated (community) population in general. Leschied points out that, "In 2006, 12 percent of men offenders were identified at admission as having diagnosed mental health problems, an increase of 71 percent since 1997. For women, the 2006 rate was 21 percent, an increase of 61 percent since 1997" (CSC Review Panel 1 cited in Leschied).

It has been noted trans-nationally that certain ethnic or racial groups are over-represented in prison. Much has been written, for example, about the over-representation of African American and Latino(a) offenders in prisons in the United States. Demographic distortions of this nature are particularly extreme in the case of women offenders. Moreover, differences in the sentencing and treatment of incarcerated women in custody based on race even when they committed a same type of crime have been also noted. In the American context, Jenni Vainik has recently explored the historical treatment of female prisoners, differentiating the rehabilitative sentences given to white women and the starkly punitive sentences received by racialized women.

Corrections policies are not generally crafted to respond to gender, let alone racial and economic inequalities. Vainik argues that while women are the fastest growing sector of the U.S. prison population, little has been done to change policies or services to accommodate them. Amnesty International published a report in 1998 about human rights abuses in American prisons as they pertain to incarcerated women, much of which reports on mothers and mothering. This report indicated that the United States has failed to ratify or fully implement various international human rights standards. Concerns were raised about the prevalence of sexual abuse in custody, the use of shackles on women during childbirth and the quality and availability of health care, especially pre-and post-natal care. It remains the case in several U.S. states that incarcerated women are routinely—and legally—shackled during labour.

Clearly, the proportion of racialized or visible minority individuals in the prison system versus in the non-criminal and general community is skewed. In Canada, the particular situation of Aboriginal people relative to the criminal law and custodial system is alarming. While Aboriginal adults represent only 4.0 percent of the total Canadian adult population, 21 percent of the total federal offender population are Aboriginal (Office of the Correctional Investigator). In the case of women, the demographic distortion whereby Aboriginal people are over-represented in the prison system is even higher. Aboriginal women represent 33 percent of all federally incarcerated women in Canada (CSC).

In summary, compared to earlier decades of criminology, nowadays we are certainly more aware, or at least more data are reported that pertain to gender, racial and other issues associated with criminality. However, in spite of that, there is also a growing number of prisons and women locked behind bars! In other words, we still have a long way to go. The schism between raised awareness, accumulated knowledge on one hand, and day to day practice of hindering growth and development on the other, continue to occur at every level; policy making, gender and racially laden advertisements, children's stories, criminalization of certain groups, unproductive, compartmentalized and individualistic approaches to "resolving" social and individual issues.

We would like to draw special attention to paradoxes and mechanisms associated with the discourse on "assisting" incarcerated individuals to re-integrate with, or re-enter the society. For the most part, those who are to be assisted with "re-entry" into the society upon their release from prison have never been part of mainstream society. Their membership and participation in society, if measured by having equal opportunities, stable housing and income, access to the educational system, and other social resources that are easily available to those who constitute the mainstream society, in fact, have never existed. Prior to incarceration, they were outsiders, residing on the margins and on the "borders" of society. As such, they assisted the "society" to identify and delineate itself. As is the case with any phenomenon, identifying the margins is necessary in order to delineate the "main" or the "central" space. Therefore, it is important to ask ourselves, where exactly are they being "assisted" to return?

ON INCARCERATED MOTHERS: THIS COLLECTION

While, as noted, it is "odd" for the popular imagination to conceive of incarcerated women as mothers, studies consistently show that *most* incarcerated women are mothers. Further, a majority of incarcerated women were living with their children as single parents prior to incarceration. As will be discussed below and further explored in the essays in this collection, issues relating to motherhood certainly add complexity to incarcerated women's circumstances. While they create challenges and adversity, in many instances, being a mother and having dependents, also represents a main reason for women to keep going (Chesney-Lind and Pasko; Comack; Elizabeth Fry Society; Sommers; Wine). However, it is important to keep in mind that not all incarcerated mothers had custody and mothered their children prior to incarceration. Moreover, not all incarcerated mothers want to maintain, establish or re-establish contact with their children during and after incarceration.

Some writing exists that provides insights about the experiences of children of incarcerated mothers. There is a growing body of literature about the best interests of the children of incarcerated parents and the rights of the child. What writing there is about incarcerated mothers has only very rarely been undertaken from a Canadian perspective. Based on our extensive research, the present collection seems to the first in the past number of decades that focuses particularly on Canadian laws, institutions, circumstances and incarcerated mothers in Canada. However, the content of the book is not limited only to the Canadian context; it also includes contributions from the international perspective and other continents.

This book seeks to contextualize the experiences of incarcerated mothers in political and social systems where the oppression of women, and in particular, of mothers, continues to significantly shape their lives. An intersectional approach is taken; mothers are discussed with reference not just to their gender or mother work but also in reference to how they are being marginalized in other ways—for example on the basis of race or socioeconomic status.

Each article presents not only what is done to mothers in and by these systems but they also examine the agency of the mothers themselves, their resistance and values that are of high importance to them. Mothers end up being incarcerated for many reasons. In this collection, incarcerated mothers are considered in many contexts: child protection/ child welfare reasons used to detain adolescent mothers, mothers incarcerated for acts of civil disobedience, mothers incarcerated for acts committed against their abusers where the defence of self-defence was not adequately raised or considered, incarcerated for thefts of food in times of hunger, incarcerated for drug crimes, for prostitution-related offences, and for the commission of crimes.

Although overlapping in many ways, depending on the main lens through which issues of incarceration and mothering are discussed, these essays could be broadly grouped in two sections. Essays in the first section situate incarceration of mothers in broader systems of social inequality and oppression, whereas essays in the second section depict lived experiences of incarcerated mothers demonstrating how these social policies and legal practices shape individuals' lives. Processes of oppression and resistance, albeit from different lenses and perspectives, are discussed and highlighted in all essays.

Incarcerated Mothers in Context: Social Systems and Inequality

Dena Derkzen and Kelly Taylor's essay depicts the Canadian context as it pertains to federally sentenced women, showing that recent survey results support findings from previous studies that the majority of incarcerated mothers were single parents prior to incarceration. They further provide an overview of the existing studies regarding mother-child contacts during mothers' incarceration. While studies in this area are regrettably sporadic, results nevertheless consistently indicate that maintaining these contacts during incarceration is highly beneficial for both the children and mothers. To that effect, Derkzen and Taylor provide a detailed description of the Correctional Service of Canada (CSC) policies that are established to ensure mothers' rights to have contact with their children, and in some cases, to have their children reside with them in the institution. However, the authors' present survey results show that, in spite of these policies, only one in five women had a weekly visit with her children. Clearly, there is a significant gap between the policy (which was reportedly established to foster mother-child contact), and the everyday practice in prisons, which render most mothers with meagre opportunity to have contact with their children.

Gordana Eljdupovic, Terry Mitchell, Lori Curtis, Rebecca Jaremko Bromwich, Alison Granger-Brown, Courtney Arseneau and Brooke Fry examine the social and financial costs of the over-representation of Aboriginal women among Canada's incarcerated population, particularly in view of the fact that the majority of these women are of child bearing and child rearing age. The authors inquire why, in spite of significant "efforts" to lower the rates of over-representation of Aboriginal peoples in prison, there is in fact an exponential increase. They identify significant gaps in the levels of intervention, funding allocation, and ultimately, in the conceptualization of the notion of justice. They discuss how current approaches have led to repeated failures to decrease the exponential growth of incarceration rates of Aboriginal people in Canada, particularly Aboriginal women. Finally, the authors provide recommendations on how to "do more with less" by situating restorative justice practices within the broader context of transitional justice. They recommend addressing both rehabilitation and prevention through greater investments in the re-development of strong Aboriginal communities rather than increasingly providing costly essential services, education, and cultural programs for Aboriginal women within prison walls.

Rebecca Jaremko Bromwich explores historical connections between the criminal and child welfare systems with respect to incarceration of adolescent mothers in Canada. Specifically, the paper problematizes the use of incarceration as a deterrent to ensure conformity and female gender role performance differentially for diversely situated women. Historically, social expectations for white adolescent young women were different than those for Aboriginal young women; working-class young women were held to different standards of behaviour than the rich. Bromwich shows how incarceration was used as a sanction to prevent and punish adolescent young women from lower social strata and racialized backgrounds from engaging in socially "unfeminine" conduct as well as work, including mother work and procreative labour. The racist and colonial historical Canadian state saw these activities to be politically and socially undesirable activities. Bromwich proceeds to examine current and proposed child protection regimes that allow for the forced detention of adolescent young women suspected of involvement in the sex trade. She problematizes the extent to which these regimes already do in some jurisdictions and would, if fully implemented in others, continue to perform under a different guise the same type of oppressive criminalization of motherhood and incarceration of adolescent mothers, which historical juvenile criminal regimes did.

Martine Herzog-Evans provides a discussion of the current situation regarding incarcerated mothers in France, situating it within an international, and more specifically, European context of child-rearing practices, values systems and human rights. Significantly, France presents a counter-example to many jurisdictions and as Herzog-Evans presents, it managed to resist the Western world increase in female imprisonment. The explosion of female incarceration that has characterised other countries has not been detected in France. While from that perspective, France seems to differ from many countries, its prison population nevertheless shares common characteristics with those from other countries, including Canada; women who are incarcerated in the French prisons are often mothers, or expectant mothers. Herzog-Evans explores how France deals with mother and baby pairs in prisons, relative to other countries, pointing out indisputable presence of Latin/Nordic and Anglo-Saxon divide in perception and interpretation of mother-child bonding and resulting practices in women's prison. Her analysis draws upon field research conducted by a team of law students researching in five prisons in several regions of France and it presents experiences of women in prison as well as the legal framework governing French prisons.

Her analysis highlights traces of colonialism reflected in the expectations regarding mothering that are imposed on women who are incarcerated in French prison system but who are of non-French origin or culture. Herzog-Evans provides thorough analysis and contrasts competing demands and issues associated with multicultural countries, as France has become, in regards to human rights and the best interest of the child.

Deseriee Kennedy provides an analysis of the current legal system in the United States, and brings to the forefront inconsistencies between the criminal justice and child welfare laws and policies. These policies punish incarcerated mothers not only for their criminal activities but also for not being available to their children due to circumstances that this very system imposed on them. She reminds us that addressing a woman's criminal activity does not and should not translate into punishing her as a mother and punishing her children. Kennedy's analysis shows how the process of sentencing does not take into account gender and family circumstances. When a single mother with young children is sentenced to prison, alternatives to incarceration are not considered in order to prevent children's trauma caused from being taken away from their homes and being separated from their mother. However, when assessing a woman's fitness to mother, being away from children due to incarceration is considered a reason to deem her unfit and for her children to become state wards. Personal stories, helplessness, pain and anguish voiced by incarcerated mothers in relation to this issue are well documented in other papers in this collection and represent testaments that these circumstances are found throughout various criminal and child welfare systems. For instance, one of the participants in Olivia Scobie's research project described how, shortly after she gave birth to her daughter, her mother and sister raced to the hospital to take the baby with them. They did so in order to "beat" the authorities and to claim custody of the baby. Had they not arrived in time, the child would have been deemed a ward of the state.

In her description of the Indian landscape, Upneet Lalli shows that being married and becoming a mother are the main sources of pride for women in India. Religious scriptures, folklore and popular culture glorify the mother image, at times comparing her to God itself and giving her ultimate respect. At the same time, this also paves the way and legitimizes women's subjugation. Although the practice of dowry in India is by legislation officially deemed unlawful, this practice still exists, often leading to violence and torture of women, suicide, crime and incarceration. Due to dowry offences it is not uncommon for a few family generations, mothers, daughters and sisters-in-law, to be simultaneously incarcerated.

Precisely because of the ingrained traditional practices that lead to committing dowry crimes, saving face and mothers' attempts to maintain contact with their children during incarceration are difficult and often insurmountable. Incarcerated women bestow shame on their family; they are highly stigmatized to the extent that they may not be allowed to contact their children or request information about their well-being. Moreover, they face multiple barriers to successful reintegration upon release and carry a burden and guilt that due to their incarceration, their daughters' prospects to get married are damaged. Consistent with practices across other countries and continents, women who are the most marginalized, poor and the least educated are overrepresented in the Indian prison system. Lalli shows that they also carry the greatest burden of traditional gender norms and have next to no prospects of being sufficiently empowered to file complaints and grievances even when this is offered to them. Lalli proceeds to demonstrate the need for current Indian legislation to be aligned with the United Nations Rules, respect human rights, become more flexible and focus on alternatives to imprisonment.

Manuela da Cunha and Rafaela Granja provide an overview of two Portuguese prison settings over the span of several decades. They remind readers that ideologies reflecting gender asymmetry inform a less frequently discussed issue, that if any efforts are directed toward salvaging parent-child bond during parental incarceration, it is referring to incarcerated mothers, not fathers. Allowing children to stay in prison with their incarcerated mothers and not their fathers is informed by stereotypical gender ideology, perpetuating the patriarchal division of labour and justifying further control of women. Historically, this is related to the tendency to reform, train and domesticate "fallen women" by forcing them to engage in their "natural" duties—childcare. Furthermore, by facilitating that children reside with their mothers in prison, a greater area for controlling and criticizing of women is created. Incarcerated mothers' accounts show the extent to which prison guards are intervening and "correcting" their interactions with children, invading the most private and sacred area of their lives. Women are being scolded in front of their own children, rendering them disempowered and hopeless, and at times, resentful of their mother role as another site of disempowerment. This chapter also shows that middle class incarcerated mothers choose to leave their children in the care of relatives, as they do not want them to grow up in prison. However, those mothers who come from poverty stricken environments do not have a choice but to keep their children imprisoned. Otherwise, they would be a burden for the family members on the outside who would have one more mouth to feed, or if living outside of prison, these children would have even less than what they get in prison. Not only does this speak of women's circumstances on the outside, but it also shows the extent to which one's oppression and lack of control is shaped by their socio-economic status and social hierarchy. Finally, da Cunha and Granja bring to our attention the emerging changes in the mother-child relationships, associated with recent mass imprisonments, due to which multiple family generations reside in prison, which often results in co-imprisonment of mothers, daughters and grand-daughters. Under these circumstances, it is not the separation but togetherness of mothers and daughters that needs to be critically examined and addressed.

Ruth McCausland and Eileen Baldry take us through historical circumstances and current policies highlighting mechanisms of perpetual marginalization and discrimination of Indigenous people in Australia, particularly women. These mechanisms are not unlike those found in the Canadian context, both historic and current. For instance, forcible apprehension of Aboriginal children in Australia is a mirror image on the "Sixties Scoop" in Canada, both justified by the "best intentions" of the white, dominant non-Aboriginal governments. Another clear parallel is the un-coincidental and distressing statistics that Aboriginal people are over-represented in the penal system. While they make only two to five percent of the Australian or Canadian population, Aboriginal women in both countries represent at least 30 percent of incarcerated women.

The authors present difficulties Indigenous women encounter both upon incarceration and in their attempts to integrate into the society. Some of these difficulties are lack of supported long-term housing and financial means. Moreover, ingrained and systemic socio-economic structures of subjugation, racism and sexism are internalized as one's own shortcomings and faults resulting in mental health and other issues. A number of these mechanisms are clearly presented in other papers in this collection. Although from a different lens, they repeatedly show how marginalization keeps certain groups of people locked away, making prison their "home."

Lived Experiences of Incarcerated Mothers

Alison, Brenda, Sarah, Martina, Tanya, Devon, Jennifer, Betty, Renee, Patricia, Mo, Kelly and Linnea weave a story about emergence and closure of the mother-child program in a women's prison in British Columbia, Canada. Accounts clearly convey short- and long- term benefits of babies staying with their mothers in prison where mothers can receive much needed assistance. Almost all narratives in this essay reflect women's opinions that they would not have made it "out there, if it weren't for prison and the assistance they received while incarcerated." Sadly, for a number of women, "prison was the best thing that happened to them" as all of us who worked in women's institutions have heard many times.

The reader is left in dismay that such a program, which evidently result-ed in a number of positive outcomes, was needlessly shut down. Further, while there is no question that most incarcerated women need considerable assistance in many domains of their lives, one cannot help but wonder why it has to be in a prison where these needs are often met for the first time. Alison Granger-Brown et al. present a story that is woven with threads of different texture, strength and backgrounds. All contributors are women and mothers. While their roles in the correctional system varied greatly, they equally valued and acknowledged the importance of facilitating the mother-child bond. In this paper, as was the case with the mother-child program itself, "opposite" sides of the prison system united; voices of the former warden of the woman's institution, clinical manager, recreational therapists and correctional officers were intertwined with the voices of incarcerated women, of whom most gave birth and cared for their babies during incarceration. The very fact that they once again united to tell their story through co-authoring this paper and in spite of the closure of the mother-child program, gives us great hope.

Olivia Scobie and Amber Gazso show how neoliberal social policies and programs intertwine and negatively shape experiences of low-income moth-ers. Notably, low socioeconomic status characterizes most of those who are incarcerated. Interviews with mothers who were incarcerated show lived ex-periences of encountering numerous social and financial obstacles that render mothers feeling inadequate, ill-equipped and unable to conduct their mother work; they feel solely responsible for circumstances that were imposed on them. Comparison of some versus none social assistance that women received in two Canadian provinces showed their significance in shaping, fostering or hindering women's mothering endeavours, often making it impossible for lone mothers to regain full custody of their children upon release from prison. Pain and disempowerment caused from an absence of support and facilitation of maintaining contact with children during incarceration, led to a drastic shift in women's mother-identity. From being joyful mothers on the outside, some women entirely disconnected from their mother role during incarceration. As one mother said, "it was easier to say I didn't have kids," in spite of the fact that having children, was and remained to be, the only hope that kept her going during incarceration.

As part of their action research project on incarceration and reintegration into the community, Christine Walsh and Meredith Crough present qualitative analysis of interviews with women residing in the community who were previously incarcerated. Consistent with other studies, lives of the women who took part in this study were characterised by hardship, lack of social support, associated guilt feelings and sense of self-doubt. However, the authors' analysis of women's narratives detected parallel emergence of another theme; women voiced a sense of personal agency that stemmed from tapping into areas where they had some control over decisions regarding their mother-work. While struggling with guilt and self-doubt, and fully aware of and owning up to their choices that resulted in incarceration, women nevertheless strengthened their personal agency by redefining their experiences. Walsh and Crough demonstrated how women took pride that they were able to acquire wisdom regarding their life hardships, which gave them strength to move on and find hope in spite of their dire circumstances. Rather than to succumb to regrets, guilt and self-punishment, women tapped into their strength by embracing healing and restoration of their lives. The authors point out the role of hope, and how women redefined their mothering in a way that allowed them to fulfill its main tasks: to encourage growth, understanding of self and others. Their resistance and determination to fulfill the mother work was evident in their renegotiating the concept of motherhood giving prominent role to personal healing and restoration of contacts with their children.

Gordana Eljdupovic explores mothering before and during incarceration as experienced from "within" by incarcerated women themselves. This qualitative inquiry, based on interviews with incarcerated women, takes us through stages of mothering from pregnancy, separation due to incarceration, to incarcerated mothers' projections of the future. It shows how women's construals of their mother-role were linked to changes in their material conditions and how incarcerated women's self-evaluations of themselves as mothers map onto their socio-economic circumstances. In the case of most women, poverty and marginalization permeated every aspect of their daily lives prior to incarceration. Their strong determination, developed during pregnancy, to make their children's lives better than their own deprived childhoods, rapidly eroded as each day went by; stress and hardship gradually rendered mothers weak, disappointed and feeling less-worthy. Of particular significance is that Eljdupovic's analysis demonstrates a clear correspondence between desires and needs associated with mothering that women developed during pregnancy and incarceration. The similarity is such that in many cases, women's narratives on mothering during incarceration and pregnancy had identical wordings expressing the same dreams. What is common in these two circumstances is the absence of the day-to-day mother-work, which created space for women to romanticize mothering.

Eljdupovic draws attention to shifts in women's construals of their mother-role, as their circumstances change, expecting that upon release, switching to a "real-life" context may render the assumptions held during incarceration less relevant. Analysis of women's pre-incarceration living environment clearly indicates a significant gap between their desires regarding mothering their children and "affordances" of their circumstances to make these intentions a reality. This gap points out the absence of supportive environments and social structures that characterize women's lives. Therefore, upon release, and in spite of their dreams regarding mothering their children, women will once again encounter the same difficult and limited circumstances they left upon incarceration. These circumstances initially precluded them to turn their dreams into realities and mother their children how they hoped they would during pregnancy. Since they are re-entering these same circumstances upon release from prison, in order for their dreams developed during incarceration to become a reality, something has to change. Consistent, on-going adequate social support needs to be put in place. Expecting only the mother to change is unjustified.

Karen Shain, Lauren Liu and Sarah DeWath depict an important alliance that has been developed in California and provides a series of narrative vignettes derived from interviews with individual mothers incarcerated in the United States. These vignettes offer the voices of incarcerated mothers themselves accompanied by a series of photographs. The women interviewed, Shante, Barbara, Brenda and Maribel, are incarcerated mothers who met with interviewers several times to talk about their lives. These accounts are both personal and political; the women talk about their experiences while, at the same time, they explain how treatment they have received as incarcerated mothers has violated their human rights as well as the rights of their children.

Ruth Elwood Martin, Joshua Lau and Amy Salmon provide a thorough overview of the evidence that establishing and maintaining mother-baby bond has multiple benefits for both incarcerated mothers and their children. They remind us that breastfeeding does not only meet a child's nutritional needs but it also represents a crucial factor in a child's psychological and social development. Moreover, a number of benefits to the mother (and ultimately to the social system as well) have been also noted. For instance, maintaining contact with the child is a strong predictor of a mother's successful transition from prison into the community as it decreases the likelihood of re-offending. The authors provide a detailed review of results obtained through multi-method studies which involved mothers who participated in the Mother-Infant Health Initiative at the provincial correctional facility in British Columbia, Canada. This initiative emerged in 2005 as a result of the partnership between British Columbia Provincial Corrections and the Ministry of Children and Family Development. It encouraged and provided opportunities for incarcerated mothers to keep and take care of their babies and infants during incarceration.

Well grounded in theory and empirical evidence, the authors provide a number of specific recommendations regarding future directions for mother-infant units in Canadian prisons. These recommendations highlight the necessity to invest resources into facilitation of the mother-child bond, which in addition to improving their well-being, also contributes to a significant and long term decrease of social, correctional and medical interventions and costs.

Danielle Poe highlights links between politics and resistance in her discussion of the incarceration of mothers for nonviolent resistance in an American context. In her analysis of Diane Wilson, who is a mother and an activist, Poe shows an example of yet another mothering practice that does not follow the prescribed mainstream rules. Wilson often took all her five children to demonstrations, exposed them to seeing her engage in hunger strikes, chained to factory walls, and to ostracism from the community. Poe portrays Wilson as an example of "mothering at its best." She praises Wilson as an example of someone who willingly exposed her children to separation and fear, precisely because she cared deeply for them, for their children, other people's children and the community at large.

Themes, Gaps and Future Research

Voices of Aboriginal women, both within Canada and across the world, have been an integral part of narratives presented in all the essays in this collection, if nothing else, than by virtue of the sheer numbers of their representation in the incarcerated population. In any Canadian discussion of incarcerated mothers, a large number of the women studied or discussed are Aboriginal.

Sadly, in Canada, 33 percent of incarcerated women are Aboriginal, and as presented by McCausland and Baldry almost identical prevalence rate is found in the Australian context. Overall, racialization and disadvantaged circumstances among incarcerated individuals, between Indigenous and other groups, are inexcusably high and alarming, particularly in the case of women. If Canadian standards of living were assessed by the average income of its Aboriginal people, Canada would quickly drop from the top ten countries in the world, to a considerably lower place. If measured by standards of living of Aboriginal women, Canada's ranking, would drop even further (O'Donnell and Wallace).

Aboriginal women in Canada are more likely to be lone parents than non-Aboriginal women. Moreover, lone parent families headed by Aboriginal women tend to be larger than those headed by non-Aboriginal women (O'Donnell and Wallace). This most likely applies to a number of incarcerated Aboriginal women as well. This in and of itself represents an imperative that specific research, consultation processes and recommendations regarding incarcerated Aboriginal women need to be conducted in the future. Specific focus, attention, care and dedication need to be given to voices of incarcerated Aboriginal women, many of whom are mothers. Considerably more research needs to be done with a specific focus on colonialism, racialization and racism and their legacy in the legal culture pertaining to incarcerated women and mothers. We hope that it will not be long before we see books, volumes and other publications and communication media specifically dedicated to a long overdue presentation and analysis of historical, political and cultural issues that create and maintain the marginalized circumstances of Aboriginal people in Canada and result too often in tragic outcomes for entire groups of people, particularly women.

Research about incarcerated mothers is timely in Canada's current social and political context. The incarceration of people, and in particular of women, is a growth industry in Canada. The country's current governmental regime and legislative agendas are redirecting funds and focus from dismantling social programs to incarcerating "criminals," and therefore increasing overall incarceration rates and building "superjails." In their thorough analysis of the existing literature, Alana Cook and Ronald Roesch clearly show that these trends are a direct result of the current political climate and that "there is no empirical support for the rationale of this policy and the related assumption that this policy will reduce crime and better protect public" (217). Nevertheless, Bill C-10, now passed into law, has been projected to result in incarcerations of vastly more people for longer periods of time and has raised the ire of provincial officials who will have to pay for prison facilities as a result. Newly constructed and soon-to-be-built large prison complexes amplify challenges to incarcerated mothers. The chances of mothers being allowed to have their children with them either full time or for regular family visits are thinning as the prison population is growing. These trends were well depicted in some of the essays in this collection.

More specifically, while viewing the issue from different lenses Alison et al.'s work as well as Derkzen and Taylor's, nevertheless uniformly showed that grave consequences of such political climate are already evident. Rana Haq has argued that the closure of 14 of Ontario's provincial jails and the opening of five "superjails" removes women from their children and families and limits the ability of women to be in proximity and maintain relationships with their children. Incarcerated mothers are, as discussed, by stereotypical patriarchal definition doubly "bad" mothers because they are "double-odd." The essays in this volume share in common a call for readers to resist viewing stereotypes about mothers as "natural." It is important to situate mothering by women who end up incarcerated in the tremendously challenging context that shapes their everyday reality. It is equally important to appreciate the need of all mothers for support, respect, autonomy and empowerment when mothering and to reject totalizing, essentializing definitions of who is a "good" or "normal" mother.

Perhaps what all of the essays in this compilation together call for most clearly is an empathetic and inclusive redefinition of motherhood from a feminist-maternal perspective when actors in the justice and correctional systems as well as members of the general public consider incarcerated mothers. Andrea O'Reilly has characterized Sara Ruddick's perspective as one of maternal empowerment. Rather than relegating mother work to the private sphere, this perspective emphasizes the political and social aspects of mother work. It challenges traditional practices of gender socialization and defines the act of motherhood as political. Some authors have identified such a feminist understanding of mothering as "outlaw" (O'Reilly 2004). The naming of feminist mothering as "outlaw" is an attempt to generally accord to mothers the agency, authority, authenticity and autonomy denied to them in patriarchal motherhood (O'Reilly 2008).

While the idea of "outlaw" motherhood is generally applicable to mothers, the notion of outlaw motherhood has particular, specific salience where incarcerated mothers are considered. If empowered mothers are ideological outlaws, then incarcerated mothers—as legal outlaws—are not inherently "odd" or excluded by definition from normal motherhood as they are from the mainstream, traditional point of view. The "outlaw" understanding of feminist motherhood helps bridge the gap between the "double odd" patriarchal construction of incarcerated mothers and the experiences of many other mothers. Further research into links between the experiences of incarcerated mothers and other mothers could shed more light on what mothers share in common than what the present collection was able to provide.

Also called for by the essays in this volume is amelioration of the living conditions faced by incarcerated mothers, not only during incarceration and upon release, but even before they are "criminalized." Essays in this collection repeatedly and consistently reference a lack of social support and the absence of necessary structures in place to assist with raising children.

Several authors make clear that mothers may engage in criminal activities as a way to provide for their children and sustain life. We could add that in many cases, they do what they learned in their environment and in their families, as evidenced by multi-generational incarceration experiences of many families.

Marginalized and unsupported circumstances only deepen and intensify upon incarceration, when women "re-enter" the "society," or more precisely, when they re-enter, the criminogenic margins of society they lived in prior to incarceration. At that moment, women are carrying yet another burden, the one of being "ex-cons" and are therefore pushed even further aside, ostracized from the mainstream society and precluded from opportunities to claim its resources.

While they might have learned and developed a number of skills through correctional programming during incarceration, incarcerated mothers nevertheless leave correctional institutions with a criminal record and considerably fewer opportunities and supports than they might have had in prison. As these essays show, under such circumstances and without a consistent and strong social support system, finding employment, stable housing, and quality childcare and health care is essentially impossible. Therefore, with some exceptions, a limitation of this collection of essays is that it does not specifically outline recommendations how to sustain and structure social supports that would assist incarcerated mothers with the transition from incarceration to community and to ensure that "ex-cons" do not return. Further research on integrating incarcerated mothers during and upon release with culturally sensitive social supports outside prisons would be well worth undertaking.

While it adds further complexity and may seem contradictory, it is equally important to keep in mind that although most of the incarcerated women and mothers come from marginalized environments and experienced unspeakable and horrendous abuse, being poor and being abused are unfortunately characteristics that are shared by many women in general. Therefore, while it is important to keep these factors in mind, it is equally important to keep in mind that if abuse and poverty were a direct cause of women's crime, the number of women who get in conflict with the law and who end up in prisons would be considerably higher; the number would by far exceed the one of male incarcerates. This however, is not the case. Therefore, in order to understand how to best assist incarcerated mothers, it would be beneficial to gain a better understanding of those mothers who share a number of same relevant characteristics but nevertheless do not end up conducting criminal acts, being incarcerated, or developing substance abuse. This approach would pave the way to understanding "resiliency" or agencies that women who share a number of similar experiences with those who are incarcerated, develop and utilize and which assist them in making different choices and navigating away from crime and prison.

Motherhood Studies is still a relatively new field of academic inquiry. We hope that this collection contributes to the vitality and growth of the field. Following in the theoretical footsteps of Ruddick and O'Reilly, we seek to promote and support mothering as intellectual and emotional work of great value. To effectively and equally promote and support mothering, it is vital that academics, activists, those employed in the justice and correctional systems and the general public examine the complexities of how mothering is affected by and functions within a wide variety of contexts. It is crucial that this consideration includes attention to the marginality, poverty, abuse and other systemic inequalities in social contexts experienced by incarcerated mothers. This book is intended to spark a dialogue amongst a diverse group of people who are invested in the relationship between mothering, incarceration, oppression and resistance, to invite others to join this conversation and, ultimately, to encourage social justice through action.

[1] See, for example, "Jury Gives $975K to Woman" and "Nebraska Woman Settles."

WORKS CITED

Ali, Jennifer and William R. Avison. "Employment Transition and Psychological Distress: The Contrasting Experiences of Single and Married Mothers." *Journal of Health and Social Behavior* 38. 4 (1997): 345-362. Print.

Amnesty International. *United States of America: Rights for All.* London: Amnesty International Publications, 1998. Print.

Atwood, Joan D. and Frank Genovese. "The Feminization of Poverty: Issues and Therapeutic Concerns." *Journal of Feminist Family Therapy* 9.2 (1997): 21-40. Print.

Boritch, Helen. *Fallen Women: Female Crime and Criminal Justice in Canada.* Toronto: International Thomson Publishing Company. 1997. Print.

Brody, Gene H. and Diane Flor. "Maternal Psychological Functioning, Family Processes and Child Adjustment in Rural, Single-Parent African American Families." *Developmental Psychology* 33.6 (1997): 1000-1011. Print.

Brown, George W. and Patricia Moran. "Single Mothers, Poverty and Depression." *Psychological Medicine* 27.1 (1997): 21-33. Print.

Canadian Association of Elizabeth Fry Society (CAEFS) of Ontario. "Facts and Figures." 2011. Web.

Chant, Sylvia. "Re-Thinking Feminisation of Poverty in Relation to Aggregate Gender Indices." *Journal of Human Development* 7.2 (2006): 201-220.

Chesney-Lind, Meda and Lisa Pasko. *The Female Offender: Girls, Women and Crime.* Thousand Oaks, CA: Sage Publications, Inc. 2004. Print.

Comack, Elizabeth. *Women in Trouble: Connecting Women's Law Violations to Their Histories of Abuse.* Halifax: Fernwood Publishing, 1996. Print.

Cook, Alana N. and Ronald Roesch. "Tough on Crime" Reforms: What Psychology has to Say About the Recent and Proposed Justice Policy in

Canada." *Canadian Psychological Association Journal* 53.3 (2012): 217-225.

Correctional Service of Canada (CSC). *Women Offender Statistical Overview: Fiscal Year 2009-2010.* Ottawa, ON: Author, 2010. Print.

Elizabeth Fry Society. *Nobody There: Making Peace With Motherhood.* Edmonton: Elizabeth Fry Society, 1994. Print.

Garcia Coll, Cynthia, Janet L. Surrey and Kathy Weingarten, eds. *Mothering Against the Odds: Diverse Voices of Contemporary Mothers.* New York: Guilford Press, 1998. Print.

Haq, Rana. "Ontario's Regressive Approach to Prisons: The Negative Impact of Superjails on Women and their Children." *Canadian Woman Studies/les cahiers de la femme* 19.1,2 (1999): 131-135. Print.

"Jury Gives $975K to Woman Who Gave Birth Alone In Floor in Jail Cell." *Seattle Times* 3 February 2012. Web.

Kazdin Schnitzer, Phoebe. "He Needs His father: The Clinical Discourse and Politics of Single Mothering." *Mothering Against the Odds: Diverse Voices of Contemporary Mothers.* Ed. Cynthia Garcia Coll, Janet L. Surrey and Kathy Weingarten. New York: Guilford Press, 1998. 151 -173. Print.

Koch, Rebecca, Mary Lewis and Wendy Quinones. "Homeless: Mothering at Rock Bottom." *Mothering Against the Odds: Diverse Voices of Contemporary Mothers.* Ed. Cynthia Garcia Coll, Janet L. Surrey and Kathy Weingarten. New York: Guilford Press, 1998. 61-85. Print.

Leschied, Alan W. *The Treatment of Incarcerated Mentally Disordered Women Offenders: A Synthesis of Current Research.* Ottawa: Correctional Service of Canada, 2011.

Maidment, Madonna R. *Doing Time on the Outside.* Toronto: University of Toronto Press, 2006. Print.

Millar, Jane and Caroline Glendinning. "It All Really Starts in the Family: Gender Divisions and Poverty." *Women and Poverty in Britain.* Ed. Caroline Glendinning and Jane Millar. Hertfordshire: Harvester Wheatsheaf, 1992. 3-11. Print.

Moghadam, Valentine. *The Feminisation of Poverty and Women's Human Rights.* Paris: UNESCO, Gender Equality and Development Section, Division of Human Rights, 2005.

"Nebraska Woman Settles Prison Toilet Birth Lawsuit." *JournalStar.com* 12 January 2012. Web.

O'Donnell, Vivian and Susan Wallace. "Women in Canada: A Gender Based Statistical Report: First Nations, Métis and Inuit Women." Ottawa: Statistics Canada, Social and Aboriginal Statistics Division, 2011. Print.

Office of the Correctional Investigator. *Annual Report of the Office of the Correctional Investigator 2011-2012.* Ottawa: Author, 2012. Print.

O'Reilly, Andrea, ed. *Mother Outlaws: Theories and Practices of Empowered*

Mothering. Toronto: Women's Press, 2004. Print.

O'Reilly, Andrea. *Feminist Mothering.* Albany: SUNY Press, 2008. Print.

Parnell, Myrtle and Jo Vanderkloot. "Poor Women: Making a Difference." *Women in Context: Toward a Feminist Reconstruction of Psychotherapy.* Ed. M. Pravder Mirkin. New York: The Guilford Press, 1994. 390-408. Print.

Polatnick, M. Rivka. "Why Men Don't Rear Children: A Power Analysis." *Mothering: Essays in Feminist Theory.* Ed. J. Trebilcot. Totowa, NJ: Rowman & Allanheld, 1984. 21-41. Print.

Ruddick, Sara. *Maternal Thinking: Toward a Politics of Peace.* Boston: Beacon Press, 1995. Print.

Sommers, Evelyn K. *Voices from Within: Women Who Have Broken the Law.* Toronto: University of Toronto Press, 1995. Print.

Vainik, Jenni. "The Reproductive and Parental Rights of Incarcerated Mothers." *Family Court Review* 46.4 (October 2008): 670-694. Print.

Valeska, Lucia. "If All Else Fails, I'm Still a Mother." *Mothering: Essays in Feminist Theory.* Ed. Joyce Trebilcot. Totowa, NJ: Rowman & Allanheld. 1984. 70-81. Print.

Weitzman, Lenore. *The Divorce Revolution: The Unexpected Social and Economic Consequences for Women and Children in America.* New York: Free Press, 1995. Print.

Williams, Rebecca. *Child, Parent or Both? Who Should Be the Focus of an Effective Parenting Program?* New York: Garland Publishing, Inc., 1995. Print.

Wine, Shelly. *A Motherhood Issue: The Impact of Criminal Justice System, Involvement on Women And Their Children.* Ottawa: Solicitor General of Canada, User Report No. 1992-03. Print.

Young, Iris Marion. *On Female Body Experiences: "Throwing Like a Girl" and Other Essays.* Oxford: Oxford University Press, 2005. Print.

PART I
Incarcerated Mothers in Context: Social Systems and Inequality

The Canadian Landscape for Incarcerated Mothers

Lessons, Challenges and Innovations

DENA DERKZEN AND KELLY TAYLOR

THE NUMBER OF INCARCERATED WOMEN in Canada has increased by 41 percent since 2002-2003 (CSC 2007: 6; CSC 2010: 7). In 2009-2010, 503 women were incarcerated in six federal regional institutions managed by Correctional Service of Canada (CSC) (2010: 7). At any given time, the proportion of incarcerated mothers consistently falls between 66-75 percent of the incarcerated female population (Barrett, Allenby and Taylor 39; Fornier qtd. in Yoong 5). Moreover, a substantial proportion (64 percent) is comprised of single mothers (Barrett, Allenby and Taylor 46). Consequently, given the growing incarcerated female population, the detrimental effects of maternal incarceration in Canada are escalating. The following chapter will examine the lessons and challenges of incarcerated mothers and a number of innovative programs and services available for this subpopulation of offenders in Canada.

This brief review will focus on the factors that mitigate or influence the negative impacts of the incarceration of mothers, including the role of the new caregiver, the impact of visitation between mother and child, and parenting and mother-child programs. The remainder of the chapter examines the context with respect to incarcerated women in Canada, their unique challenges and the types of programming available while incarcerated.

MITIGATING AND MODERATING FACTORS OF MATERNAL INCARCERATION

The existing body of literature in this area tends to focus on the multitude of negative impacts of having an incarcerated mother on a child (e.g. impact on emotional development, attachment, academic performance). Interested readers should refer to authors such as Danielle Dallaire or Julie Poehlmann for comprehensive reviews of the impacts of maternal incarceration. Factors that assist in alleviating the impact of incarceration are critical to our understanding of this issue and assist in building and improving the relationship between mother and child. Such areas include regular contact between mother and child, role of caregiver, parenting programs and institutional mother-child programs.

Mother-Child Contact While Incarcerated

It is intuitive that the length of separation from one's child would impact the mother-child relationship; that is, the longer a woman is incarcerated the more difficult it becomes to fulfil and maintain her role as a mother. Given that women are relational and their maternal sense of identity is challenged while incarcerated, role strain is a major aspect contributing to this disconnect. Role strain results in feelings of inadequacy, depression, and guilt (Baunach 48; Berry and Eigenberg 104). This greatly impacts the psychological well-being of the mother while incarcerated and the longer the separation, and limited direct contact, the greater the strain (Berry and Eigenberg 114).

In considering frequency of contact, children who had little or no contact with their incarcerated parent report negative feelings toward this parent, express feelings of alienation and uncertainty regarding further contact (Shlafer and Poehlmann 410). Adolescents with frequent and varied contact with their incarcerated mothers experience fewer suspensions and school dropouts (Trice and Brewster 34); however, contact during maternal incarceration has been linked to increased apprehension and anxiety in children (Hissel, Bijleveld and Kruttschnitt 357; Poehlmann 2005b: 687).

The frequency of phone calls during mothers' incarceration relates to the quality of the mother-child relationship prior to incarceration as well as the age of the child (Poehlmann 2005a: 355). Age is likely a contributing factor to a more positive relationship, as an older child presumably would have had greater amounts of time, prior to incarceration, to develop an existing relationship with their mother. As well, an older child has the cognitive capacity to understand the complexity of the situation resulting in potentially better outcomes between mother and child (Poehlmann 2005a: 356).

In one of only a few studies examining Canadian federally incarcerated women who are mothers, Gordana Eljdupovic-Guzina (2001: 74) examined the impact of the quality of the mother-child relationship while incarcerated on the mother's well-being. Results suggest that a positive relationship between mother and child while incarcerated provided the mother a sense of hope, regardless of her self-perception of herself as a mother.

Conversely, when the mother-child relationship was not adequate, a sense of hope was only present when a woman had a positive self perception of herself as a mother. These findings demonstrate the importance of maintaining the mother-child bond and the factors that influence these relationships.

Role of Caregiver

Various sources suggest that when mothers are incarcerated, grandparents are most often given the responsibility of providing care for the children (El-jdupovic-Guzina, 1999: 20; Mumola 4; Poehlmann 2005a: 205). To a lesser extent, children may live with their father, other family members, relatives or foster cares (Eljdupovic-Guzina 1999: 20; Mumola 4).

The function of the caregiver on the maintenance of a mother-child relationship during maternal incarceration is considerable. The quality of the relationship between the caregiver and the mother significantly impacts the frequency of contact between mother and child. Specifically, a mother-caregiver relationship viewed as poor, lacking in warmth, and immersed with conflict was associated with few visits between mother and child (Poehlmann 2005a: 356). Further, caregivers restricting the contact between mother and child can destabilize the dynamic (Poehlmann 2005a: 356). Given the reliance on caregivers to regulate contact between mother and child, their role is not to be diminished and should be considered as as another avenue for positive relationship building while incarcerated.

Parenting Programs

Parenting programs, for both men and women, are commonly offered in a correctional setting. The objectives of such programs include improving skills related to parental decision-making, self-esteem, effective parenting techniques, understanding one's parenting style, and improving capacity to develop a healthy mother-child bond (Browne 218; Loper and Tuerk 2006: 410).

Ann Booker Loper and Elena Hontoria Tuerk (2006) provided a review of current research on parenting interventions for incarcerated parents. They noted that intra-individual change in program participants and changes in attitudes towards parenting (i.e. parenting acceptance, parenting stress) have been demonstrated (Wilczak and Markstron qtd. in Loper and Tuerk 2006); as well as improvements in self-esteem (Browne; Kennon; Thompson and Harm qtd. in Loper and Tuerk 2006).

Further in terms of skill development and interpersonal gains, participation in parenting programs resulted in less parenting distress and anxiety in anticipation of upcoming prison visits with their children, relative to a comparison group (Loper and Tuerk 2011: 99). Additionally, significantly lower levels of symptomology related to mental distress and parenting stress were evident post-program. Increases in the frequency of contact (letter-writing) and improvements in relationships with caregivers, an area known to impact the quality of the mother-child relationship, (Enos qtd. in Poehlmann 2005a: 356) were also reported (Loper and Tuerk 2011: 89). Despite the paucity of research on the efficacy of parenting programs, existing studies offer promise and offer an opportunity for incarcerated mothers to improve the mother-child bond while incarcerated.

Mother-Child Programs

Mother-child programs, prison nurseries, or mother-baby units, all have a similar program objective: to foster positive relationships between mothers and their children while incarcerated. In recent years, there has been increasing interest in implementing programs whereby an infant is authorized to spend their first few years with their incarcerated mother.

Such programs offer an opportunity for children and mothers to form a bond or an attachment during the most critical period of their development. If no such relationship is formed, with either an appropriate caregiver or mother, the child may have difficulties in subsequent relationships and further social development (Dallaire 17; Pollock 38-39; Zeanah and Fox qtd. in Dallaire 17). There is tremendous variability in approaches among mother-child programs in terms of length of child's stay with the mother, institutional, security level of the institution, inclusion/exclusion criteria for involvement in the programs (e.g. offence types), and age-limits for children (Kauffman 62-65).

Outcomes studies for mother-child type programs are limited in number and quality; however, of those available, results are promising. Studies have demonstrated positive gains with respect to facilitating secure attachments with infants (Byrne, Goshin and Joestl 386), and decreasing reoffending for those released mothers who have participated in nursery programs relative to a comparison group of non-participants (Carlson 1998: 81-81; Carlson 2001: 86-87; Drummond). Similarly, results have demonstrated lower rates of institutional misconducts for mothers during program involvement have also been noted (Carlson 2001: 85).

Upon release, several mothers who have participated in mother-child programs and who retained custody of their children reported feeling a stronger bond with their child as a result of program involvement (Carlson 2001: 92; Gabel and Johnston qtd. in Holland 3411). Additional benefits include: a) increased opportunities for children to socialize; b) adequate nutritional and health care support and supplies; and c) opportunities to participate in parenting classes (Gabel and Johnston qtd. in Holland 3411).

These findings, although limited in numbers, demonstrate consistency in benefits for incarcerated mothers. Not examined to date, is the extent to which these favourable programs have been implemented in a Canadian context.

We will now turn our review to the Canadian context and describe the Correctional Service of Canada's current research and approaches to alleviate the impact of maternal incarceration.

MATERNAL INCARCERATION IN CANADA

In research replicating the research of Margaret Shaw et al., a survey conduct-ed with 178 federally sentenced women (Barrett, Allenby and Taylor 46-48) indicated that just over three quarters of the women surveyed (77 percent) were mothers with children ranging in age from seven months to 45 years of age. Of these mothers, three-quarters reported having at least one child under the age of 18 and over half (57 percent) indicated that they were the primary caregiver of minor children prior to their incarceration. Notably, the results also demonstrated that a large proportion of the women (64 percent) were single mothers. Many of these women (42 percent) indicated that throughout their incarceration, they were in touch with their children, at least weekly; however, one-third of the women reported that they had little or no contact with their children. The women surveyed indicated that they would appreci-ate more consistent opportunities for general visits, private family visits,[1] and temporary absence[2] options to keep in touch with their family. Most women (63 percent) indicated that they were able to maintain weekly contact with friends, family, and community supports; however challenges highlighted by the women included costs (53 percent), transportation (20 percent), and emotional difficulties (28 percent).

The 2009 survey conducted by Correctional Service of Canada was undertaken to inform decision-making and policy development. In total, 56 incarcerated mothers responded to this survey from both institutional and community set-tings (notably, over 90 percent were in the institution). Fewer than 70 percent of the women were single mothers, not that different from the 64 percent reported by Barrett and colleagues (46). Approximately three in five of these women reported that they were the primary caregiver of their child prior to their sentence (similar to the results discussed above from Barrett et al.) and over three-quarters of the women anticipated caring for their child after their release. This certainly provides context around the reality incarcerated mothers face as the majority are single parents without the consistent support of a partner in their parenting responsibilities. Just over half of these women were Caucasian with approximately 30 percent identifying as being of Aboriginal decent.

Over half of these women were serving a sentence of less than three years, approximately one-quarter were serving a sentence of three to five years, while the remaining women were serving between six and fifteen years. With this in mind, just fewer than 40 percent of the women anticipate caring for children between three and five years of age and approximately equal numbers anticipate caring for children nine to twelve years of age. This rep-resents approximately 80 percent who anticipate caring for children less than twelve years of age. Recall that Barrett and colleagues indicated 75 percent of the incarcerated mothers from their sample had children under the age of 18. This highlights the relevance of the ability to maintain contact with these children during the period of incarceration, in hopes of maintaining, or enhancing, the development of the mother-child bond and facilitating reconnection upon release.

Respondents indicated that they retained contact with their children primarily through telephone or mail. Furthermore, just over one-quarter indicated that they had monthly visits with their children; while approximately 1 in 5 women reported weekly visits with their children. These numbers are promising in terms of maintaining some form of contact with the child; however, just over one-quarter of the women also indicated that they did not have the opportunity to visit their children.

In terms of parenting programming, roughly three in five of the women had participated in a parenting program in the past. Over 90 percent of the women indicated that they would like to understand more about child development, felt that it was possible (and they would like) to have a better relationship with their child, and would like to learn how to manage their time as a mother. Furthermore, the survey inquired about their interest in understanding emotions (their own and those of their child), discipline, nutrition, community resources, learning to deal with being separated from their child, legal and administrative processes around custody, and childrearing. In each of these areas, the women expressed overwhelming support for a need for more knowledge.

It is beyond the scope of this chapter to cover all areas of the survey but those issues outlined above certainly speak to the demographics of these incarcerated mothers, their intention to parent a child upon release, their methods for retaining contact during incarceration, and their interest in learning more about parenting and parenting related issues. Furthermore, it provides some evidence for the validity or reliability of findings from Barrett et al. Nevertheless, there are certainly limitations to this survey, in that the sample size is quite small and therefore not necessarily reflective of the population as a whole; furthermore, the methodology utilized for this survey had certain limitations (e.g response options, phrasing of questions) that lead to difficulties in the interpretation of some of its findings. The next sections of this chapter will begin to focus on the maintenance of contact between mother and child (e.g., visitation) and the opportunities available for incarcerated mothers to learn more about parenting (e.g., programming).

In considering the relevance of opportunities for visitation between incarcerated women and their families it is prudent to highlight research outcomes in this regard. Dena Derkzen, Renee Gobeil and Justin Gileno (14) found positive associations between receiving visits and a lower likelihood of readmission after release. Visits from children were associated with a decreased likelihood of readmission. Additionally, research examining protective factors, support that women identify their relationship with their children as a positive factor in the promotion of successful community reintegration (Gobeil 22). These findings reinforce the value of correctional visitation programs but also speak to the importance of maintaining this key familial bond, not only from the obvious perspective of the woman and child's well-being, but from the perspective of contributing to breaking the "cycle of crime" and the success of women upon their release from an institution as one of the most important factors in remaining crime free.

The 1990 Task Force Report, *Creating Choices*, examined the disadvantages that incarcerated women face including separation from their children and families, isolation from their cultures and communities, and the lack of appropriate women-centred programs and services. This report set forth five principles which guide CSC's programming strategies and interventions for federally sentenced women and include: empowerment, meaningful and responsible choices, respect and dignity, supportive environments, and shared responsibility.

In line with the principles of *Creating Choices*, CSC has implemented programs to support incarcerated mothers and provide them with the knowledge, confidence and skills to: 1) cope with the reality of being separated from one's child; 2) deal with the guilt of this separation; 3) maintain a relationship during the period of incarceration; and 4) improve parenting skills for use both during, and post, incarceration. Different programs, policies, and interventions contribute to efforts in this regard. The following section of the chapter will provide an overview of these interventions.

CSC has a parenting skills program for federally sentenced women. This program is regarded as a key component in CSC's strategy to support incarcerated mothers in their parenting efforts. The primary goal is to strengthen the capacity of federally sentenced women to provide for, and nurture, their children. The program strives to ensure that upon release, the women are better equipped with the skills and knowledge to ensure that their children are raised in a safe, secure and nurturing environment and to make parenting an enriching and affirming experience for the women involved in the program. Objectives of the program include: 1) providing women with the necessary child development knowledge and skills to parent effectively; 2) helping the women to make healthy lifestyle choices for both themselves and their children; 3) supporting the women in maternal decision-making, including the decision to take responsibility for parenting, and for making decisions that will be in the best interests of the child; and 4) assisting the women in accessing community resources and networks which can help them and support them in their efforts to parent effectively. Issues and themes that are considered throughout programming efforts may include, but are not limited to:

- •taking care of oneself;
- •parenting and self-esteem;
- •parenting styles;
- •modelling behaviour;
- •effective coping strategies;
- •parenting, stress and frustration;
- •dealing with children with special problems;
- •the need for mutual support;
- •helping mothers explain their incarceration to their children;
- •a focus on everyday problem-solving; and
- •dealing with reintegration and marginalization.

The parenting skills program is not only important for those mothers who will be reuniting with their children upon release, or preparing for visitation or temporary release options that will include their children, but also for mothers who are involved in CSC's Institutional Mother-Child Program. This program, as outlined in CSC's Commissioner's Directive (CD) 768, strives to provide a supportive environment that fosters and promotes stability and continuity for the mother-child relationship. Not surprisingly, this policy describes the best interests of the child as the pre-eminent consideration in all decisions relating to participation within the program. The safety and security, along with the physical, emotional, and spiritual well-being of the child are at the forefront of the decision making process when considering an incarcerated mother's involvement in the program.

CSC, for this, and other policy relating to situations implicating incarcerated mothers, defines mother as biological, adoptive, legal guardians, or step-mothers. The Mother-Child Program has two possible levels of participation. The first being a full-time residency in which the child lives with the mother within the institution on a full-time basis. The second being part-time residency meaning that the child does not live with the mother on a full-time basis but may live with the mother within the institution on weekends, holidays, or school vacations, for example. The policy on this program stipulates that inmate accommodation takes priority over the Mother-Child Program in both the long and short term. In other words, if there is not enough space for a federally sentenced woman to have her own single occupancy accommodation, options for involvement in the Mother-Child Program may need to be restricted.

As with any policy, there are many parties implicated in ensuring it is respected. In the case of the policy around the Mother-Child Program, institutional heads, institutional staff, and the programming board[3] all play a key role in implementing and monitoring the program. In terms of eligibility for participation, only women classified as minimum or medium security,[4] who are housed in institutions that offer the program, are eligible to participate. The oldest a child can be to be eligible for full-time residency is four years of age and the upper age limit for part-time residency eligibility is twelve years of age. Policy around the program stipulates that alternate age limits may be considered; however, requests with appropriate rationale must seek higher levels of approval (i.e., outside of the institutional approval process and with regional and national management).

There are strict expectations around the on-going monitoring and assessment of women and children involved in the Mother-Child Program. Please refer to CD 768 for an in-depth description of the required parenting agreement and the monitoring and assessment process. The process requires the Program Board to review each case one month after the program has commenced and then every six months thereafter to ensure that the program continues to be in the best interests of the child. These reviews consider how the mother is responding to the child's needs, if needs are being attended to in a timely manner, whether the time spent with the child is considered to be of quality, and finally, whether the mother is responding appropriately to the child's behaviour.

The above summary of the Mother-Child Program and the related CD 768, provides only a general overview and it is important to note that the policy also provides critical information around processes around health care, conducting searches of the child, mother, and/or their room, monetary assistance, consent to involvement, termination of involvement in the program, management of emergencies, and transitioning the child and mother from the institution to the community. The level of detail required to adequately describe each of these areas goes beyond the scope of this chapter; however, the reader is directed to CD 768 for a more in-depth description of the program and all related policy.

A preliminary implementation evaluation of the CSC Mother-Child Program was conducted in 2000/2001 after the pilot program began at Okimaw Ohci Healing Lodge in 1996. Other regional institutions began offering the program in 1997. On the whole, results of the evaluation were positive, and recommendations centred on operational concerns, such as ensuring provisions were available for proper care and monitoring child development; ensuring adequate financial resources and operational costs and ensuring the environment is safe and secure for mother and child (CSC's 2002).

Certainly, it is beneficial to have these types of programs in place for incarcerated mothers; however, the fact that the majority of incarcerated mothers in Canada will be released from prison and in some instances return to their parenting responsibilities, or simply be seeking to re-establish a relationship with their children does not go unrecognized. In support of ensuring the successful reintegration efforts of women and supporting their goals with respect to reconnecting with their children, CSC's Commissioner's Directive (CD 715-5): The Community Supervision of Women with Children, seeks to direct and support the work of staff in their supervision of women with children in the community.

Principles outlined within CD 715-5 include:

> •respecting the significance of a women's parenting role in the post-release period as key to her stabilization and community reintegration;
> •recognizing the need to link women who have parental responsibilities with appropriate community services and resources during this critical period of time;
> •ensuring the best interests of the child is the paramount consideration in all decisions; and
> •the establishment of relevant community connections during pre-release planning and continuing throughout the period of release.

In implementing pre-release planning, there is recognition that planning must include consideration of accommodation requirements for women who are pregnant or with child while in custody to support a day parole release at the earliest appropriate time. A variety of staff are considered to be directly implicated in ensuring this CD is respected including district directors,[5] institutional parole officers, and community parole officers. As per the *Creating Choices* philosophy, there is a focus on shared responsibility and recognition of the significant contributing role of community-based residential facilities[6] and private home placement[7] options. Finally, parental support is a key component of this policy and acknowledgement of financial considerations of women with children in the community are noted.

Given the increasing number of incarcerated women in Canada, the detrimental effects of maternal incarcerations are of growing concern. Only recently are academics beginning to investigate factors that have a role in influencing the impact of maternal incarceration; such as regular prison visitation and the quality of the mother-caregiver relationship. Since the inception of *Creating Choices*, 20 years ago, the Correctional Service of Canada has introduced a number of innovative programs such as mother-child or parenting programs. However, such programs are seldom evaluated with respect to their ability to assist in maintaining a healthy mother-child bond and assisting with transition upon release.

Advancements made and lessons learned will permit both operational staff and researchers alike to continue to advance their practices and knowledge as it pertains to incarcerated mothers. The continued challenge in documenting empirically based outcomes will be that these programs are rarely used and the numbers therefore remain relatively small; however, qualitative research initiatives and the implementation of systematic data collection efforts around said programs will contribute to our ability to conduct on-going research in this area. Furthermore, there are excellent examples of best practices occurring both nationally and internationally. An effort to conduct an environmental scan of these best practices would go far in facilitating positive outcomes for incarcerated mothers, their children, and their families. With time, what correctional systems should strive for is the elimination of cyclical crime patterns and the opening of doors for children to have access to their incarcerated mothers. Canadian initiatives outlined in this chapter certainly represent steps in that direction. As previously mentioned, and with many mother-child interventions, the best interests of the child are the main priority in determining participation, including their safety and security as well as physical, emotional, and spiritual well-being. Furthermore, as outlined in related policy documents, the requirement to offer the mother-child interventions to eligible offenders is based on long-term accommodation availability. If current and projected increases in incarceration rates continue, and the demographics and nature of correctional populations continue to change, correctional establishments offering mother-child interventions may be forced to consider new and varying options for on-going interventions.

[1]Private family visits (PFV) have been established by the Correctional Service of Canada in hopes of encouraging offenders to develop and maintain family and community ties in preparation for their eventual return to the community. It is also argued that PFV will lessen the negative impact of incarceration on family relationships.

[2]Temporary absences allow an offender to be absent from the institution and can be with or without an escort. They are granted for a defined period of time and are viewed as an opportunity for the offender to prepare for their release to the community. Temporary absences may be granted to assist with rehabilitation efforts and successful reintegration into the community or for medical or humanitarian reasons.

[3]A programming board assesses the individual programming requirements for a given offender, identifies appropriate program assignments based on the offenders' needs, develops and maintains appropriate programming scheduling systems and is responsible for the general monitoring of programming assignments, terminations, and successes.

[4]There are three levels of Security Level Classification within the Correctional

Service of Canada: minimum, medium, and maximum security. For women, security classification is determined by the Custody Rating Scale upon intake and then by the Security Reclassification Scale for Women upon reassessment. For more detail on security level classification, please refer to Commissioner's Directive 710-6.

[5]District Directors focus their energy and expertise on community corrections and related priorities including but not limited to the operational needs and priorities of community parole offices and community correctional centres.

[6]CSC partners with non-government organizations that manage approximately 200 community-based residential facilities (CBRF) across the country. These CBRF provide important programs and services to offenders who are on conditional release to the community.

[7]Private home placements provide residency options for offenders upon release. These placements are typically arranged in partnership with non-government organizations and have strict and comprehensive selection and placement criteria. They provide an alternative residency option to ensure that an offender is receiving appropriate support upon release thereby contributing to successful reintegration efforts.

WORKS CITED

Barrett, Meredith R., Kim Allenby and Kelly Taylor. *Twenty Years Later: Revisiting The Task Force on Federally Sentenced Women*. Research Report R-222. Ottawa: Correctional Service Canada, 2010. Print.

Baunach, P. J. *Mothers in Prison*. New Brunswick, NJ: Transaction Books, 1985.

Berry, Phyllis E. and Helen M. Eigenberg. "Role Strain and Incarcerated Mothers: Understanding the Process of Mothering." *Women and Criminal Justice* 15.1 (2003): 101-119. Print.

Browne, Dorothy C. H. "Incarcerated Mothers and Parenting." *Journal of Family Violence* 4.2 (1989): 211-221. Print.

Byrne M. W., L. S. Goshin and S. S. Joestl. "Intergenerational Transmission of Attachment for Infants Raised in a Prison Nursery." *Attachment and Human Development* 12.4 (2010): 375-393 Print.

Carlson, Joseph R. "Evaluation the Effectiveness of a Live-in Nursery Within a Women's Prison." *Journal of Offender Rehabilitation* 27 (1998): 73-85. Print.

Carlson, Joseph R. "Prison Nursery 2000: A Five Year Review of the Prison Nursery at the Nebraska Correctional Centre for Women." *Journal of Offender Rehabilitation* 33.3 (2001): 75-97. Print.

Correctional Service of Canada (CSC). "Institutional Mother-Child Program." Performance Assurance Sector, (User report 394-2-015). Ottawa: Correctional Service of Canada, 2002. Print.

Correctional Service of Canada (CSC). "Commissioner's Directive 768: Institutional Mother-Child Program." Ottawa: Correctional Service of Canada, 2003. Print.

Correctional Service of Canada (CSC). *Women Offender Statistical Overview: Fiscal Year 2006-2007.* Ottawa: Correctional Service of Canada, 2007. Print.

Correctional Service of Canada (CSC). "Commissioner's Directive 715: Community Supervision Framework." Ottawa: Correctional Service of Canada, 2008. Print.

Correctional Service of Canada (CSC). *Women Offender Statistical Overview: Fiscal Year 2009-2010.* Ottawa: Correctional Service of Canada, 2010.

Dallaire, Danielle H. "Children with Incarcerated Mothers: Developmental Outcomes, Special Challenges and Recommendations." *Journal of Applied Developmental Psychology* 56 (2007): 440-453. Print.

Derkzen, Dena. "Review of Literature on Mother-Child Programs." Unpublished Research Brief. Ottawa: Correctional Service of Canada, 2008. Print.

Derkzen, Dena, Renee Gobeil and Justin Gileno. "Visitation and Post-Release Outcome Among Federally-Sentenced Offenders." Ottawa: Correctional Service of Canada, 2009. Print.

Drummond, Tammerlin. "Mothers in Prison." *Time* 156.19 (November 6, 2000):106-108 Print.

Eljdupovic-Guzina, Gordana. "Parenting Roles and Expectations of Abuse in Women Offenders: Review of the Offender Intake Assessments." Ottawa: Correctional Service of Canada, 1999. Print.

Eljdupovic-Guzina, Gordana. *Mothering During Incarceration: Connecting the Past and Present Experiences.* Unpublished doctoral dissertation, Carleton University, Ottawa, 2001. Print.

Gobeil, Renee. "Staying Out: Women's Perceptions of Challenges and Protective Factors in Community Reintegration." Ottawa: Correctional Service of Canada, 2008. Print.

Hissel, Sanne, Catrien Bijleveld and Candace Kruttschnitt. "The Well-Being of Children of Incarcerated Mothers: An Exploratory Study for the Netherlands." *European Journal of Criminology* 8.5 (2011): 346-360. Print.

Holland, T. L. *A Theoretical Model for a Prison Nursery Based on Infant Mental Health Principles.* Dissertation Abstracts International: Section B: The Sciences and Engineering, Vol. 66(6-B), 2005: 3411. Print.

Kauffman, Kelsey. "Mothers in Prison." *Corrections Today* 63.1 (2001): 62-65. Print.

Loper, Ann Booker and Elena Hontoria Tuerk. "Parenting Programs for Incarcerated Parents: Current Research and Future Directions." *Criminal Justice and Policy Review* 17.4 (2006): 407-427. Print.

Loper, Ann Booker and Elena Hontoria Tuerk. "Improving the Emotional

Adjustment and Communication Patterns of Incarcerated Mothers: Effectiveness of a Prison Parenting Interventions." *Journal of Child and Family Studies* 20 (2011): 89-101. Print.

Mumola, Christopher. "Incarcerated Parents and their Children." (Report No. NCJ 182335) Washington, DC: U.S. Department of Justice, Bureau of Justice Statistics, 2000. Print.

Poehlmann, Julie. "Incarcerated Mothers' Contact with Children, Perceived Family Relationships, and Depressive Symptoms." *Journal of Family Psychology* 19 (2005a): 350-357. Print.

Poehlmann, Julie. "Representations of Attachment Relationships in Children of Incarcerated Mothers." *Child Development* 76.3 (2005b): 679-696. Print.

Pollock, J. M. "Parenting Programs in Women's Prisons." *Women and Criminal Justice* 14 (2002): 131-154. Print.

Shaw, M., K. Rodgers, J. Blanchette, T. Hattem, L. Seto Thomas and L. Tamarack. (1991) "Survey of Federally Sentenced Women: Report to the Task Force on Federally Sentenced Women on the Prison Survey." Ottawa: Ministry of the Solicitor General of Canada, User Report No., 1991-4. Print.

Shlafer, R. J. and J. Poehlmann. "Attachment and Caregiving Relationships in Families Affected by Parental Incarceration." *Attachment and Human Development* 12 (2010): 395-415. Print.

Task Force on Federally Sentenced Women (TFFSW). *Report of the Task Force on Federally Sentenced Women: Creating Choices.* Ottawa: Ministry of the Solicitor General, 1990. Print.

Trice, A. D. and J. Brewster. "The Effects of Maternal Incarceration on Adolescent Children." *Journal of Policy and Criminal Psychology* 19 (2004): 27-35. Print.

Yoong, Sabrina. "The Needs of Incarcerated Mothers and Their Children: Implications for Parenting Programs in Women Offender Institutions." Women Offender Programs, Ottawa: Correctional Service of Canada, 2007. Print.

Incarcerating Aboriginal Mothers

A Cost Too Great

GORDANA ELJDUPOVIC, TERRY MITCHELL, LORI CURTIS, REBECCA JAREMKO
BROMWICH, ALISON GRANGER-BROWN, COURTNEY ARSENEAU AND BROOKE FRY

I N THIS CHAPTER we examine the social and financial costs of the over-representation of Aboriginal people in the Canadian prison systems with acknowledgement of the concerted efforts, consultations and financial investments that have already been made to address this serious issue. We discuss why, rather than the desired outcome of lowering the rates of over-representation of Aboriginal peoples, there is an exponential increase in both costs and incarceration rates. While we are aware that the issue of over-representation affects both Aboriginal males and females, this chapter focuses on Aboriginal women as we wish to highlight the social, cultural and political implications of incarcerating an over representative number of Aboriginal women of child bearing age. Lastly, we will provide recommendations and propose practices that emerge from an intersection of both restorative and transitional justice which will guide current investments in a more promising direction. We agree that for Aboriginal women, who for many well-documented historical, social, and economic reasons, find themselves in conflict with the law, "more of the same simply is not good enough" (Office of the Correctional Investigator 36).

SOCIAL PORTRAIT

The drastic socioeconomic conditions of Aboriginal peoples are apparent to anyone in Canada who reads the social literature and to those who simply watch the news or read a newspaper. The percentage of Aboriginal families living in poverty is almost twice that of non-Aboriginals; 21 percent vs. 12 percent, respectively. Crowded living conditions exist for eleven percent of Aboriginal families compared to three percent of non-Aboriginal families (Statistics Canada 2008: 24); 25 percent live in houses needing major repairs compared to seven percent of non-Aboriginal families (Statistics Canada 2008: 7). While school completion rates are improving for Aboriginals, gross gaps in educational attainment persist with a 69 percent high school graduation rate and eight percent university completion ("Aboriginal Living Conditions"), compared to the non-Aboriginal high school and university completion rates of 87 percent and 24 percent respectively ("High School Completion"). Aboriginal populations are much younger than the Canadian population; almost one third of Aboriginal people are children living in very different family situations than non-Aboriginal children. Over seven percent of Aboriginal children do not live with either parent as compared to one percent of non-Aboriginal children. Over one-third of Aboriginal children live with a lone parent: 26 percent with a lone mother and six percent with a lone father. The proportions are half that for non-Aboriginal children.

The appalling socioeconomic circumstances of Aboriginal people are recognized as pathways to crime (TFFSW; La Prairie 235-46; Wesley 19) and thus have been recognized by the Supreme Court of Canada as crucial factors leading to Aboriginal over-incarceration, as is discussed in the *Gladue* and *Ipeelee* cases below (*R v. Gladue*). Recent trends show a substantial increase in the incarceration rates of Aboriginal people with a particularly alarming increase in the proportion of Aboriginal women in Canadian prisons (Office of the Correctional Investigator). While four percent of the Canadian population is recognized as Aboriginal, 21 percent of the inmate population is of Aboriginal decent (Office of the Correctional Investigator) and 33 percent of incarcerated females are Aboriginal (CSC 2010b: 2). The past five years has seen an 18 percent increase in female offenders; 23 percent housed in prisons, and 13 percent in the community. The percentage of offenders living in the community has consistently been higher than the percentage of offenders who are incarcerated at 53 percent vs. 47 percent for non-Aboriginals. Significantly, the trend is very different for Aboriginal women with a 28 percent increase in incarceration and a one percent decline in community dwelling. The percentage of Aboriginal women sentenced to incarceration consistently outranks those given community sentences (currently 62 percent vs. 38 percent, respectively). Sixty-two percent of Caucasian women offenders are currently under community supervision while only 17 percent of female Aboriginal offenders are (61).

Aboriginal women are almost 50 percent more likely to be in a maximum-security setting, 20 percent more likely to be in a medium security setting and 50 percent less likely to be in a minimum-security setting than non-Aboriginal women. Aboriginal women are less likely to be released on parole and thus, more likely to obtain statutory release than non-Aboriginal women. Day parole accounts for 54 percent of the releases of non-Aboriginal women, full parole for five percent and 40 percent are statutory releases. Statutory release accounts for 66 percent of Aboriginal women's releases while day parole accounts for 33 percent and full parole only one percent (CSC 2010b: 62).

While the differential in Federal statistics is alarming, the provincial numbers are even worse. For every person in Federal prison there are 16 in provincial jails. The percentage of Aboriginal people in the provincial and territorial facilities is extremely high. In Nunavut where the Inuit represent 78 percent of the population they represent 98 percent of the prison population. The territories of NWT and the Yukon have Aboriginal prison populations of 88 percent when they are 45 percent of the population and 80 percent where they are 22 percent of the population respectively. The over-representation of Aboriginal people in prairie prisons is of particular concern with 71 percent in Manitoba where Aboriginal people represent twelve percent of the population and a high of 88 percent in Saskatchewan where the Aboriginal population is only eleven percent of the total provincial population (Statistics Canada 2010). While we do not have figures for women it would be reasonable to assume that the 80 percent or more of the population of the new women's prison in the Yukon would be Aboriginal women.

The picture painted here is quite disturbing. Not only are Aboriginal women over-represented in the penal system in general, but compared to non-Aboriginal federally sentenced women, they are considerably more likely to be housed in prisons rather than serving their sentences in the community. Some may view this disparity as necessary given reports that Aboriginal women are convicted of more violent crimes than non-Aboriginals, 74.7 percent vs. 46.7 percent, respectively (Native Counselling Services of Alberta 125). However, further investigation shows that the statistics are driven by Aboriginal offenders convicted for substantially more Schedule I offences but a slightly smaller proportion of murders. Aboriginal females are 0.3 percentage points less likely to be convicted for murder than non-Aboriginal females (16.6 percent vs. 16.9 percent) while Aboriginal females are almost twice as likely to be convicted for Schedule I offences compared to their counterparts (58 percent vs. 30 percent) (125).

Significant to our argument on the impacts of the over-representation of Aboriginal women is the reality that approximately 60 percent of incarcerated women have children under the age of 18 years (Barrett, Allenby, and Taylor). On average, the incarcerated Aboriginal population is younger than the non-Aboriginal population but, more importantly, the vast majority are in the typical childbearing and childrearing ages. Over 50 percent of Aboriginal inmates are under the age of 30 and another 32 percent are between the ages of 30 and 45 years (Wesley 10). Aboriginal women have more children at substantially younger ages than non-Aboriginals, thus they are more likely to be young mothers (O'Donnell and Wallace 20) and, as stated previously, they are more than twice as likely to be lone mothers (Galarneau). Since Aboriginal women are much more likely to serve their entire sentences, and to serve them in prison rather than in the community (CSC 2010b: 7), a higher proportion of incarcerated Aboriginal women than non-Aboriginal women are separated from their children.

For incarcerated women with children, the separation from their child is very stressful, leading to feelings of isolation, loneliness and a fear of losing the bond with their child (Barrett, Allenby and Taylor). Barbara Bloom et al. claim that successful reintegration into the community and reduced recidivism can be assisted by a strong bond between incarcerated mother and their child (57). The following is a quote from an Aboriginal woman we interviewed about her experiences as an incarcerated mother.

> *We basically look down on ourselves enough as it is, you know in everyday life. And to be incarcerated and to have kids out there is that much harder on us, you know. And once you're inside, there's not a whole lot you can do, your hands are tied. It's uh, so you see, that it's like we're fighting that much more harder, I guess, to try to keep our children.*

Through the Indian Residential schools (1876-1996), child welfare practices, and the over-representation of Aboriginal people in Canadian prisons, there has been an ongoing separation of Aboriginal children from their families, communities, and culture. Growing up separated from one's parents, without the support of one's cultural community renders Aboriginal children vulnerable in the same manner as their parents were at their age. This creates the conditions for the intergenerational transmission of cycles of poverty and violence, with a higher likelihood of related criminality and imprisonment. In view of the fact that almost a third of Aboriginal mothers are lone parents, with a higher number of children than the general population, the over-representation of Aboriginal women in prison is of particular concern. Aboriginal children are disproportionately represented in foster care in Canada. Data from provincial and territorial ministries of child and family services for 2000–2002 suggest that 30 percent to 40 percent of children and youth placed in out-of-home care were Aboriginal, yet Aboriginal children made up less than five percent of the total child population in Canada. The number of First Nations children from reserves placed in out-of-home care grew rapidly between 1995 and 2001, increasing by 71.5 percent. In Manitoba, Aboriginal children made up nearly 80 percent of children living in out-of-home care in 2000 (Gough et al. 1). The number of Aboriginal women who are incarcerated contributes to the number of children in care and the number of Aboriginal children who in turn find themselves in prison. Another woman who was incarcerated when she was a mother noted the following concerns.

Well, uh, of course, I hope that they wouldn't you know follow in my footsteps
and uh unfortunately one did ... at least one ended up ... uh not getting
into trouble and being in and out of jail. You know and I just pray daily
that my oldest one just comes to his senses and stops that cycle as well. You
know like I do feel like I failed as a mother you know and um ... and now
that they're older I still look at them as being (pause) my little boys.

It is well established in historical records, in principle, and in law, that pathways to crime for Aboriginal peoples emerge out of specific social, economic, and historical contexts (TFFSW; La Prairie 235-46; Wesley 19). There has also been recognition that gender specific issues need to be addressed as "Aboriginal women experience not only the injustices suffered by women generally in our society they also suffer from the displacement and inequities which have been endured over many years by Aboriginal men, women and children" (TFFSW 112).

In order to address the over-representation of Aboriginal women in Canadian prisons these realities must be reasonably addressed. Improving the socioeconomic conditions of Aboriginal peoples will reasonably lead not only to lower levels of incarceration but to better outcomes in general. In fact, the 1996 Report of the Royal Commission on Aboriginal Peoples estimated "the cost of doing nothing"—failing to fundamentally change federal government policy toward Aboriginal peoples—was $7.5 billion per year (43). The figure included $5.8 billion in lost productivity and the remainder in increased remedial costs due to poor health, greater reliance on social services and related program expenditures.

The Canadian Government currently spends about $5 billion dollars a year in international aid for developing countries (Fitzpatrick). Given that many Aboriginal people live in conditions ranked worse than those in some developing countries, the Canadian Government could consider providing additional funding to address the gaps in education, housing, water, and health as targeted by the Kelowna Accord: an agreement signed by all First Ministers with Aboriginal leaders in 2005. The Kelowna Accord, aptly named Closing the Gaps, was a commitment to invest five billion dollars over ten years to bring high school completion rates on par with the non Aboriginal population, to reduce suicide rates by 50 percent and to provide potable water and improved housing conditions to First Nation reserves. The health targets were to reduce infant mortality, youth suicide and childhood obesity and diabetes by 20 percent in five years and 50 percent in ten years. Two-hundred-million dollars were also ear marked for investment in community economic development (Government of Saskatchewan 2-19).

If the levels of educational attainment and labour market outcomes for the Aboriginal population were increased to the levels of the non-Aboriginal population in 2006, the federal and provincial governments would benefit from a total of $3.5 billion (2006 dollars) in additional tax revenue in the year 2026. Considering both fiscal savings and increased tax revenues, the government balance would improve by $11.9 billion (2006 dollars) in Canada in 2026. It is estimated that the cumulative benefit for the consolidated Canadian government of closing the gap between Aboriginal and non-Aboriginal education and social well-being would be $115 billion over the 2006-2026 period (Sharpe et al. vii).

Clearly, improving the socioeconomic circumstances of Aboriginal peoples is estimated to produce huge social and economic gains for Aboriginal communities and Canada in general. However, even if we start the improvement process tomorrow it will likely take at least a decade or two to come to fruition. While a number of advances have occurred in the past, incarceration rates of Aboriginal people, particularly women and mothers continue to grow because of poor planning and poor implementation. It is becoming ever more evident that tinkering at the margins is not improving the situation. New and innovative approaches including substantial institutional change must be implemented.

THE NEED FOR INSTITUTIONAL CHANGES
AND COMMUNITY INVESTMENTS

Section 718.2(e) of the *Criminal Code of Canada* seeks to address the over incarceration of Aboriginal people in Canada. The Section requires courts to take alternatives to incarceration into account, particularly when sentencing Aboriginal offenders. However, problems with the legislative approach became starkly visible in a watershed case, when sentencing Jamie Gladue,[1] a young First Nations woman who committed a serious crime on the eve of her nineteenth birthday; the presiding judge claimed Section 718.2(e) did not apply as she lived off-reserve. Upon appeal of the case, the Supreme Court of Canada ruled that sentencing judges were required to consider the circumstances and heritage, of any Aboriginal offender, which may have played a role in their appearance in the judicial system.[2] While the *Gladue* decision was widely hailed as a progressive move in Canada, it did not result in the anticipated dramatic changes to sentencing practices. It was narrowed by subsequent precedent.[3] In 2012, the Supreme Court of Canada, in *R v. Ipeelee*[4] rendered an important decision on appeals by two separate Aboriginal people who were declared long-term offenders.[5] The Supreme Court of Canada held, in a six-to-one majority: Courts must take judicial notice of such matters as the history of colonialism, displacement, and residential schools and how that history translates into lower educational attainment, lower incomes, higher unemployment, substance abuse and suicide rates, and related higher levels of incarceration for Aboriginal peoples. While these matters, on their own, do not necessarily justify a different sentence for Aboriginal offenders; they provide the necessary context for understanding and evaluating the case-specific information presented by counsel.[6]

The Supreme Court acknowledged that *Gladue* failed to effect change for Aboriginals in Canada's justice system. The Court stated: "Over a decade has passed since this Court issued its judgment in *Gladue*. As the statistics indicate, section 718.2(e) of the Criminal Code has not had a discernible impact on the overrepresentation of Aboriginal people in the criminal justice system."[7] As a result of *Ipeelee*, the Canadian justice system has newly reinvigorated instructions to treat Aboriginal accused in a way that appreciates the historical and contemporary realities of their lives. However, it is unclear whether this new mandate will be any more consequent than previous ones, as the vicious circle continues. The response of the criminal justice system is contingent on the presence of appropriate infrastructure and resources as well as nuanced analysis. It is a stark reality that the continuing conditions of adversity (lack of infrastructure and resources) faced by Aboriginal people in the community, both on and off reserve, contribute to courts' too-frequent perceptions that custodial sentences are the only viable options for Aboriginal offenders.

Pro-active social remedies would reasonably be more effective, than legal accommodations after a conviction has been entered, at reducing incarceration rates. It is important, therefore, to eliminate the conditions that lead to incarceration. Investing resources in communities to significantly increase access to education, training, and employment, as well as basic services such as housing and water, would constitute substantive commitments to crime reduction and to addressing the over-representation of Aboriginal women in Canadian prisons.

INITIATIVES TO IMPROVE OUTCOMES OF INCARCERATED ABORIGINAL WOMEN

Correctional Service of Canada (CSC) developed a number of initiatives to address the over-representation of Aboriginal people within the correctional system. For instance, in 2003, the Aboriginal Continuum of Care Model was developed which was intended to lead "…to paths of healing in institutions, and works toward the safe and successful reintegration of Aboriginal offenders" (CSC 2010a: 22). As well, Commissioners' Directives and correctional programs were developed for Aboriginal offenders based on "approaches that incorporate Aboriginal values, cultures and traditions in our correctional operations" (CSC 2011: 4). Significant funds were associated with these initiatives. For example, CSC received $18.6 million over five years (2000 to 2005) to address Aboriginal issues. Evidence indicated that reconnection with families and communities would improve outcomes and reduce recidivism for Aboriginals, therefore the bulk of funds ($11.9 million) were initially dedicated to the development of Aboriginal healing lodges (CSC 2011: 7).

Aboriginal communities were interested in the progressive initiative but limited training in running contemporary community-based justice programs in combination with poor living conditions, and the lack of programs within CSC to prepare Aboriginal offenders for release to a healing lodge, set the alternative justice initiative up for failure. In addition, the focus of many Aboriginal communities, given their established third world status, was on more basic needs such as potable water, housing, health and the complex challenges arising from colonization and social marginalization. As a result, early evaluations of the healing lodges indicated that the outcomes of offenders who had been released from the lodges were worse than Aboriginal offenders released from CSC minimum-security institutions (e.g., higher recidivism rates) (CSC 2011: 7).

A significant shift also emerged in Canadian federal women's corrections with a document called *Creating Choices: The Report of the Task Force on Federally Sentenced Women* (TFFSW). This report, developed through a consultation process with federally and provincially sentenced women, conveyed their voices, concerns, lived experiences and needs. *Creating Choices* provided guidelines for the Canadian correctional system to design programs, services, and facilities for women offenders. It identified that many Aboriginal women felt uncomfortable dealing with non-Aboriginal people who do not understand their culture and experiences, and that incarcerated Aboriginal women wanted access to Elders and more Aboriginal programs for substance abuse, and physical and sexual abuse. *Creating Choices* identified five guiding principles summarized in the following guiding statement:

> The Correctional Service of Canada with support of communities, has the responsibility to create the environment that empowers federally sentenced women to make meaningful and responsible choices in order that they may live with dignity and respect. (TFFSW 117)

Since the release of this report, the development of federal correctional interventions and programming for women has been informed by these principles. The Prison for Women in Kingston, Ontario, which had been officially operational since 1934, closed its doors in 2000. For decades this was the only prison in Canada for federally sentenced women thus, was geographically distant from most Aboriginal women's homes and communities. In 1995, new regional facilities started to open across Canada (CSC 2010b: 2), including the Okimaw Ohci Healing Lodge that was specifically designed to address the needs of Aboriginal women following their traditions and culture. The intention of building these new facilities was to allow federally sentenced women to be geographically closer to their families and in some instances to have children on the facilities with them. Specific policies supporting mother-child contact, such as Commissioner's Directive on the Institutional Mother-Child Program, were also developed (CSC 2003). This investment in and focus on cultural, therapeutic, educational, and parenting programs for women after they enter the correctional system does nothing, however, to change the social inequities, displacement, and injustices suffered by Aboriginal women which bring them into the prisons at disproportionally high rates. Pointedly, the recent changes in Canadian legislation which have been referred to as "tough on crime" policy reforms (Cook and Roesch 217), have resulted in increases in the incarcerated population, particularly females, leading to overcrowding of women in these regional facilities. Women are being double bunked, placed "in common spaces, such as gymnasiums and private family visiting units in order to temporarily accommodate rising inmate numbers" (Office of the Correctional Investigator 40).

While initially there were and continue to be, specific policies designed to assist incarcerated women to maintain contact with their children, and possibly to reside with them in prison, the current inflation in women's incarceration rates is likely preventing implementation of these mother-child programs. In 2008, Stockwell Day, then Minister of Public Safety, changed the eligibility requirements for the mother-child program excluding women convicted of serious crimes involving violence, children, or crimes of a sexual nature. As well, the age of child participants was reduced from twelve to six and further child and family services were required before they could enter the program. These changes effectively eliminated participation of Aboriginal mothers, further isolating them from their children (Wesley 21).

REBUILDING CULTURE IN THE WRONG PLACE: RECONSIDERING JUSTICE

As presented, there have been a number of initiatives targeting the over-representation of Aboriginal people in the penal system as well as issues specific to women offenders that were associated with significant budget allocations. However, while the government recognizes that social conditions contribute to elevated levels of distress and crime it currently addresses the over-representation of Aboriginal people in prison mainly by providing treatment at the individual level after offences have occurred. Ironically, Aboriginal women sometimes gain access to essential services such as housing and potable water as well as educational training, addiction counselling, and parenting programs only after being incarcerated.

The Canadian Government needs to address the injustices that Aboriginal peoples historically and currently endure that are associated with their over-representation in court and prison systems and under representation in schools, universities and employment. An Aboriginal woman we interviewed spoke of the enduring intergenerational impacts of Indian Residential Schools:

> *...Especially for Aboriginal people, it's a lot different two or three generations above me, you know they suffered from residential schools and residential school is brought on through their children, and their children are taught it, and with today's generation, it's up to us to break that cycle. You know, and for Aboriginal people it is hard, because people don't know how to get rid of that.... You know so, it's yeah, if there is anything to know about Aboriginal women, the message is, you know we all have a different story to tell right?*

In order to address both rehabilitation and prevention, correctional services should consider addressing the over-representation of Aboriginal women in prison in terms of restorative justices practices within the larger context of transitional justice. The focus of restorative justice is "to repair the torn community fabric" in keeping with the values and customs of Indigenous communities and collectivist cultures (Van Ness 2). Transitional justice includes political apologies, reparation, truth and reconciliation processes, institutional reform, social development investments and a guarantee of non-repetition of harm. Canadian judicial and correctional systems need to be restructured such that the government is not continuing to separate Aboriginal children from their parents at the same degree or higher than during the residential school period, and therefore continuing to repeat the harm. Rather than providing essential services to Aboriginal people in prison we need to resource Aboriginal communities to provide basic services in education, health, employment and cultural renewal in their own communities.

The Hollow Water First Nation Community Holistic Circle Healing (CHCH) strategy is an example of a restorative justice process where considerable investments were made in keeping with the larger framework of transitional justice. The CHCH strategy integrated elements of a number of government-funded services (policing, justice, corrections, health and social services), Aboriginal spirituality, victims and victimizers and their families into its healing process in a participatory approach. An evaluation of the process indicated that it led to improved health, higher levels of education, better parenting skills, and increases in community empowerment, responsibility, safety, as well as an overall reduction in violence and lower recidivism rates than average. The evaluation also concluded that the $2.4 million dollars provided by government sources over ten years would have been 2.6 to 6.6 times as much if conventional programs had been used with conventional programs providing fewer benefits for all. For every $2 the government invested the community received between $6.21 and $15.90 worth of services and value-added benefits (Native Counselling Services of Alberta iv). Given that CSC plans to spend over $30 million in two years on 152 prison beds for women perhaps a more traditional strategy like CHCH would provide better outcomes at a lower cost. Incarceration is a very expensive undertaking economically and socially. Government could consider transitional justice approaches to social investments where less is more.

It costs approximately $312 per day or $13,880 per year, on average, to keep a person in prison (excluding capital costs, buildings etc.). The costs for females are more than males at $578 per woman per day ($210,970 per woman per year) compared to $303 per man per day ($110,595 per man per year) in 2010 (Office of the Correctional Investigator). Given current incarceration rates, the estimated cost of incarceration for Aboriginal women and men was $50,613,726 and $436,518,465 in 2010, respectively, for a total of close to $0.5 billion. The current trend of increasing incarceration rates will drive the figures higher.

The cost figures include only those costs pertaining to keeping the person in prison. Costs to children and/or families, communities, or the taxpayers such as caring for the children of the incarcerated are not included. For example, Alison Cunningham and Linda Baker provide a conservative estimate of 20,000 children per year affected by their mother's incarceration (2).[8] Current figures would be substantially higher given the recent increase in the incarceration rate of women. The surveyed mothers reported approximately 20 percent of their children were in foster care (Cunningham and Baker 7). Ontario taxpayers pay approximately $44,830 a year to keep a child in foster care (Hilborn). If costs are similar across Canada, taxpayers could be paying up to $180 million per year for foster care for incarcerated mothers. If we assume the rates of motherhood and foster care are similar for incarcerated Aboriginal women, approximately $60 million would be spent on Aboriginal children (one third of incarcerated women are Aboriginal). This would bring the costs of incarcerating Aboriginal women to just over $110 million. Add that to the costs of incarceration of male Aboriginals and the government is looking at approximately $0.6 billion per year to incarcerate Aboriginal men and women.

Tolga R. Yalkin and Michael Kirk explore changes to the criteria for conditional sentence of imprisonment (CSI) that lowers the number of individuals who would be eligible to serve their sentence in the community (3). They propose that not only costs of incarceration, but court, parole boards and other administrative costs will increase as alleged offenders will be less likely to plead guilty, more likely to go to trial, and more likely to use the parole system. They estimate the changes will cost the government almost 13 times more as offenders serve their sentences in prison rather than the community and 16 times as much if court, parole and administration costs are added in. The authors estimate community costs in the range of $2,757 per offender ($7.40/day), corrections costs of $37,022 per offender ($165.54/day) for total costs of $41,006 per offender ($182.22/day) on average.[9] The authors claim that not allowing offenders to serve their sentences in the community will increase the over-representation of Aboriginals in prisons as 20 percent of CSI participants are Aboriginal (71). The CSI program allows individuals to serve their sentence in the community; it saves the justice system about $175 per day or just under $64,000 per person year for lower risk offenders. An extensive review of the literature reveals that the current reforms while increasing prison sentences do not reduce recidivism and have been proven to be ineffective at deterring individuals from committing crimes. In contrast, there is an extensive, often overlooked body of evidence on the effectiveness of rehabilitation and prevention programs (Cook and Roesch 219).

The Hollow Waters CHCH (HWCHCH) program offers proof that higher-risk offenders benefit from serving their sentences in the community. In addition to lower risk offenders, over ten years, HWCHCH treated 72 males and seven females that would have otherwise been incarcerated in a federal prison. Males would have been incarcerated for an average of two years and women for two-and-a-half years. The costs to the federal government would have been $15,925,680 for the males and $3,691,975 for the females for just under $20 million (excluding capital costs) over the ten years at Public Safety Canada cost estimates (Office of the Correctional Investigator). In the year 2000 the HWCHCH program employed a manager ($30.37/hr in 2011 = $74,027/year including benefits), five counsellors ($22.25/hr in 2011=$54,234 including benefits), an administrative assistant ($17.00/hr in 2011=$41,438 including benefits) (*Living in Canada*) and 3,500 hours of volunteer time ($10.25/hr—minimum wage in Ontario, British Columbia, and Manitoba). Labour costs would be $386,635/year, volunteer time $35,875 for a total salaries and benefits of $422,510. Other costs were 18.5 percent of labour costs that would be $78,164 in 2011 for a total program cost of $500,674/ year or $5,006,740 over 10 years. At today's costs, the HWCHCH program would save the government approximately $15 million over the ten years (cost about $5 million and save the correctional system about $20 million). Given that CSC plans to spend over $30 million in only two years on 152 prison beds for women, investing some of those funds into programs like HWCHCH would lead to better outcomes for the women at a lower cost. Mothers would be living in the communities with their children, recidivism rates would be lower, and the participating communities would likely experience improved health, higher levels of education, better parenting skills, increases in community empowerment, responsibility, safety and an overall reduction in violence (Native Counselling Services of Alberta 58).

The evaluation of Hollow Waters provides an economic as well as a moral argument for greater investments in community infrastructure and related prevention and rehabilitation programs versus spending increasing amounts of public tax dollars on the expansion of prison infrastructure. The "Tough on Crime" direction of recent and proposed justice policy in Canada is resulting in greater numbers of incarcerated as well as longer periods of incarceration despite the reality that crime rates in Canada have been declining for the past 20 years (Cook and Roesch 217). We need to consider the manner in which prevention, rehabilitation, reintegration and reconciliation are intricately tied together.

The separation of Aboriginal mothers and children as confirmed in the over-representation of Aboriginal women in Canadian Prisons and the corollary of an over-representation of Aboriginal children in child welfare is a largely unrecognized if unintended extension of the failed assimilation project with predictable outcomes for Aboriginal communities and Canada. The current overrepresentation of Aboriginal women in prison, the majority of whom are mothers, is a critical social issue that can be addressed by increasingly ensuring the provision of essential services for Aboriginal women in their communities rather than in prison.

Incarceration is a very expensive undertaking both economically and socially. To address the over-representation of Aboriginal mothers in prison and the grave concern of the continual separation of Aboriginal children from their parents and their cultures, we propose commitments to transitional justice practices. A commitment to reconciliation would include institutional reform to child welfare and corrections services, a guarantee of non continuance of harm, and further investments in community re-development as identified in the abandoned Kelowna Accord. Greater investments in community infrastructure and education as well as investments in community based restorative justice practices would contribute to the prevention of social inequities and crime while supporting the healing and community re-integration of Aboriginal women and their children.

Acknowledgements: We wish to thank the women who participated in our research for providing rich and important perspectives on the experiences and impact of the incarceration of Aboriginal mothers.

[1]*R. v. Gladue*, 1 S.C.R. 688. Supreme Court of Canada
[2]It is particularly salient from feminist perspectives and from a perspective

grounded in maternal thinking that the intersectional aspect of Jamie Gladue's embodiment that she is a *woman Aboriginal* is virtually absent from, and not considered within the judgment.

[3]In 2000, in the case of *R v. Wells*, 1 S.C.R. 207, the Supreme Court of Canada unanimously clarified the impact of *Gladue* by stating that the significance of s. 718.2(e) on sentencing will decrease as the seriousness of the offence increases. Further, courts continued in many instances, to hesitate to take judicial notice of systemic and background factors affecting Aboriginal people in Canadian society (see, e.g., *R v. Laliberte*, 2000 SKCA 27, 189 Sask R. 190).

[4]*R. v. Ipeelee.* S.C.J. 13. Supreme Court of Canada.

[5]The central issue on each appeal was determining a fit sentence for a breach of a long-term supervision order. The Supreme Court explicitly cited issues such as cultural oppression, poverty, and a history of abuse in the residential school system must factor heavily into sentencing Aboriginal offenders.

[6]At paragraph 60 of the judgment.

[7]At paragraph 63 of judgment.

[8]Native Women's Association of Canada report survey results claiming 27/39 Aboriginal women who served federal sentences were mothers when doing so.

[9]Although the cost data from the last few paragraphs may seem at odds, note that offenders eligible for the CSI program are facing lighter sentences than those housed in federal prisons thus the costs of incarceration are less than half on average.

WORKS CITED

"Aboriginal Living Conditions." Aboriginal Affairs. Ontario Ministry of Aboriginal Affairs, n.d. Web. 2 Dec. 2012.

Barrett, Meredith Robeson, Kim Allenby and Kelly Taylor. "Twenty Years Later: Revisiting the Task Force on Federally Sentenced Women." Ottawa: Correctional Service Canada, 2010. Web. 29 Nov. 2012.

Bloom, Barbara, Barbara Owen, Stephanie Covington and Myrna Raeder. *Gender-Responsive Strategies: Research Practice and Guiding Principles for Women Offenders.* Washington: U.S. Department of Justice, National Institute of Corrections, 2003. Print.

Cook, Alana N. and Ronald Roesch. "Tough on Crime Reforms: What Psychology Has to Say About the Recent and Proposed Justice Policy in Canada." *Canadian Psychology* 53.3 (2011): 217-25. Web. 4 Dec. 2012.

Correctional Service of Canada (CSC). *Commissioner's Directive 768: Institutional Mother-Child Program.* Ottawa: Correctional Service of Canada, 2003. Print.

Correctional Service Canada (CSC). *Revised National Community Strategy for Women Offenders.* Ottawa: Correctional Service of Canada, 2010a. Web. 10

November 2012.

Correctional Service of Canada (CSC). *Strategic Plan for Aboriginal Corrections; Innovation, Learning & Adjustment, 2006-07 to 2010-11.* Correctional Service of Canada, 2011. Web. 25 November 2012.

Correctional Service of Canada (CSC). *Women Offender Statistical Overview: Fiscal Year 2009-2010.* Ottawa: Correctional Service of Canada, 2010b. Print.

Cunningham, Alison and Linda Baker. *Waiting For Mommy: Giving a Voice to the Hidden Victims of Imprisonment.* London, ON: Centre for Children & Families in the Justice System, 2003. Web. 30 Nov. 2012.

Fitzpatrick, Meagan. "Foreign Aid Could Be Better Spent." *CBC News,* 2011. Web. 24 Nov. 2012.

Galarneau, Diane. "Education and Income of Lone Parents." *Perspectives on Labour and Income* 18.1 (2006): n. pag. Statistics Canada. Web. 29 Nov. 2012.

Gough, Pamela, Nico Trocmé, Ivan Brown, Della Knoke, and Cindy Blackstock. *Pathways to the Overrepresentation of Aboriginal Children in Care.* Toronto: Centre of Excellence for Child Welfare, 2005. Web. 4 Dec. 2012.

Government of Saskatchewan. *First Ministers and National Aboriginal Leaders: Strengthening Relationships and Closing the Gap (Kelowna Accord).* Meeting of First Ministers and National Aboriginal Leaders, 2005. Web. 29 Nov. 2012.

"High School Completion." *How Canada Performs.* The Conference Board of Canada, n.d. Web. 2 Dec. 2012.

Hilborn, Robin. "Save Money: Get Kids Out of Foster Fare, Says Adoption Council of Canada. *Familyhelper.net.* n. p., 2011. Web. 4 Dec. 2012.

La Prairie, Carol. "Aboriginal Women and Crime in Canada: Identifying the Issues." *In Conflict with the Law, Women and the Canadian Justice System.* Eds. Ellen Adelberg and Claudie Currie. Vancouver: Press Gang Publishers, 1993. 235-246. Print.

Livingin-canada.com. Living in Canada, 2012. Web. 24 Nov. 2012.

Native Counselling Services of Alberta. *A Cost-Benefit Analysis of Hollow Water's First Nation Community Holistic Circle Healing Process.* Public Safety Canada: Aboriginal Peoples Collection, 20, 2001. Web. 10 Nov. 2012.

Native Women's Association of Canada. "Survey of Federally Sentenced Aboriginal Women in the Community." *Correctional Service Canada,* 1990. Web. 25 Nov. 2012.

O'Donnell, Vivian and Susan Wallace. "First Nations, Métis and Inuit Women." *Women in Canada: A Gender-Based Statistical Report 6.* Ottawa: Statistics Canada, 2011. 89-503-X. Web. 2 Dec. 2012.

Office of the Correctional Investigator. *Annual Report of the Office of the Correctional Investigator 2011-2012.* Ottawa: 2012. Web. 1 Dec. 2012.

R. v. Gladue. 1 S.C.R. 688. Supreme Court of Canada, 1999. Web. 29 Nov. 2012.

R. v. Ipeelee. S.C.J. 13. Supreme Court of Canada, 2012. Web. 4 Dec. 2012.

Report of the Royal Commission on Aboriginal Peoples. *Renewal: A Twenty-Year Commitment.* Vol. 5. Ottawa: Canada Communication Group Publishing, 1996. 21-49. Print.

Sharpe, Andrew and Jean-Francois Arsenault. *The Effect of Increasing Educational Attainment on the Labour Force, Output and the Fiscal Balance.* Centre for the Study of Living Standards, 2009. Web. 2 Dec. 2012.

Statistics Canada. *Aboriginal Peoples in Canada in 2006: Inuit, Métis and First Nations, 2006 Census.* Ottawa: Minister of Industry, 2008. 97-558-XIE. Web. 29 Nov. 2012.

Statistics Canada. "Characteristics of Adult Offenders Admitted to Correctional Services 2008/2009." Ottawa: Statistics Canada, 2010. Web. 28 Nov. 2012.

Task Force on Federally Sentenced Women (TFFSW). *Creating Choices: The Report of the Task Force on Federally Sentenced Women.* Ottawa: Ministry of the Solicitor General, 1990. Web. 2 Dec. 2012.

Van Ness, Daniel W. "An Overview of Restorative Justice Around the World." *Eleventh United Nations Congress on Crime Prevention and Criminal Justice,* 2005. Web. 4 Dec. 2012.

Wesley, Mandy. *Marginalized: The Aboriginal Women's Experience in Federal Corrections.* Public Safety Canada: Aboriginal Peoples Collection, 33, 2012. Web. 30 Nov. 2012.

Yalkin, Tolga R. and Michael Kirk. *The Fiscal Impact of Changes to Eligibility for Conditional Sentences of Imprisonment in Canada.* Ottawa: Office of the Parliamentary Budget Officer, 2012. Web. 29 Nov. 2012.

When Motherhood Is the Crime

Incarcerating Adolescent Mothers in Canada

REBECCA JAREMKO BROMWICH

WHEN INCARCERATED MOTHERS are considered, it is often assumed that mothering is a socially celebrated, or at least culturally permitted, task that forms a context over which criminalization may be overlain. Motherhood is often assumed to be something that incarceration for something generally recognized as criminal tragically interrupts. However, mothering has intersected with incarceration in another important way in Canadian law. Adolescent young women were historically incarcerated for sexual "impropriety." Such impropriety could include becoming pregnant with illegitimate children by socially undesirable fathers. As a result, historically, some adolescent young women in Canada were locked up for becoming, and incarcerated for being, mothers.

It has historically been, and remains the case that, there are only a small minority of adolescent young women who are criminalized. Compared to adolescent men, there are proportionately far fewer adolescent young women who encounter the youth justice system. Those adolescent young women who are criminalized tend to be an especially marginalized group. Adolescent mothers who are incarcerated are an even smaller group. They tend to be disproportionately Aboriginal or otherwise racialized, hail from low socioeconomic backgrounds and have experienced instability in their homes (Sprott and Doob). Adolescent young women dealt with under Provincial Child Protection legislation are more obviously a vulnerable group. By definition, they are deemed "at risk" and fall within the jurisdiction of these statutes.

This paper will examine historical regimes that criminalized motherhood on the part of adolescent girls in Canada. It first explores historical situations and selective enforcement of historical laws to reveal that racist and classist agendas shaped the criminalization of motherhood. Second, it looks critically at contemporary contexts in which mothering by adolescent young women has been criminalized, or, if not treated criminally in name, used as a rationale to constrain girls' liberty. It highlights and raises questions about the extent to which, under current child welfare laws in Canada's provinces, the situation has changed.

Throughout the history of Canadian youth justice law, there has been a troubling relationship between the regulation of morality, sexual behaviour and adolescent maternity. Incarceration has been used to deal with conduct that would not be considered criminal were it undertaken by a male or an older woman. More specifically, a more rigid set of rules has been enforced harshly against socially non-compliant teenage girls. The particular focus of this paper is when social non-compliance takes the form of motherhood. Put another way, this paper problematizes the use of incarceration to channel the labour of adolescent young women away from mother work in nurturing and caring for socially undesired children in a racist, patriarchal social order.

From this discussion, I argue that criminal law was historically used as means for moral regulation and retrenchment of patriarchal sexual control that channeled vulnerable adolescent young women's labour into socially accepted tasks. In doing so, these laws, and the tactic of incarceration, channeled adolescent young women's work away from unpaid mothers who cared for children and who were not seen as socially desirable in a racist, classist, colonial social order. I then problematize to what extent current child welfare regimes may continue to effectively incarcerate some adolescent young women for becoming mothers.

MOTHERHOOD AND MOTHER WORK

The key to understanding motherhood being criminalized by the statutes discussed in this paper is understanding motherhood and maternal thinking. These will be respectively introduced and elucidated by feminist theorists Sara Ruddick and Andrea O'Reilly.

"Maternal thinking" (Ruddick preface) is a particular genre of feminist theory developed in large part by philosopher Sara Ruddick (1995) and recently expanded upon and clarified by Canadian academic Andrea O'Reilly. Andrea O'Reilly, Sara Ruddick, Patricia Hill Collins and Adrienne Rich are key thinkers who have thus far developed feminist motherhood theory. Ruddick sees maternal thinking as a discourse or discipline analogous to the discourses of religion or science, with particular dimensions as a practice. Although traditionally understood as women's work, it is not essentially female. It is a kind of caring labour that is engaging, physical and involves "protection, nurturance and training ... care and respect" (Ruddick xi). Ruddick identifies the "maternal standpoint" (Ruddick xviii) as a way of looking at all children and other people as human.

Mothering is, for Ruddick, "work, not an identity" (Ruddick xi) Ruddick therefore disaggregates "maternalism" from any particular embodied subject. She focuses not on static personal attributes but on themes characteristic of maternal thinking. Similarly, Andrea O'Reilly draws together Judith Butler's notions about the performativity of gender with Ruddick's maternal thinking to further advance a non-essentialist understanding of maternal activism. She writes that, far from being essentially feminine, "drawing upon Judith Butler's theory of the performativity of gender … motherhood is similarly performed by maternalist activists" (O'Reilly 16). Maternal thinking is performed rather than "biologically inhabited."

HISTORICAL CRIMINALIZATION

Until quite recently, statutes across Canada provided for the criminalization and incarceration of adolescent young women most often in relation to allegations of sexual promiscuity or impropriety with a socially undesirable partner, particularly as evidenced by pregnancy. Until 1982, when the *Young Offenders Act* (R.S.C. 1985 c. Y-1) came into force, adolescent young women were routinely criminalized for "status" offences. Most commonly, the status offence for which young women would be incarcerated was "incorrigibility," predominantly found in allegations of sexual impropriety and allegations of sexual activity outside of a socially sanctioned marriage. This was the offence for which adolescent young women were most often incarcerated for nearly a century. Allegations of sexual promiscuity were evidenced by pregnancy and the birth of an "illegitimate" or deemed socially undesirable child and resulted in motherhood becoming itself a crime.

From 1908 onwards, the *Juvenile Delinquents Act* (JDA) (R.S.C. 1908 C-40), with its regime of status offences, criminalized teen motherhood in certain circumstances for adolescent young women up to sixteen or eighteen years of age depending upon the jurisdiction. From 1897 to 1958, in Ontario, the *Female Refuges Act* (R.S.O. 1897) provided at Section 17 for young women up to age 21 to be incarcerated for incorrigibility. The *Indian Act* provided for charges for adolescent young women in provisions that prohibited things such as the consumption of alcohol and a general offence of "profligacy" (Sangster). Delinquent status as a result of these general status offences could be evidenced by pregnancy.

Incarceration of adolescent young women for sexual impropriety and for motherhood of "illegitimate" children took place in the context of white European Imperialism. Performance of femininity was enforced by the criminal law as it related to adolescent young women. As Joan Sangster has pointed out, incarceration of adolescent young women in Canada was undertaken in ways that were similar to practices across North America whereby adolescent young women's sexual conduct was a central concern of the courts. Allegations of sexual promiscuity were a major reason that judges resorted to closed custody sentences (Sangster). Allegations of sexual misconduct would often become the central issue, no matter what the original charge or concern of the charging authorities, whether those authorities gained jurisdiction under the *Indian Act*, provincial legislation, police powers, or the allegations were raised by someone from the adolescent young woman's family. This focus on young women's sexual behavior was related to broader social contexts of eugenics (McLaren) and white supremacy (Stoler 634-9).

Passed in 1908, revised in 1929 and remaining in force until 1982, the JDA was very euphemistic in its tone. It applied generally to both males and females but adolescent young women were arrested and incarcerated under its auspices for very different reasons than were adolescent young males.

Filled with platitudes, the JDA presents a cautionary tale about how patriarchal systems can distort compassionate advocacy and motherhood statements (Platt 4). Acting in the "best interests" of an adolescent was the highest priority under the legislation. The JDA saw the state as a sympathetic, patriarchal guardian whose actions were intended to treat the juvenile as a misguided child in need of care and supervision. The JDA contained a definition of delinquency that went beyond codified adult crimes specified in the *Criminal Code* to include "sexual immorality or any similar form of vice." Jurisdiction of the Juvenile Court under the JDA also extended to cases that concerned neglected, abused or otherwise "incorrigible" or uncontrollable children. After a finding of delinquency, the state's open-ended jurisdiction over them lasted until their 21st birthdays.

Adolescent young women across Canada did not receive equal treatment under these historical laws. The operation of the JDA was by no means uniform across jurisdictions and time. Provincial legislation was even more obviously divergent across Canada. Jurisdictional inconsistencies were a problem that compounded its difficulties in operation.

The vague offence of "incorrigibility" was enforced selectively. Race and social class, especially Aboriginal heritage, were other complicated factors leading to differential treatment of adolescent young women across Canada. For instance, anti-Chinese racism was a particularly virulent motivating force behind defining some adolescent young women's relationships as criminal in Canada (Backhouse 315-68). As Joan Sangster has noted, Aboriginal young women were stereotyped as wild and out of control before any conduct on their part specifically evidenced "incorrigibility", a systemic bias that contributed to high levels of incarceration of Aboriginal young women under the JDA (Sangster).

In general, too often under the JDA, moral regulation and sexual control as well as performance of proscribed gender roles were rigidly enforced against

Canadian adolescent young women. The JDA "dealt with" adolescents labeled as delinquents expressly in the "best interests of the child." Forcible confinement (that was actually incarceration) was euphemistically termed "training." It was imposed on girls most commonly for the status offence of "incorrigibility" which often meant alleged sexual promiscuity, sometimes evidenced by pregnancy. Other times, "incorrigibility" meant running away from a battering father, step-father or male relative, or sexual and physical abuse in their homes (Valverde).

Perhaps the most famous case of an adolescent young Canadian woman criminalized for a sexual liaison and resultant motherhood is that of Velma Demerson. Demerson was arrested at her father's request for being "incorrigible" under the *Female Refuges Act*. A recounting by "delinquent" Velma Demerson of her story (Demerson) and Professor Constance Backhouse's chronicling of it in her book *Carnal Crimes* (Backhouse) brought to public prominence problems related to incarcerating young women for "incorrigibility" as relating to sexual activity and pregnancy. It also highlighted abuse of adolescent young women within carceral institutions (Backhouse).

Demerson's incorrigibility was founded on her romantic relationship with, and pregnancy by, a Chinese man named Harry Yip. Demerson offered to marry the father of her child at her trial. This suggestion was rejected by the Court. Harry Yip was never charged with anything. Demerson was incarcerated for this incorrigibility, during which time she gave birth at the Mercer Reformatory. Before giving birth, Demerson underwent sadistic experiments by a physician at the reformatory. These experiments included performing tactics on her genitals and abdomen while she was pregnant and involved the injection of chemicals; these likely compromised her son's health. After his birth, her son Harry Junior was taken from her once he was three months old. Once she was released, Demerson eventually regained custody of her son.

In this case, it is evident that racism too played a considerable role in deter-minations as to which teen pregnancies and sexual behaviours by girls might give rise to a finding of delinquency and which might instead be *corrigible* by a swift marriage or a discreet absence and adoption.

The JDA and provincial legislation like the *Female Refuges Act* created a highly discretionary youth justice system that left police, judges and probation officers to do whatever they thought was in a young woman's "best interests." The fact is that under these historical laws, girls were locked and sometimes even medically tortured and sexually assaulted ostensibly *for their own good*.

The JDA lacked legislative guidelines governing jurisdiction and sentencing. Statutory language and court practices not only failed to afford but actively discouraged representation of young accused girls by counsel. In turn, these problems led to disparities and injustices across Canada regarding who was under juvenile court authority and in what ways they were treated.

What was understood to be "good" for adolescent young women was defined in the interests of what were perceived to be greater than their individual autonomy or liberty. What was considered most important was the moral development of Canada's children in general and the creation of a morally pure nation (Valverde), contemplated as a white one.

Adolescent young women were rigidly regulated by juvenile justice law as it existed in Canada historically. Adolescent young women were forced into socially desirable activities, socially sanctioned relationships and required to comply with subordinate gender roles by threat of criminal sanction. The labour of adolescent young women was channeled by the JDA, the *Female Refuges Act,* and related statutes into working-class paid employment, and to the bearing of, and caring for, socially sanctioned white children. Inter-racial unions, like Demerson's, were seen as undesirable. Further, Aboriginal women's mother work was consistently derogated and discouraged in a society that simply did not value Aboriginal children being born. Society actively prevented transmission of culture, language and traditions by Aboriginal mothers to their children by apprehending children at young ages and sending them to residential schools. (Kline 118-41).

State actors crafting and administering the JDA, as expressly stated under the legislation, believed they were acting in the best interests of these adolescent young women. Problematically, under this regime, protection of the adolescent young women's moral virtue and socialization into appropriate (and subordinate) gender roles were understood to be things like "light soap and water" that were integral to the building both of Canada as a nation and the moral development of teenage girls. (Valverde). What was considered to be *best* for adolescent young women was referential to what, under a patriarchal social order, were *distorted* understandings of the good (Gavigan 283-95). Critics ultimately attacked the JDA for paternalism, informality of processes and failure to protect the basic legal rights of adolescents.

In response to these and other criticisms, the *Young Offenders Act* (YOA) (S.C. 1985 C-Y-1) eliminated all status offences (such as truancy, incorrigibility and sexual immorality). Delinquency is no longer a legal status in Canada. Culpability for the purposes of the criminal law is confined to only criminal offences. The *Young Offenders Act* also provided young offenders with the right to legal representation and established strict rules of evidence and proof throughout court proceedings. The YOA reframed criminal law with respect to youth and formed a youth justice system that stresses the offender's accountability and the protection of society while still recognizing special needs of youths. As a reflection of this, its dispositions ranged from reprimands, fines, probation and community service to secure custody to a maximum carceral term of ten years.

The contemporary *Youth Criminal Justice Act* (SC 2002 C.1) (YCJA) came into force in 2003. It retained much of the structure of the YOA. The current legislative regime continues to deal with adolescents by means of a criminal justice model system and does not re-establish status offences.

CONTEMPORARY CHILD PROTECTION LAWS

As noted previously under the JDA and related provincial laws, until 1984, the lines between child protection and youth criminal justice were blurred in Canada. With the enactment of the YOA and then continuing with the YCJA, legal discourses of child protection and youth criminal justice have been formally differentiated. It has been noted that, under current youth criminal justice law, it is no longer permitted to incarcerate adolescent young women for sexual impropriety, or "for their own good."

However, whether adolescent young women continue to be incarcerated for sexual impropriety and putatively socially undesirable motherhood under current child protection regimes is questionable. Where female adolescents are concerned, values that inform interpretation of "best" in the "best interests of the child" standard has historically been fraught with patriarchal assumptions and problematic racial and class biases in the context of child welfare law (Reitsma-Street). Just as administration of the JDA and related statutes was problematic in that it treated adolescent young women differently depending upon their class, race and particularly Aboriginal heritage, there is scholarship and statistical evidence supporting the contention that contemporary child welfare legislation continues to disproportionately affect the lives of racialized and economically marginalized young women generally, especially Aboriginal young women (Monture).

Within the child welfare systems of Canada's provinces and territories, there remain problematic contexts in which adolescent young women continue to be effectively incarcerated as a result of allegations about their sexual behaviour. Where sexual activity is regulated and criminalized, so too do motherhood and mother work end up having the potential to lead to incarceration.

Detention under the auspices of child protection legislation is a prevalent but controversial method of regulating child prostitution and of controlling illicit drug use by teens. Child protection laws are used to coercively detain—effectively to incarcerate—adolescents for protective reasons related to sexual behaviour in several provinces. A number of tactics have been used to facilitate this. Some jurisdictions simply include prostitution among the criteria for classifying a child as in need of protection. Others have enacted "secure care" legislation that authorizes *involuntary detention* of minors engaged in prostitution or who are suspected of involvement in drug use (Busby et al.).

Protection legislation in many provinces provides social services authorities the power to remove children at risk of prostitution and place the adolescents into the child welfare system. British Columbia, Alberta, Saskatchewan, and Prince Edward Island explicitly refer to prostitution in their child welfare legislation. These Provincial laws allow a child to be found in need of protection and be involuntarily detained if he, or, more commonly *she*, has been or is likely to be sexually abused or exploited.

In addition to the basic provisions noted above, courts in British Columbia and Alberta can issue a restraining order if reasonable grounds exist to believe that a person has encouraged or coerced (or is likely to encourage or coerce) a youth involved in the child welfare system to engage in prostitution.

Alberta has enacted the *Protection of Children Abusing Drugs Act* (PCAD). (R.S.A.). Saskatchewan's parallel law is called the *Youth Drug Detoxification and Stabilization Act* (S.S.) and Manitoba has passed the *Youth Drug Stabilization (Support for Parents) Act* (S.M.). All of this legislation provides for involuntary detention of youth who are involved in substance abuse. British Columbia's legislature has assented to legislation that deals with both drug abuse and prostitution, but has indicated it will not be proclaimed in force (*Secure Care Act*).

Similar laws exist respecting child prostitution. Alberta passed the *Protection of Sexually Exploited Children Act* (R.S.A. 2000). This law provides for the involuntary detention of youth who are involved in prostitution. Saskatchewan (*Emergency Protection for Victims of Child Sexual Abuse and Exploitation Act)*, Ontario (*Rescuing Children from Sexual Exploitation Act*), and British Columbia have introduced or effected similar legislation.

Critics of these laws often focus on the efficacy of the legislation. They contend that forcibly confining an adolescent young woman who is suspected to be involved in prostitution has little efficacy and in fact may be counter-productive in ending her involvement with the sex trade in the long run. The argument often is that offering help when adolescent young women want or need it, such as assisting with unplanned pregnancies and providing access to social assistance, will be more helpful to them than creating a climate of fear by state incarceration. Provision of appropriately designed voluntary community and social services is arguably far more effective in providing a woman a path out of prostitution in the long-term. Addressing her poverty and victimization by various kinds of abuse could be much more effective than forcibly confining her (Busby et al. 89).

In addition to providing ineffective protective measures to adolescents, child protection regimes that forcibly detain adolescent young women are also problematic in that they impinge on a young woman's rights to liberty and autonomy. A determination may be made under child protection statutes, which results in a long period of what is tantamount to incarceration without the procedural safeguards or presumption of innocence that would be afforded her in a criminal court. While a child protection order is levied in language that sounds benevolent, it can result in the same sort of forced confinement that a woman would face in jail and that is tantamount to incarceration.

The end result of provincial child protection laws that detain adolescent young women due to allegations of their involvement in the sex trade may be to legitimize precisely what was made illegal by *YOA's* enactment. It may be that these statutes create a new status offence of incorrigibility, albeit by another name, in the pursuit of a patriarchal distortion of what constitutes the "best interests" of the adolescent young woman or child.

CONCLUSION

This paper has presented a discussion of historical criminal justice contexts in which adolescent young women's expression of their sexuality and related motherhood, were criminalized. This would be a double penalty, because, in many cases, pregnancies would have resulted from sexual abuse, prostitution or rape. It has shown how incarceration was historically made a direct consequence of motherhood in juvenile justice legislation and related provincial laws. This paper has also problematized the extent that a similar pattern of incarceration of adolescent young women for motherhood, mother work and even maternal thinking continues under contemporary child protection legislation. It argued that current child protection laws that coercively detain adolescents for suspected involvement in child prostitution or the drug trade may continue to do indirectly what historical status offence sentences did overtly: incarcerate marginalized adolescent women for becoming mothers "for their own good."

More generally, Canada's historical incarcerations of adolescent mothers are predicated on understandings of a young woman's "best interests." What has been understood as "best" has been interpreted as what is good from within an agenda of white nation building. This patriarchal agenda posits moral regulation, sexual control, regulation of the reproductive and caregiving labour involved in mothering as well as more general gender subordination for girls and young women as virtuous and beneficial. As discussed, consequences for individual adolescent young women who do things *for their own good* have historically been, from the perspective of their rights and autonomy, very bad indeed.

Canada's youth justice and child protection systems need to be scrutinized and more carefully mobilized in ways that appreciate the often oppositional roles of the state, no matter how benevolent its self-understanding and intentions, and an adolescent young woman's agency. Criminal justice in regards to the conduct of adolescent young women should only be administered in the context of a full appreciation of a girl's rights to reproductive choice and physical autonomy under s. 7 of the *Canadian Charter of Rights and Freedoms* (Constitution Act)—rights that include both the entitlement *not* to carry unplanned pregnancies to term and the right to choose to labour to give birth to, and perform the caregiving labour necessary to, mother children.

WORKS CITED

Backhouse, Constance. *Carnal Crimes: Sexual Assault Law in Canada, 1900-1975.* Toronto: Irwin Law, 2010. Print.

Busby, Karen, Pamela Downe, Kelly Gorkoff, Kendra Nixon, Leslie Tutty, E. Jane Ursel and Resolve Research Network. "Examination of Innovative Programming for Children and Youth Involved in Prostitution." *In the Best Interests of the Girl Child: Phase II Report.* Ed. Helene Berman and Yasmin Jiwani. London, ON: Alliance of Five Research Centres on Violence, January 2002. 93-118. Web.

Canadian Charter of Rights and Freedoms Part 1, *Constitution Act,* 1982.

Collins, Patricia Hill. "Shifting the Center: Race, Class, and Feminist Theorizing About Motherhood." *Mothering: Ideology, Experience, Agency.*Ed. Evelyn Nakano Glenn, Grace Change, and Linda Rennie Forcey. New York: Routledge, 1994.

Demerson, Velma. *Incorrigible.* Toronto: Laurier Press, 2004. Print.

Gavigan, Shelley. "Law, Gender and Ideology." *Legal Theory Meets Legal Practice.* Ed. Anne F. Bayefsky. Edmonton: Academic Publishing, 1988. Print.

Emergency Protection for Victims of Child Sexual Abuse and Exploitation Act, S.S. 2002.

Female Refuges Act R.S.O. 1897.

Juvenile Delinquents Act R.S.C. 1908.

Indian Act R.S., 1951, c. I-5.

Kline, Marlee. "Complicating the Ideology of Motherhood: Child Welfare Law and First Nations Women." *Mothers in Law: Feminist Theory and the Legal Regulation of Motherhood.* Ed. Martha Albertson Fineman and Isabel Karpin. New York: Columbia University Press, 1995. 118-141. Print.

McLaren, Angus. *Our Own Master Race: Eugenics in Canada, 1884–1945.* Toronto: McClelland and Stewart, 1990. Print.

Monture, Patricia. "A Vicious Circle: Child Welfare and the First Nations." *Canadian Journal of Women and the Law* 3.1 (1989): 1-17. Print.

Ontario Hansard. 1999. Web. 16 November 1999.

O'Reilly, Andrea. *The Twenty-First Century Motherhood Movement.* Bradford Ontario: Demeter Press, 2011. Print.

Platt, Anthony M. *The Child Savers: The Invention of Delinquency.* Chicago:

The University of Chicago Press, 1969. Print.

Protection of Sexually Exploited Children Act R.S.A. 2005.

Reitsma-Street, Marge. "More Control than Care: A Critique of Historical and Contemporary Laws for Delinquency and the Neglect of Children in Ontario." *Canadian Journal of Women and the Law* 3.1 (1989-90): 510–30. Print.

Rescuing Children from Sexual Exploitation Act, S.O. 2002 [not yet in force].

Rich, Adrienne. *Of Woman Born: Motherhood as Experience and Institution.* New York: Norton and Norton, 1976.

Ruddick, Sara. *Maternal Thinking: Toward a Politics of Peace.* Boston: Beacon Press, 1995. Print.

Sangster, Joan. "'She Is Hostile to Our Ways': First Nations Girls Sentenced to the Ontario Training School for Girls, 1933–1960." *Law and History Review* 20 (2002): 59-96. Print.

Sprott, Jane and Anthony Doob. *Justice for Girls: Continuity and Change in the Justice Systems of Canada and the United States.* Chicago: University of Chicago Press, 2009. Print.

Stoler, Anne. "Making Empire Respectable: The Politics of Race and Sexual Morality in Twentieth-Century Colonial Cultures." *American Ethnologist* 16.4 (1989): 634-59. Print.

Valverde, Mariana. *The Age of Light, Soap, and Water: Moral Reform in English Canada, 1885-1925.* Toronto: McClelland & Stewart Inc., 1991. Print.

Young Offenders Act R.S.C. 1985, c. Y-1.

Youth Criminal Justice Act R.S.C. 2002, C-1.

Mothers and Babies in French Prisons

Cultural and Legal Variables

MARTINE HERZOG-EVANS

FRANCE HAS BEEN SPARED the explosion of female incarceration, which has characterised other countries. Over the last three decades (Ministère de la Justice), it has retained its extremely low number of female inmates—below four percent. Like in most countries, however, incarcerated women are often mothers or expectant mothers. In 2009, there were 58 available mother and baby cells located in 23 different prisons, and 20 children were present with their mothers as of the 1st of January 2009 (Huet). When it comes to allowing these women to keep their children with them, there are abyssal policy differences among European countries. Some jurisdictions choose to remove the child from the prison setting, regardless of his age; other jurisdictions allow mothers to keep their babies for a short period of time; others allow the child to stay for long periods, ranging from three to six years. France, like England, has chosen a middle of the road response: it allows mothers to keep their baby until he is eighteen months old. In this chapter, we shall reference and update previous legal studies pertaining to inmates' children in general (Herzog-Evans 2002) and to mothers and babies in particular (Herzog-Evans 2010). We shall also draw upon field research conducted with a team of four fifth-year (Master Plus) law students[1] during the 2009-2010 term year during which five prisons were investigated: Gradignan and Seysses in the South of France; Fleury-Mérogis in the Paris region; Rennes and Nantes, on the West coast. The students spent a few days in the units and attended the commission meetings which makes decisions regarding mothers and their babies. They conducted interviews with prison staff, judges, psychologists and doctors who operated in these units. However, we were partly unsuccessful when we tried to interview mothers. First, because it is consistently difficult to conduct research in French prisons and related administrations. This is particularly true when it comes to interviewing prisoners. After all, the institution is consistently reprimanded by European Human Rights Institutions and by the French prison ombudsman.

Another more positive reason can also explain this difficulty: the principles of reinsertion and privacy are very strong in France and there is a prevailing idea that inmates should be left in peace. Another reason is that most women serve short sentences (except in Rennes) and spend the majority of their detention on remand. Consequently, our team needed to obtain an authorisation from the prosecutor in charge of the ongoing investigation and from Fleury-Mérogis, which is unfortunately the biggest prison with the highest number of mothers and babies. The prosecutor only allowed us to distribute written questionnaires (in French and English). Many mothers could not read it and only two were returned. Eventually, only the student who had access to Gradignan and Seysses managed to speak to all the detainees. Despite all this, the team managed to collect interesting data which gave some backbone to our legal research.

WHY ALLOW INCARCERATED MOTHERS TO KEEP THEIR INFANTS WITH THEM?

One of the first reasons why women may be allowed to keep their babies with them stems from a long overdue recognizance of women's specific needs. Feminism in general and feminist criminology in particular (Walklate) have contributed to an awareness about the special consequences of incarceration for female offenders who are also mothers. There is an increased trauma that these women endure when they are separated from their children (Stanton; Enos). In the Anglophone world, in particular, such awareness has generated specific policies (Corston). Unfortunately, in France, gender diversity is virtually ignored and, but for a recent Parliamentary report (Huet), gender specific criminal justice policies are unheard of. Despite consistent progress in inmates' conditions over the last 25 years, very little attention has been paid to female prisoners and their specific needs (Huet; Cardi). One of the reasons for this is that France believes in legal equality rather than real equality. As a result, French laws typically declare that women and men are or should be equal, but fail to ensure that equality actually happens. Another reason may be that French feminists have adopted a rather collaborative view of feminism whereby women should tend to be... men. On the positive side, a child awareness factor is indeed at play when it comes to incarcerating mothers (Cario) or when considering early release.

Attachment theories (Bowlby) have revealed how a secure attachment (in particular an infant's attachment to its mother) is essential to the development of human offspring. Such theories show that separation from the mother at an early age induces a trauma from which a child may not recover. It is true that a lot of female prisoners have a history of loss and problems with attachment (Biondi); they should therefore be supported as mothers rather than deemed unfit on principle. Detrimental consequences for the child's psyche and social environment of incarcerating mothers have also been widely studied. Moreover, studies show that babies' physical long-term well-being is dependent upon breastfeeding (WHO).

Allowing babies to stay with their incarcerated mothers can also claim criminological support. For indeed, parental (and in particular a mothers') incarceration has serious both short and long term detrimental effects on offspring. It first has an immediate impact on children's behaviour. Some authors have suggested that children of incarcerated fathers show "acting out"behavioural problems, whereas children of incarcerated mothers show "acting in" difficulties (Fritsch and Burkhead, 1981). In one research study, 44 percent of the children developed severe behavioural problems (Bendheim-Thoman Center; Murray and Murray). The outcome for these children is rather ominous. A host of research has showed that there is a clear link between incarceration of a parent and later in life juvenile violence, delinquency (MacLanahan and Bumpass; Robins, West and Herjanic), alcoholism and drug abuse (Murray, Farrington, et al.).

Children of incarcerated mothers may well be at greater risk than children of incarcerated fathers. With very small children, from an evolutionary and primal health point of view (Trevathan), this may be due to the fact that mothers are the first figure of attachment. It has also been shown that the child of an incarcerated mother has a higher risk of being placed in foster care than the child of an incarcerated father, who is usually taken care of by his mother or relatives (Glick and Neto).

From a legal point of view, the universal concept of the "best" or "superior" interest of the child is that the child should remain with his mother. Insisting on the rights of the child makes it more difficult for law-makers to adopt a purely punitive stance. When the standpoint is based on the mothers' legal rights, it is easy to say that she has committed an offence and should be denied any advantage. However, when the standpoint is based on a vulnerable baby or toddler, it is harder to uphold this opinion.

International treaties do not address this issue per se. However, article 7 of the International Convention on the Rights of the Child does state that children have a right to be brought up by both parents, whilst article 9-1 states that they should not be separated from their parents unless it is in their best interest, in particular where abuse or neglect are present. Article 9-3 goes on to declare that states should protect children from parental separation. Recommendations sometimes address the question of mothers and babies in prison. Thus, a recent UN recommendation known as the Bangkok Rules (Rules for the Treatment of Women) contains article 49, which recommends that the decision to allow a child to stay with his mother should be based on his/her best interest.

In Europe, the Convention on Human Rights is silent about this issue and the European Human Right Court has showed a regrettable lack of courage and vision. In the case of *Helen and Wilfred-Marvin Kleuver v. Norway* (April 30, 2002, application n° 45837/99), the applicant (who acted with her son, a Dutch national) had been detained on remand in Norway and had, as a result, been separated from her son at birth and for the following three months. The court ruled that: "According to information supplied by the applicants in a number of Contracting States, there exist detention centres offering facilities for a mother and a newborn baby to stay together. The Court notes, however, that this concerned mainly open institutions; it does not permit the conclusion that in the vast majority, or at least the majority, of the Contracting States, there are such facilities in closed detention centres of the kind at issue in the present case." It then concluded that an "applicant could not legitimately claim that the competent national authorities ought to have taken any special measures in order to secure her interests in having the child with her in prison."

National French law contains a similar rule to article 7 of the New York Convention. Article 373-2-6 of the Civil Code states that courts should take adequate measures in order to make sure that a child effectively maintains his ties with his parents and article 371-4 adds that a child has a right to have a personal relationship with his parents and grandparents.

In spite of the above mentioned international guidelines, European nations have enacted surprisingly diverse policies.

WHY SUCH A BIG DIVIDE IN EUROPE?

Comparative law reveals an ocean of differences within the European continent. In cultures such as Latin countries, where motherhood is praised and viewed as being essential, children are usually allowed to stay in prison with their mother for several years: in Portugal and Italy (Biondi) they can stay up to three years; in Greece, up to four years; in Spain, up to six years. Germany, which is also very protective of the mother-child bond, allows children to stay for up to three or four years in one prison (Aichach) and in two open prisons (Vechta and Fröndenberg) for up to six years. The Netherlands also allows children, in more open settings, to stay up to four years.

In countries where, conversely, motherhood is not deemed as central, where fathers and mothers may be seen as interchangeable and also, where social services and the state may be more interventionist, children can only stay for short periods of time. Such is the case in Scandinavian countries (with the exception of one prison in Denmark, Horserod, and Finland). In all countries, children and their mothers stand a stronger chance not to be separated when they are in open prisons.

France, England and Wales and Ireland are typically at the crossroads of this European divide; depending on the prison setting, children can stay up to 12 or 18 months. Comparing England and Wales, on the one hand and France, on the other, may provide some insight into the deeply seated cultural grounds of the aforementioned European divide (Caddle). Partly Latin in culture, France may encourage primal mothering during the very first months of a child. It also aims at protecting the family unity. Conversely, its atypical form of feminism has led it to see mothers and fathers as being entirely identical. Such a nexus of opposed influences sets France apart from other European countries and may explain the legal choices it has made. Article D 401, paragraph 1, of the Penal Procedure Code (PPC) states that the maximum length of time a child can remain in the prison is eighteen months. However, before 1946, France was more on par with Latin countries as it allowed children to stay up to four years. After WWII, resistants who had formerly been imprisoned, campaigned in favour of better prison conditions. Many believed that prisons presented unacceptable environments for children and the law was changed. The prevailing influence of psychoanalysis in France throughout the twentieth century and beyond has also created a culture whereby mothers are systematically deemed suspicious of wanting to "devour" or "castrate" their offspring. To this day, the dominant idea in the population and with psychologists is that "the cord" between a child and his mother should be cut as early as possible. In opposition to this, attachment theories supported by human rights and contemporary reforms have slightly improved children's fate. In 1998, article D 401-1 was inserted into the PPC, which allowed a prolongation of the previous eighteen months limit by an additional six months. Paragraph 3 inserted into article D 401 stated that a child who had to leave the prison could come back for short sojourns, this during six additional months. In 2007, a Human Rights commission attached to the Ministry of Justice (CNCDH), recommended that the eighteen month limit should be raised to three years. As a result, another decree (Dec. 23, 2010) prolonged article D 401-1's six month extension to one year. In summation, today, a child can stay with his mother for two and a half years and then return for short sojourns during an additional six months. After several decades of being closer to its Nordic influences, France is now returning to its Latin origins.

However, the decision to allow a mother to prolong her child's sojourn in prison is subject to an evaluation by a pluridisciplinary commission, which is comprised of prison staff, a probation officer, a psychologist, a medical doctor, and a psychiatrist. Central to these meetings is an evaluation of whether the inmate is a "good" mother. Such a notion is bound to be culturally relative. Given that a lot of incarcerated mothers are foreigners, this may lead to discrimination. For instance, France traditionally opposes prolonged breastfeeding and views cosleeping with Freudian eyes as being seriously deviant. Other cultures may, on the contrary, consider this the norm. Thus, in France, it may well lead to a "bad mother" label. Indeed, France is not a communautarist country and it assimilates foreigners by asking them to bcome fully French (Guichard and Noriel; Costa-Lascoux) at the risk of negating their own culture. On the positive side, this suggests that France will not be totally blind to the child's perceived best interests, which is usually to remain with his attachment figure.

Conversely, the disadvantage of communautarism is that it leads to a greater emphasis on the culture of origin of the child and less to his intrinsic interest. Such may be the case in England and Wales. In this regard, the P and Q case (Court of Appeal, *P and Q*, 20 July 2001, [2001] EWCA Civ 1151, Case No: C/2001/1114 & v/2001/1110) is topical. Two foreign female inmates wanted to keep their child longer than the maximum limit of eighteen months. Lords C. J. Woolf and J. Lightman rejected one mother's application but not the other. In France, judges would have wondered whether the mother had a strong—but not too strong—bond with her child and was a good enough mother, viewed through their culturally-tinted lenses. They would also have tried to assess whether the baby would be happier with his mother or with foster parents. Even though Lord Woolf and Lightman examined all the relevant parameters, they essentially based their ruling on the cultural and ethnic compatibility of the available foster families: in one case, the foster family was of the same ethnic origin and had the same religion as the mother; in the other, no such connection was found. The first mother lost her case; the other kept her child. Seen from a French perspective, it seems extraordinary that such criteria would be seen as essential for a child of such a young age.

In 2000, the Council of Europe's Parliamentary Assembly tried to determine whether a given European state could decide this matter. Its Social, Health and Family Affairs Committee reviewed the literature. It concluded that, on the one hand, separating babies and young children from their mothers had serious and sometimes irreversible psychological consequences; on the other hand, keeping the child in the prison setting could delay its development. However, in the latter case, it was determined that such a developmental delay was not irreversible. The report concluded that mothers should not be incarcerated at all unless they were dangerous, and if they were, they should be released as soon as possible. Only when this was impossible should the child remain with his mother. The report also recommended that states should offer appropriate living conditions to the mothers and their children and endeavour to stimulate children's cognitive and social faculties—and to train the prison staff accordingly. The Parliamentary Assembly adopted the committee's conclusions (Recommendation 1469 [2000] *Mothers and babies in prison*). The recommendation is thus more pugnacious than the European Prison Rules (2006), which merely state that "infants may stay in prison with a parent only when it is in the best interest of infants concerned" (Rule 36-1), that they should be in adapted settings (Rule 36-3) and should be taken to day-care during the day (Rule 36-2).

The EPR refer to "a parent"; not merely to a "mother." In practice, children are only allowed to stay in female prisons. Several reasons may explain this. First, incarcerated mothers are usually single parents (Corston; Stanton; Alejos). Also, female delinquency is typically much less violent, diverse and serious than males delinquency (Carlen; Walklate; Cario), which means that children's security is easier to guarantee in a female prison.

Whether children should remain in prison with their mothers has generated a host of research. Conversely, the rules governing their status and conditions have drawn little attention from social scientists. In their studies, these children seem to have little importance (Pösö, Enroos and Vierula).

RULES GOVERNING THE CHILD'S STATUS WITHIN THE PRISON

In France, institutional invisibility is confirmed by the very legal nature of the rules governing children's sojourn in prison: whereas, according to the French constitution, such questions should have warranted a Parliament Act, a mere sub-decree (Circulaire AP, August 18, 1999, NORJUSE 9940062C)—and as such only binding for the prison institution and staff—regulates such issues.

The UN Bangkok Rules state that children incarcerated with their mother "shall never be treated as prisoners" (Rule 49). An identical rule had been inserted into the EPR (n° 36-1) and in the above mentioned French sub-decree.

In practice, however, prison regulations will always prevail over general principles. As a striking example, the sub-decree states that a child who goes to the visitation room or leaves the prison (e.g. to go to day-care) is subjected to a before and after body search. If the child were outside the walls of the prison, only a high ranking police officer would be allowed to search him or her and only if there were a reason to believe he/she had committed an offence (Court of cassation, Criminal Chamber, *Isnard*, Jan. 22, 1953, D. 1953, jurisp.: 533 ; *JCP* 1953, II, 7456). Extraordinarily, the sheer illegality of a prison officer imposing this on a non-offender baby or toddler, this, on the non-binding basis of a mere sub-decree has not yet raised criticism. Conversely, the sub-decree reminds the mother that the prison institution should not fund her child's stay. In practice, she contributes via the single mother benefits that she receives. More rarely, the father is asked to pay alimony.

Because the child is not an inmate, in principle his mother has full parental rights, unless a court has declared her unfit, which is exceptional. However, the very place where her child is detained does not allow her to make all the choices a mother would normally exercise. For instance, she may want her child to be seen by a particular pediatrician. However, as she is detained, she can only refer him to the prison General Practitioner—who is detached from a local hospital. She may want to choose a specific birthing method, but in reality she depends on what is available in the prison. The research has also shown that some medical teams make birth induction mandatory as they are concerned they might have to deal with a night birth.

Given the French cultural context, the main preoccupation that the sub-decree assigns to prison staff is to avoid the dangerous "fusion" between mother and child that Freudian thinking abhors. Another unmentioned reason is that the child may have to leave if his mother's sentence exceeds the provisions of article D 401 of the PPC Prison staff and probation officers consequently make sure that children go to day-care as regularly as possible, using a wide range of local agencies (Deze and Marti). They also organise his release into foster care or into the hands of a family member.

Separation, as can be expected, is extremely traumatic for mother (Celinska and Siegel) and child and, as our research has shown, for staff. This may explain why recent decrees have tried and delayed the inevitable. Luckily, few women serve long enough sentences to have to endure a separation from their child. Also, whenever possible, courts use all available tools to release children when implementing sentencing.

WHAT ARE THE RULES CONCERNING PRISON RELEASE ?

In France, a variety of measures are available to courts who consider releasing a mother before she has served her entire prison sentence, in order to avoid mother-child separation. Providing a sufficient proportion of the sentence has been served, "semi-freedom" (day-leave), an equivalent measure called "placement in the community," or electronic monitoring can be granted, inter alia, for a person whose "participation" to "family life" is "essential" (PPC, art. 132-25 and 132-26-1). The same rules apply to ordinary conditional release (PPC, art. 729). However, a specific "parental" conditional release has been created in 2000 (PPC, art. 729-3). It allows the parent of at least one child up to ten years of age, who has parental authority over said child and is sharing his life, who has to serve a sentence of up to four years, or, for a longer sentence, has up to four years left to serve, and who is not a recidivist, to be conditionally released. In such a case, traditional criteria for conditional release such as having a convincing release plan are viewed more compassionately (Criminal chamber, Court of cassation, 24 Jan. 2007, no 06-82.217 and 24 Jan. 2007, pourvoi n° 06-82217, and 7 Nov. 2007, pourvoi n° 07-82.598).

In creating a parental conditional release, legislators were inspired by both the Italian legal system (see Gualazzi and Mancuso, 2010) and by the Council of Europe aforementioned 2000 Recommendation. There is no doubt that their intention was not to be overly lenient with inmates who happened to be parents, but that they wanted to protect the children's best interests. Still, at first, sentence implementation courts struggled with the apparently contradictory demands that the law assigned them (Herzog-Evans 2012; Rodier-Guilpar). Recently, the criminal chamber of the French highest court, the Court of Cassation, has clearly stated that the need for a release plan comprising of the elements that the law would require for a regular conditional release (such as a job, housing, treatment, etc.) was not mandatory in the case of parental conditional release, as long as the mother met the requirements of article 729-3 (Criminal chamber, Court of cassation, 3 Feb. 2010, pourvoi n° 09-84.850). This then supported the applicant's argument that the court should base their ruling on the "children's best interest." This ruling will fit in easily with French judges implementing sentences and whose professional culture is strongly pro-rehabilitation, reinsertion and desistance.

CONCLUSION

France has resisted the Anglophone Western world's increase in female imprisonment. Both the chivalry factor and the "best interest of the child" standard seem to be still protecting women and their children during the penal process' sentencing and release phases. However, when women are incarcerated, prison regulations do prevail even though children are not legally prisoners. Also, mothers and babies are subjected to the pressure of French ideas on mothering and education, which is particularly challenging when it comes to foreign mothers.

We have also seen that France is at the crossroads of many beliefs. Culture dictates the choices that are made regarding whether babies should stay with their incarcerated mothers, for how long, on what grounds and how. France is a multicultural country with various and often opposite influences; it presents a strikingly complex and sometimes contradictory image, a complexity which is reenforced by the influence of human rights law.

[1]Marion Le Moine, Cindy Laubin, Gwendoline Richard and Marie Faguet, Universities of Nantes, Reims and Pau/Bordeaux IV.

WORKS CITED

Alejos, Marlene. *Babies and Small Children Residing in Prisons*. Geneva: Quaker United Nations Office, 2005. Print.

Bendheim-Thoman Center for Research on Child Well-Being, Princeton University and Columbia Population Research Center, Columbia University. "Parental Incarceration and Child Wellbeing in Fragile Families." *Fragile Families Research Brief* 42 (2008). Print.

Biondi, Gianni. *Lo sviluppo del bambino in carcere*. Collana, Serie di psicologia. Milano: Franco Angeli, 1994. Print.

Bowlby, John. *Attachment and Loss*. New York: Basic Books, 1969. Print.

Caddle, Diane. *Age Limits for Babies in Prison, Some Lessons From Abroad*. Home Office Research, Development and Statistics Directorate, 80, 1998. Print.

Cardi, Coline. *La déviance des femmes. Délinquantes et mauvaises mères : entre prison, justice et travail social*. Ph.D. thesis (Thèse Paris 7), 2008. Print.

Cario, Robert. *Les femmes résistent au crime*. Paris: L'Harmattan, 1997. Print

Carlen, Pat. *Women and Punishment. The Struggle for Justice*. Cullompton: Willan Publishing, 2002. Print.

Celinska, Katarzyna and Jane A. Siegel. "Mothers in Trouble: Coping with Actual or Pending Separation From Children due to Incarceration." *The Prison Journal* 90.4 (2010): 447-474. Print.

CNCDH. "Sanctionner dans le respect des droits de l'homme. Tome I, Les droits de l'homme dans la prison, 11 mars 2004." La Documentation française, 2007. Print.

Council of Europe, Parliamentary Assembly. *Mothers and Babies in Prison*. 2000a. Recommendation 1469. Print.

Council of Europe, Parliamentary Assembly. Social, Health and Family Affairs Committee. *Mothers and Babies in Prison*. June 9, 2000b. Doc. n° 8762. Print.

Corston, Jean. *The Corston Report, A Report of a Review of Women with Particular Vulnerabilities in the Criminal Justice System*. Home Office, UK, March 2007. Print.

Costa-Lascoux Jacqueline. *République et particularismes*. Paris: La Documentation française, Problèmes économiques et sociaux, Dossiers d'actualité mondiale, n° 909. 2005. Print.

Enos, Sandra. *Mothering from the Inside. Parenting in a Women's Prison*. New York: State University of New York Press, 2001. Print.

Deze, Antoinette and Brigitte Marti. "L'accompagnement d'un bébé à l'extérieur de la maison d'arrêt." *Rester parents malgré la détention*. Ed. Jean Le Camus. Paris: Erès, 2000. 119-137. Print.

European Prison Rules. Committee of Ministers, Council of Europe, 11 January 2006. Web.

Fritsch, Travis A. and John D. Burkhead. "Behavioral reaction of children to parental absence due to imprisonment." *Family Relations* 30.1 (1981): 83-88. Print.

Glick, Ruth M. and Virginia V. Neto. *National Study of Women's Correctional Programs*. Washington, DC: U.S. Department of Justice, 1977. Print

Gualazzi, Alessandra and Chiara Mancuso. "Italy." *Release from Prison: European Policy and Practice*. Ed. Nicola Padfield, Dirk van Zyl Smit and Frieder Dünkel. Cullompton: Willan Publishing, 2010. 266-299. Print.

Guichard, Eric and Gérard Noriel. *Constructions des nationalités et immigration dans la France contemporaine*. Paris: Rue d'Ulm, 1997. Print

Herzog-Evans, Martine. "Droit civil commun, droit européen et incarcération. *Droit au respect de la vie familiale au sens de la Convention européenne des droits de l'homme*. Ed. Frédéric Sudre. Paris: Bruylant, 2002. 241-285. Print.

Herzog-Evans, Martine. "Le séjour du petit enfant avec sa mère en détention.» *Figures de femmes criminelles de l'Antiquité à nos jours*." Ed. Loïc Cadiet, Frédéric Chauvaud et al. Paris: Publications de la Sorbonne. 2010. 205-222. Print.

Herzog-Evans, Martine. *Droit de l'exécution des peines*. 4th ed. Paris: Dalloz, 2012. Print.

Home Office Research, Development and Statistics Directorate. London. 80. 1998. Print.

Howard League for Penal Reform. *The Voice of a Child: The Impact on Children of their Mother's Imprisonment*. London. 1993. Print.

Huet, Guénhaël. "Rapport d'information fait au nom de la délégation aux droits des femmes et à l'égalité des hommes et les femmes sur le projet de loi pénitentiaire (n° 1506)." Assemblée Nationale. n° 1900, 2009. Print.

International Convention on the Rights of the Child. United Nations General Assembly, 1989. Web.

MacLanahan, S. and L. Bumpass. "Intergenerational Consequences of Family Disruption." *American Journal of Sociology* 94 (1988): 130-152. Print.

Ministère de la Justice. *Séries statistiques des personnes placées sous main de justice*, 1980-2011. Administration pénitentiaire, 2011. Print.

Murray, Joseph, David Farrington, et al. "Effects of Parental Imprisonment on Child Antisocial Behaviour and Mental Health: A Systematic Review." *Campbell Systematic Review* Sept. 2009. Web.

Murray, Joseph and Lynne Murray. "Parental Incarceration, Attachment and Child Psychopathology." *Attachment and Human Development* 12.4 (2010): 289-309. Print.

National Offender Management Service and National Probation Service. *The Offender Management Guide to Working with Women Offenders*. May 2008. Print.

Pösö, Tarja, Rosi Enroos and Tarja Vierula. "Children Residing in Prison with their Parents: An Example of Institutional Invisibility." *The Prison Journal* 90.4 (2010): 516-53. Print.

Robins, Lee, Patricia A. West and Barbara L. Herjanic. "Arrests and Delinquency in Two Generations: A Study of Black Urban Families and Their Children." *Journal of Child Psychology and Psychiatry* 16.2 (1975) : 125-140. Print.

Rodier-Guilpar, Chantal. "La prise en compte de l'intérêt de l'enfant dans l'application des peines." *Les liens familiaux à l'épreuve du droit pénal.* Ed. Alain Bouregba. Paris: Erès, 2002. 57-70. Print.

Rules for the Treatment of Women and Non-Custodial Measures for Women Offenders, the Bangkok Rules. United Nations General Assembly, 2010. Web.

Stanton, Ann M. *When Mothers Go to Jail.* Lexington, MA: Lexington Books, 1980. Print.

Trevathan, Wenda R. *Human Birth: An Evolutionary Perspective.* New Jersey: Aldine Transaction, 1987. Print.

Walklate S. *Gender, Crime and Criminal Justice.* 2nd ed. Cullompton: Willan Publishing, 2010. Print.

World Health Organization (WHO). "Innocenti Declaration on the Protection, Promotion and Support of Breastfeeding." Résolution WHA 45.34, 1990. Print.

Love Behind Bars

The Darker Side of Incarcerating Mothers

DESERIEE A. KENNEDY

A CONVICTION, stigmatization, imprisonment, and separation from families and communities are well-known consequences of criminal activity. However, one of the more enduring effects of criminal justice and child welfare policies is the fracturing of families and communities. Incarcerated mothers are at great risk of having their parental rights terminated as a consequence of incarceration, the conviction of a crime, or due to behaviors related to their conviction. Criminal justice and child welfare laws intersect in ways that far too easily increase the likelihood that incarcerated women may lose the legal right to mother their children (Genty). Although the rationale for terminating parental rights is based on a notion of stability of care for children, the result instead is to divorce children from their mothers and their communities. Parental terminations fall most heavily on women and seem tied to stereotypes about their ability to mother. In fact, the termination of parental rights may be a de facto punishment not only for their crimes but also for living contrary to mainstream ideals of motherhood. Current approaches to families of incarcerated women fail to adequately address the myriad issues facing incarcerated mothers who are dealing with complex, interlocking personal and social issues, which can cycle them in and out of prison making it difficult for them to provide for their children (Austin, Bloom, and Donahue). Society does too little to help these families stay together despite studies showing many of these women and children hope to maintain their familial bonds. This chapter asserts that, United States' policies have been slow to respond to the needs of these families and have maintained a punitive stance with regard to what are economic, social, and psychosocial problems. It suggests that incarcerated women, by challenging common understandings of what a "good mother" is and how she should behave, experience higher rates of parental terminations. This is due, in large part, because of widely-held stereotypes about women living on the margins of society. It concludes that current approaches to parental rights unfairly penalize incarcerated mothers and their children, fracturing families and destroying communities. As a result the chapter proposes that United States laws and policies prohibit relying on incarceration in parental termination decisions and focus on proof of harm to a child. Moreover, programs designed to facilitate and maintain the bond between incarcerated parent and child should be readily available.

The termination of parental rights has become a critical issue for women in light of the dramatic increase in incarceration rates in the United States. At the same time when overall crime rates in the United States have dropped, the rates of female incarceration have increased dramatically and, between 1991 and 2007 the number of mothers in prison grew by 131 percent (Glaze and Maruschak; Mauer; Kruttschnitt and Gartner). Women serving time may be doing so as a result of committing crimes relating to their efforts to provide for themselves and their children (Ferraro and Moe; Loper; Richie). It is not surprising, therefore, that Kathleen Ferraro and Angela Moe assert that, "The crimes for which they are most often arrested and incarcerated are suggestive of their gendered and raced social positioning" (Ferraro and Moe 12). Incarcerated women are more often poor, undereducated, under or unemployed before their conviction, African-American or Latina, and the majority were convicted of property and drug related crimes and were less likely than men to have committed a crime of violence (Luke; Greenfeld and Snell; Mumola 2000; Travis). FBI crime data suggests that in the period from 1980 to 2009, women experienced a higher arrest rate for larceny and theft while the arrest rate for men for similar crimes experienced a decline (Snyder). The greatest increase in the female prison population is due, however, to a rise in drug offense convictions (Kruttschnitt and Gartner).

Many of the women in the criminal justice system have been caught in a political and criminal justice morass in which politicians try to show that they are "tough on crime"—although these efforts have had a disproportionate effect. Part of the effort in the United States in the 1980's to lower crime rates was targeting illegal drug activities and the adoption of federal sentencing guidelines that increased sentences for drug related crimes and reduced judicial discretion in sentencing (Thompson). Law enforcement refocused its energies on drug possession and use rather than drug sale and manufacture. This change had the effect of pulling proportionately more women into the criminal justice system than men. For the period 1980 to 2009, overall arrests for drug possession and use in the United States more than doubled while arrests for drug sale and manufacturing experienced a decline from 1989 to 2009 (Snyder). By 2009, "about 4 of 5 drug abuse violation arrests in the U.S. ... were for drug possession or use" (Snyder 61). During the same period, the male rate of arrests for drug use and possession doubled while the female rate of arrests tripled (Snyder).

A collateral effect of these efforts was to sweep far greater numbers of women into the criminal justice system than ever before. Women became pawns in the War on Drugs and were used by law enforcement and prosecutors to reduce illegal drug activity. In fact, "During the ten-year period after the passage of mandatory drug-sentencing laws, the number of women in [U.S.] prison[s] rose by 888 percent" (Thompson 48). Professor Thompson, in his work on prisoner reentry into society, asserts, "From the law enforcement standpoint ... turning the woman into a cooperating witness, prosecutors strengthen their case against the more serious male offender. In the mind of law enforcement, these women deserve no special consideration. Those who have children are perceived as bad parents who should not be raising children" (Thompson 47; Schram). In addition, the federal sentencing guidelines severely limit judicial discretion and make gender and family ties irrelevant factors in sentencing (Thompson; Kruttschnitt and Gartner 10). Thus, the impact on women of the War on Drugs has been so great that some have coined it the "unannounced war on women" (Chesney-Lind 1998: 68; Celinska and Siegel; Dalley).

The result is that women are not only in prison in greater numbers but that they are serving longer sentences farther from home than has been true historically and this trend is likely to continue. Although recent U.S. Supreme Court cases allow judges greater discretion in sentencing, this loosening of the sentencing guidelines relies on an ad-hoc approach rather than adopting a broad policy[1] (Abramowicz). Judges may create exceptions to a general rule of a punitive response to drug use and possession but the approach falls short of adopting a systemic approach to dealing with the underlying causes of behaviors that result in arrest (Abramowicz). It is not surprising, therefore, that there has not been any significant change in the length of sentences for women since the Supreme Court cases were decided (Mauer). Thus, mothers in prison, many of whom having been convicted of drug related crimes, are typically still serving sentences of more than two years, a fact which can directly affect parental rights under mandates which push for parental terminations for children in foster care (Mumola 2000). Upon release, these women are subject to probation conditions that frequently result in their returning to prison for violations (Austin, Bloom and Donahue; Ferraro and Moe). Twenty-seven percent of the women in a study of incarcerated mothers conducted by Kathleen Ferraro and Angela Moe "had been incarcerated because of minor probation violations, such as failing to inform a probation officer of one's whereabouts or missing an appointment because of work, sickness, or lack of transportation" (21).

As rates of female incarceration have increased the rates of parental terminations have skyrocketed (Travis; Genty; Bernstein). This may be due in part to the complicated and not entirely consistent relationship between criminal justice goals and child welfare law and policy. Criminal sentencing and prison policy are guided primarily by a desire to punish, deter future criminal behavior, and to maintain security of the institution. Child welfare policies seek to protect children but there is little agreement about how to do so and what policies best serve children's developmental needs. Ideally, the state serves to protect children from harm serving as a substitute parent in situations in which a parent or relative is unfit. At the same time, families are entitled to a level of privacy and protection from unwarranted state intervention. In many instances these goals are complimentary, however, in others they conflict and there is little guidance as to where lines are to be drawn. Decisions about parenting rights and children are left to individual judges in case-by-case determinations.

Child welfare laws allow for a child to be removed from a parent's care if a child is abused or neglected. In a significant number of states the decision to terminate parental rights can be based on a combination of factors including conviction of a crime, the length of the sentence, the ability of the parent to maintain contact with the child while incarcerated as well as other matters a court deems relevant to the ability of the mother to parent including drug and alcohol use and the presence of domestic violence in the home (Ferraro and Moe; Kennedy). However, cases are not limited to those in which the parent has been convicted of a crime that demonstrates a clear danger to the child and include consideration of convictions unrelated to a parent's ability to raise their child, such as the property and drug crimes for which most women are incarcerated. The length of sentences on which a termination can be based varies and can be as short as two years or left to a judge's view of how to define a "substantial time."

Court action in parental termination cases may be triggered by federal law which mandates that children in state care be moved "toward permanency" if held in state care for fifteen out of the last 22 months (*Adoption and Safe Families Act*, 1997 [ASFA]). This policy of terminating parental rights of parents' whose children are in state care is designed to create stability and permanency by making children available for adoption. However, the approach is flawed insofar as adoption may not result for a great number of these children. Studies show that older children and African American children are adopted at lower rates, are more likely to remain in foster care for longer periods and to age out of the system (Seymour; Moses). The policy also fails to adequately account for the bond between the child and parent, the child and her larger and extended family and her community (Bernstein). Moreover, since for many incarcerated mothers, their status as a mother is a source of self-esteem and critical to their identity; they dream of being reunited with their children upon release. For these women, child removal, parental termination, and adoption can be devastating and can be the catalyst for resuming drug and alcohol use (Ferraro and Moe). An incarcerated woman whose parental rights were terminated made this comment about her children being placed up for adoption in the Ferraro and Moe study, "Until they're eighteen they've been sentenced to adoption" (27-28).

The decision to permanently sever parental rights is, in essence, a judgment about whether the parent is "fit" to raise the child and whether parental termination is in the child's best interests. Whether a parent has neglected or abandoned their child and is "unfit," and whether termination is in a child's "best interests" involve a level of subjective judgment. The high rate of parental terminations among this population, the ease with which courts can terminate parental rights, and the lack of serious and sustained efforts to support these families may reflect a view among many criminal justice and child welfare personnel that these are "throw-away" families. The nature of the assessment makes it possible for negative perceptions about these women and their lifestyles to seep into the decision making process. The judgmental stance with regard to the families of incarcerated women may occur, in part, because families are seen as the primary site for the socialization of children and despite changes in the structure of families and increased gender equity in childrearing, mothers (and not fathers) continue to be held primarily responsible for the socialization of children (Ferraro and Moe; Ganong and Coleman; Collins 2000). Women who adhere to mothering ideals are rewarded and those who differ are stigmatized (Ganong and Coleman).

Lawrence Ganong and Marilyn Coleman note, "Because of idealization, mothers are expected to have nearly super-human capacities to nurture and guide. Signs of imperfection in her children or even that she may have goals beyond motherhood ... can cause her to fall rapidly from the pedestal" (496). Incarcerated women and their behavior frequently run counter to motherhood ideals and to the belief that mothers should be self-sacrificing and put their families' needs ahead of their own (Ferraro and Moe). The myriad issues imprisoned women face fuel assumptions that these women are not "good" mothers thereby absolving any societal responsibility to redirect resources and efforts focused on keeping these families together.

At base, "Institutionalized and incarcerated women are perceived as "bad": violent, irresponsible, undependable, and unstable" (Stefan 454; Schram). Moreover, the veneration of motherhood is grounded in class-based and racial and biases with women of color and poor women seen as less able and deserving of assistance (Ferraro and Moe; Collins 2000). Incarcerated mothers are also adversely affected by their lack of education and employment histories since a majority of them did not have full time employment prior to their arrest and many made poverty level wages (Greenfeld and Snell). Their lack of economic resources, which may have influenced their decisions to engage in crime, is also used as evidence of their inability to care for their children prior to and after prison in a fitness determination. Furthermore, most incarcerated mothers are single parents and given the demonization of single mothers it is not surprising that the parents most in danger of losing their parental rights as a result of incarceration are single mothers. According to the Ganong and Coleman study, never married mothers are seen as having "poor childrearing abilities," of being "impoverished" and as "unhappy and troubled deviants from society" (Ganong and Coleman). It further revealed that they "are seen as more likely than other mothers to be 'irresponsible,' 'stupid,' 'drug abusers' who are 'unable to successfully raise children'" (Ganong and Coleman). Societal views of single mothers are also intimately linked to negative biases about poor women and women of color as mothers (Roberts).

A fitness analysis can be further complicated by the fact that incarcerated women suffer high levels of drug and alcohol dependency, mental illness, and abuse. More than half the women in state prisons and 43 percent of women in federal prisons report being drug dependent prior to incarceration and parents in prison report higher levels of drug use than nonparents (Mumola and Karberg; Mumola). Although children of addicted mothers share a number of risk factors, substance abuse alone does not necessarily mean bad parenting since factors such as poverty and a lack of support can play a role in a parent's ability to competently fulfill that role (Suchman and Luthar). Parenting problems among addicted mothers are the result of a numerous factors including insufficient social support systems (Suchman and McMahon). Female inmates also have higher rates of mental health problems than male inmates with more than 70 percent of state prisoners and 60 percent of federal prisoners exhibiting signs of mental illness (James and Glaze). In addition, more than half of all incarcerated women report having been a victim of abuse (Richie; Spatz-Widom). Of those women in prison for a violent act, a significant number were victims of domestic abuse and their abusive boyfriend or husband were their victims (Chesney-Lind).

The issues facing incarcerated women appear, therefore, to be overlapping. Thus, "Drug dependent or abusing inmates were more likely than other inmates to report troubled personal backgrounds, including experiences of physical or sexual abuse, homelessness, unemployment, parental substance abuse, and parental incarceration" (Mumola and Karberg 8). Moreover, drug and alcohol use may be related to mental health and abuse issues, reflecting efforts by the women to self-medicate. Yet the connection between childhood and domestic abuse, mental illness and illegal activity, including drug use, individually and as they relate to parenting ability has been understudied and inadequately addressed leaving judges and child welfare workers to rely on assumptions and stereotypes about these women and their parenting ability

(Ferraro and Moe; Richie; Spatz-Widom; Celinska and Siegel; Schram; Ganong and Coleman).

The contradictions inherent in idealized notions of motherhood involve an element of blaming women who fail to live up to those ideals and may fuel legal decisions that incarcerated women are incapable of caring for their children and unworthy of aid. In this way, stereotyped views of mothers in prison may affect the availability of resources and programs to assist mothering from prison as well as judicial judgments about whether to terminate parental rights. For example, the level and extent of communication between the incarcerated parent and the child can be used as evidence of child abandonment and are important factors in determining whether their rights should be terminated. However, in judging whether parents have maintained adequate contact with their children, courts are not required to assess the number of physical barriers that make ongoing contact with their children so difficult and expensive that the majority of incarcerated women reported very few visits with their children (Celinska and Siegel; Genty). The cases fail to deal with the fact that imprisoned mothers are dependent on others to bring their children to prison for visits, and visits are difficult and expensive since women's prisons are typically located more than 100 miles from an inmate's home, security protocol for visitors can be humiliating, and visiting rooms are often not "family friendly" (Travis; Mumola). Criminal justice and child welfare policies that fail to prioritize family preservation and social workers and child-caretakers who fail to aggressively foster the mother-child bond may be unconsciously reflecting a stereotyped view of incarcerated mothers that deems them unworthy of the extensive support they need to parent from prison. As one commentator has noted, "the clash between the stereotypes and stigma surrounding institutionalization and incarceration and our social vision of motherhood may result in automatic assumptions that they have no capacity to be mothers, or even in a desire to punish them for being mothers" (Stefan 454; Ganong and Coleman; Bernstein). In fact, one report on female offenders wryly states, "It is said that 'When a man goes to prison, he loses his freedom, but when a woman goes to prison, she loses her children'" (Austin, Bloom and Donahue 5).

The layers of issues with which incarcerated women frequently are dealing require multiple programs over a significant period of time as well as long-term assistance after release. While some notable programs exist their availability is far less than the demand. There are insufficient programs both in and out of prison to deal with the issues of the need for education, job training, drug and alcohol dependency, the ongoing effects of childhood and domestic abuse, depression, and mental illness faced by many imprisoned women (Austin, Bloom and Donahue). Moreover, critics maintain that many current therapeutic programs and assessment tools were designed for men and their use with women fail to adequately address their needs and may, in fact, be "discriminatory and unethical" (CAEFS; Ferraro and Moe). Despite large percentages of women in prison who are mothers, most criminal justice and child welfare systems provide few programs focused on maintaining a positive parent-child bond and family preservation (Ferraro and Moe).

Unfortunately, this failure to provide adequate assistance for this population can directly contribute to parental terminations. In addition, the lack of sufficient treatment can impact recidivism rates and the recycling of women in and out of prison, which, in turn, affect a mother's chances of retaining legal custody of her children. The complex problems incarcerated women face and the accelerated timetable under the ASFA make it difficult to meet the goals set for them by child welfare agencies to address their drug, alcohol, abuse, and mental health issues and in order to retain custody of their children, which is a significant factor in parental termination determinations. It has become easier to take a punitive approach, engaging in blaming and stereotyping in a way that supports a conclusion that imprisoned mothers are incapable of caring for their children and that termination of their parental rights would serve their children's best interests, than to support their families. Parental termination decisions fail to adequately address the reality that, as researchers Ferraro and Moe assert, "The ability to mother one's children according to social expectations and personal desires depends ultimately on one's access to the resources of time, money, health and social support" (Ferraro and Moe 14; Celinska and Siegel; Ellis, Malm and Bishop; McRoy).

States should be prohibited from weighing incarceration as a relevant fact in deciding parental terminations and programs assisting incarcerated women with their complex psychosocial problems should be uniformly available. Moreover, the United States should move towards minimizing or eliminating prison as a response to non-violent property and drug offenses and setting up community based rehabilitation programs and treatment. The United States should model the Canadian 1980s sentencing reform, which adopted an approach to sentencing that permits offenders to "serve their sentence in the community" and adopt a policy of "harm reduction" that focuses on drug use as a public health problem. Doing so would move the United States to a less punitive approach to crime, provide systemic efforts to keep mothers in their communities while providing holistic services and support in order to help preserve families and reduce parental terminations. Doing so would be consistent with seeing these women as valuable parts of their families and their communities who are in need of and deserving of assistance.

[1] *Blakely v. Washington*, 542 U.S 296 (2004); *United States v. Booker*, 543 U.S. 220 (2005); *Kimbrough v. United States*, 552 U.S. 101 (2007).

WORKS CITED

Abramowicz, Sarah. "Rethinking Parental Incarceration." *University of Colorado Law Review* 82 (2011): 793, 831-32. Print.

Adoption and Safe Families Act of 1997. Pub. Laws 105-89.111 Stat. 2115 (1997) (codified in scattered sections of Title 42 of the United States Code). Print.

Austin, James, Barbara Bloom, and Trish Donahue. *Female Offenders in the Community: An Analysis of Innovative Strategies and Programs.* San Francisco, CA: National Institute of Corrections, U.S. Department of Justice. Sept. 1992. Web.

Bernstein, Nell. *All Alone in the World.* New York: The New Press, 2005. Print.

Canadian Association of Elizabeth Fry Societies (CAEFS). "CAEFS Fact Sheets: Human and Fiscal Costs of Prison, Importance of Community Options, Women in Prison, Aboriginal Women." Ottawa: Author, 2011. Web.

Celinska, Katarzyna and Jane A. Siegel. "Mothers in Trouble: Coping with Actual or Pending Separation from Children Due to Incarceration." *The Prison Journal* 90 (2010): 447-474. Web.

Chesney-Lind, Meda. "The Forgotten Offender." *Corrections Today* 1 (Dec. 1998): 66-73. Web. 17 Oct. 2011.

Chesney-Lind, Meda and Lisa Pasko. *The Female Offender: Girls, Women, and Crime.* Thousand Oaks, CA: Sage Publications, Inc., 2003. Print.

Collins, Patricia Hill. "Producing the Mothers of the Nation: Race, Class and Contemporary U.S. Population Policies." *Women, Citizenship and Difference.* Eds. Yuval-Davis and Webner. London: Zed Books, 1999. 118-119. Print.

Collins, Patricia Hill. *Black Feminist Thought: Knowledge, Consciousness, and the Politics of Empowerment.* New York: Routledge, 2000. Print.

Dalley, Lanette P. "Policy Implications Relating to Inmate Mothers and Their Children: Will the Past Be Prologue?" *The Prison Journal* 82.2 (2002): 234-268. Web. 17 Oct. 2011.

Ellis, Raquel, Karin Malm, and Erin Bishop. "The Timing of Termination of Parental Rights: A Balancing Act for Children's Best Interests." *Child Trends* (September 2009): 1-13. Print.

Ferraro, Kathleen J., and Angela Moe. "Mothering, Crime, and Incarceration." *Journal of Contemporary Ethnography* 32.1 (2003): 12-13. Print.

Ganong, Lawrence H. and Marilyn Coleman. "The Content of Mother Stereotypes." *Sex Roles* 32 (1995): 495-497, 507-510. Print.

Genty, Philip M. "Damage to Family Relationships as a Collateral Consequence of Parental Incarceration." *Fordham Urban Law Journal* 30 (2003): 1671. Print.

Glaze, Lauren E, and Laura M. Maruschak. *Parents in Prison and Their Minor Children.* U.S. Department of Justice, Office of Justice Programs (NCJ 222984). 30 March 2011. Web.

Grant, Judith. "Incarcerated Women and Drug Abuse: An International Perspective." *The Journal of the Institute of Justice and International Studies* 7. (2007): 129-42. Print.

Greenfeld, Lawrence A. and Tracy L. Snell. *Women Offenders.* U.S. Department of Justice, Office of Justice Programs (NCJ 175688). 3 Oct. 2000. Web.

James, Doris J. and Lauren Glaze. *Mental Health Problems of Prison and Jail Inmates.* Washington, DC: U.S. Department of Justice, Office of Justice Programs, Bureau of Justice Statistics (NCJ 213600). 14 Dec. 2006. Web.

Kennedy, Deseriee. "Children, Parents, and the State: The Construction of a New Family Ideology." *Berkeley Journal of Gender, Law, and Justice* 26 (2011): 78-138. Print.

Kruttschnitt, Candace, and Rosemary Gartner. "Women's Imprisonment." *Crime and Justice* 30 (2003): 1-80. Print.

Loper, Ann B. "How Do Mothers in Prison Differ from Non-Mothers." *Journal of Child and Family Studies* 15 (2006): 82-95. Print.

Luke, Katherine P. "Mitigating the Ill Effects of Maternal Incarceration on Women in Prison and Their Children." *Child Welfare* 81 (2002): 929, 931-32. Print.

Mauer, Mark. "Sentencing Reform Amid Mass Incarcerations—Guarded Optimism." *Criminal Justice* 26 (2011): 27-36. Print.

McRoy, R. "Acknowledging Disproportionate Outcomes and Changing Service Delivery." *Child Welfare* 87.2 (2008): 205-10. Web. 18 Oct. 2011.

Moses, Marilyn C. "Correlating Incarcerated Mothers, Foster Care, and Mother-Child Reunification." *Corrections Today* (Oct. 2006): 98-100. Print.

Mumola, Christopher J. *Incarcerated Parents and their Children.* Washington, DC: U.S. Department of Justice, Office of Justice Programs (NCJ 182335). Aug. 2000. Web.

Mumola, Christopher J., and Jennifer C. Karberg. *Drug Use and Dependence, State and Federal Prisoners, 2004.* Washington, DC: U.S. Department of Justice, Office of Justice Programs (NCJ 213530). 19 Jan. 2007. Web.

Richie, Beth E. "Exploring the Link Between Violence Against Women and Women's Involvement in Illegal Activity." *Research on Women and Girls in the Justice System: Plenary Papers of the 1999 Conference on Criminal Justice Research and Evaluation – Enhancing Policy and Practice Through Research* 3. (2000): 4-6. Washington, DC: U.S. Department of Justice, Office of Justice Programs Bureau, National Institute of Justice. Web.

Roberts, Dorothy E. "Racism and Patriarchy in the Meaning of Motherhood." *America University Journal of Gender and the Law* 1 (1993): 6. Print.

Schram, Pamela J. "An Exploratory Study: Stereotypes About Mothers in Prison." *Journal of Criminal Justice* 27 (1999): 411- 426. Print.

Seymour, Cynthia. "Children with Parents in Prison: Child Welfare Policy,

Program, and Practice Issues." *Child Welfare* 77.5 (1998): 469-493. Print.

Snyder, Howard N. *Arrest in the United States, 1980-2009*. Washington, DC: U.S. Department of Justice, Office of Justice Programs (NCJ 234319). Sept. 2011. Web.

Spatz-Widom, Cathy. "Childhood Victimization and the Derailment of Girls and Women to the Criminal Justice System." *Research on Women and Girls in the Justice System: Plenary Papers of the 1999 Conference on Criminal Justice Research and Evaluation – Enhancing Policy and Practice Through Research* 3 (2000): 29-30. Washington, DC: U.S. Department of Justice, Office of Justice Programs Bureau, National Institute of Justice. Web.

Stefan, Susan. "Whose Egg Is It Anyway? Reproductive Rights of Incarcerated, Institutionalized and Incompetent Women." *Nova Law Review* 13 (1989): 405, 454-55. Print.

Suchman, Nancy E. and Suniya S. Luthar. "Maternal Addiction, Child Maladjustment and Socio-Demographic Risks: Implications for Parenting Behaviors." *Addiction* 95.9 (2000): 1417-1428. Web.

Suchman, Nancy E. and Thomas J. McMahon. "How Early Bonding, Depression, Illicit Drug Use, and Perceived Support Work Together to Influence Drug-Dependent Mothers' Caregiving." *American Journal of Orthopsychiatry* 75(3) (2005): 431-445. Web.

Thompson, Anthony C. *Releasing Prisoners, Redeeming Communities*. New York: New York University Press, 2008: 21-26. Print.

The Expert Committee Review of the Correctional Service of Canada's Ten-Year Status Report on Women's Corrections 1996–2006. *Moving Forward with Women's Corrections*. Ottawa: Correctional Service of Canada, 2006. Web.

Travis, Jeremy. "Families and Children." *Federal Probation* 69.1 (2005): 31-42. Print.

Mitigating the Plight of Incarcerated Mothers in India

Issues and Policy Interventions

UPNEET LALLI

O NE OF THE HARSHEST penal sanctions the state can impose upon an individual who has broken the law is imprisonment. Incarceration has irrevocable economic, social and psychological consequences. Incarceration has costs to the individual as well as to the individual's family and society at large.

Efforts undertaken in India the last few decades to humanise the penal system have primarily focused on issues faced by the predominantly male general prison population. Women, however, constitute around 5.04 percent of more than 10.1 million held in penal institutions throughout the world ("World Prison Brief"). Women's issues have not been given due consideration in Indian research regarding incarceration. They are held in a system conceived, designed and organised primarily for men. This chapter i) examines some issues relating to women, crime and incarceration of women in India; ii) provides a demographic profile of female inmates in India; iii) analyzes unique stresses and mental health issues related to incarcerated mothers in the Indian socio-cultural context; and iv) delineates policy implications and interventions pertaining to issues faced by incarcerated mothers in India.

The profile of women prisoners in India is different from that of men. Women may be in prison for offences ranging from petty theft to violent crimes and drug trafficking. Their pathways to crime and life circumstances differ from those of men and the biggest punishment is separation from their children.

Over the last two decades, the imprisonment rate of women has seen a dramatic increase in countries like the U.S., Hong Kong and Thailand (around 20 percent). However, it has remained stable in others (e.g. India). In Asia and Pacific regions, women constitute around 5.5 percent of the total prison population ("World Prison Brief").

The small number of women prisoners in itself can be the reason for several discriminations. Imprisonment impacts women differently than men and can be more devastating for women's families and identities than it is for men due to the negation of their culturally ascribed nurturing role. Female incarceration imposes many constraints and adverse effects on the mother-child bond, the family unit, and the development of children born to women while they are incarcerated. Incarceration of women imposes tremendous familial, social and economic costs.

THE STATUS OF MOTHERS IN ANCIENT INDIAN CULTURE

In Indian cultural traditions, the mother is placed on a pedestal, next to God. Motherhood is considered the greatest glory of Hindu women. The Taittiriya Upanishad teaches, "Matridevobhava" — "Let your mother be God to you."

The significance of mother is further amplified in this verse from the epic Mahabharata:

> There is no shelter like the mother. There is no refuge like the mother.
> There is no defense like the mother.... The mother is one's own body.

WOMANHOOD IN CONTEMPORARY INDIAN SOCIETY

The position of women in contemporary Indian society is paradoxical. While on the one hand they may be the most empowered, they may also be the most oppressed. There are obvious dualities in the perceived role of women in the ancient and modern cultural scenario. While women are guaranteed equality under the Constitution, legal protection has little effect in the face of prevailing patriarchal traditions. Indian society is passing through fundamental changes in socio-economic and cultural spheres. A daughter is still viewed as a liability in some Indian families (mainly due to dowry) and is reflected in the adverse sex ratio. At the same time, globalization and urbanization lead to increased mobility and increased participation of women in professional areas. India has the largest number of professionally qualified women, and they have excelled in fields ranging from politics to literature. Many women are occupying high positions of power and decision-making. However, many others may silently suffer violence and subjugation. A vast majority of women may be impoverished in terms of decision making and may be living in a constricted space.

Marriage and dowry go hand in hand in Indian society. Dowry is the money and other valuable items, like jewelry, which parents give away to their daughters at the time of marriage. Initially, the practice of dowry started as a means to give girls their due in ancestral property as all physical property was inherited by the sons. Later on, it was used as "seed money" or property for establishing a new household. The amount given was decided by the girl's parents and was voluntary. However, over a period of time, the practice degenerated and the groom's family started demanding money for marriage. This custom is prevalent in varying degrees in all sections of Indian society. Today, due to a globalized consumerist economy, the demand for money and material goods continues, sometimes even after marriage.

The dowry tradition can have extremely negative consequences for women. It often results in various forms of domestic violence, including cruelty, torture and in extreme cases, even the bride's death. Sometimes the girls commit suicide when their in-laws pressure them to bring more money from their parents. Deaths of newly married women (i.e. "dowry deaths") may take place through hanging, poisoning and sometimes through bride burning.

To eradicate social problems that result from the dowry tradition, strict laws in the form of the 1961 *Dowry Prohibition Act* and provisions in the Indian Penal Code (section 498A, 304B) were introduced. The law's intention is to punish the husband and his relatives who torture and harass the woman with a view to coerce her or her relatives to meet the unlawful demand of dowry. Section 498-A of I.P.C. provides a sentence of three years imprisonment and fine for the husband or relatives who subject the woman to cruelty. Any unnatural death of a woman within the first seven years of her marriage is investigated. If it is perceived that the woman was subjected to cruelty, on account of dowry, it is deemed as a dowry death, which is punishable with not less than seven years imprisonment, extendable to life. There have been 8,391 dowry deaths and 89,546 cases of torture for dowry during 2010; 4,529 sentenced prisoners were convicted for causing dowry deaths. Culture becomes a significant factor in understanding the nature of women's crimes, including dowry crimes, under which both older and younger women (mostly mothers and their daughters) have been imprisoned.

However, enacting a law is a limited solution to deep rooted social problems, and the practice of dowry continues. Moreover, a misuse of the law in relation to dowries by families has also been reported. Its strict provisions have been abused in some cases by the girl's family. Merely alleging the name of a relative in the complaint is enough to arrest the entire family. A number of dowry complaints from the bride's side have also been aimed at settling personal scores. As a consequence, there are a number of older mothers in law, sisters in law, and sometimes three generations in prisons, charged with dowry offences. Many may be innocent. Many are probably not. Unfortunately, in Indian patriarchal family systems, women may not only be victims but also silent collaborators in dowry crimes. Ultimately the instigators of her crime are by and large nested in their immediate familial and societal life space. Dowry crimes by women emanate from stressful family situations, marital maladjustments, and conflict prone relationships with husbands and other family members (Ahuja).

From religious scriptures to folklore and popular culture as depicted in Hindi films, a mother is glorified in various ways. The role ascribed to her by scriptures, and prescribed by society and internalized through socialization is that of a 'mother'. Hence the pleasures and pains of fulfillment and non-fulfillment of that role are equally severe. A loss of that role can negate a woman's sense of self.

Indian women construct their identities mainly in terms of relationships—as mothers, daughters, wives. In prison, too, they form these informal relationships. They know they have lost the divine image, right from the moment of arrest, and will now have to bear the severe ignominy and shame of breaking the social norms. A woman in custody has to abruptly encounter a hostile world with unpredictable, ambiguous events of the trial period and then an alien, insensitive prison system. These mothers' primary concern is to protect, care and nurture their children, even when they are undergoing their own tribulations.

PRISON SYSTEM IN INDIA AND PROFILE OF WOMEN PRISONERS

India has a low imprisonment rate of 31 per 100,000 and women constitute 4.1 percent of the total prison population of 376,969 inmates (Government of India 2009). Prison administration is the state's responsibility, hence some variations exist across different federal states. There are four substantive prison laws in India, namely, the *Prison Act,* 1894; *Prisoners' Act,* 1900; *The Transfer of Prisoners' Act,* 1950 and the *Prisoners (Attendance in Courts) Act,* 1955. Prisoners sentenced to a longer period of confinement are lodged in Central Prisons, which have a larger capacity in comparison to District and Sub jails. The other types of prisons include the Women Prison, Borstal Schools, Open Jails, and Special jails. Out of the total 1,374 prisons, there are only 18 exclusive female prisons in which 2,758 inmates are accommodated. The total population of the female prison inmates in India was 15,406, including 702 foreign women inmates.

Over the last two decades the trend in the female criminality has been almost constant, i.e. around three to four percent (Government of India 2010). The female percentage for arrested persons under the Indian Penal Code was at 6.2 percent (181,699 females) and 3.1 percent (149,735 females) under the Special and Local Laws. The percentage of women arrested was higher for those crimes that are perpetrated on women such as cruelty by husbands and relatives followed by the importation of girls and dowry deaths. More women were arrested for offences of public morality like *Immoral Trafficking and the Prohibition Act.* The majority of the arrested women fell within two age groups (18-30 and 30-50 years) with almost 75 percent being mothers. Most of those arrested are likely to be remanded in prison for at least a week until they are granted bail or are otherwise released. The average trial period is around three years. There were 4,588 women convicts (29.8 percent), 10,687

Table 1a–Age and Legal Status of Indian Women Inmates

Category	16 to 18 years	% share	18 to 30 years	% share	30–50 years	% share	Above 50 years	% share	Total
Convicts	0	0.00	1236	28.55	2235	51.62	859	19.84	4330
Undertrials	3	0.03	3747	36.52	5008	48.81	1503	14.65	10261
Detenues	0	0.00	16	16.00	68	68.00	16	16.00	133
Others	0	0.00	4	30.77	9	69.23	0	0.00	13
Total	3	0.02	5003	34.02	7320	49.78	2378	16.17	14704

(Source: NCRB Statistics, 2009)

women undertrials, (69.4 percent) 101 detenues and 30 others. The age and legal status of Indian women inmates is provided in Table 1a, while Table 1b exhibits the data regarding the number of women inmates who have children with them in the prison.

As can be seen from Table 1a, undertrials constitute a majority of the prison population. Women convicts are predominantly around the 30-50 years age group. And Table 1b indicates that 1.5 percent of these women inmates had children with them in prison, who were below the age of six years.

As is evident from Table 1b a total of 1,705 children were living with their mothers inside the prison. The legally permissible age for women to keep their children with them inside the prison is six years. A large proportion of incarcerated women is married and are mothers but most have children living outside the prison. The issue of incarcerated mothers in India has not been holistically addressed so far. Some issues related to mothers like (i) those who are expecting or those who have just given birth; and (ii) those having children living with them inside the prison, have been touched upon. However, norms governing mothers whose children are outside the prison system are still grey areas and ignore the specific needs of such mothers and their children. For Indian mothers whose total life revolves around the children, imprisonment is a devastating experience.

Table 1b: Women Prisoners with Children

Categories of Women Prisoners with Children	Number	No. of Children
Convict Women Prisoners with Children	428	497
Undertrials Women Prisoners with Children	1063	1166
Other Women Prisoners with Children	19	35
Detenues Women Prisoners with Children	05	07
Total No. of Women Prisoners with Children	1515	1705

(Source: NCRB Statistics, 2010)

STRESS, STIGMA AND RELATED ISSUES OF INCARCERATED MOTHERS

While some of the stressors and problems of incarceration are universal, there are also unique oppressions due to socio-cultural peculiarities of women in Indian society. Arrest and imprisonment generate many social and mental health problems and exacerbate existing ones. The severity of the stigma for incarcerated women depends upon the nature of their crime and the surrounding community's attitude (Murray 2005). Crimes viewed as particularly abhorrent by the community seem to attract a greater stigma (such as the violent crime-murder of husband/partner or close family member). Incarcerated mothers have to bear the brunt of societal and familial ostracism for failing in their motherly duty.

It has been found that the trauma associated with the separation can impose emotional, psychological and physical problems for not only those children, but also for incarcerated mothers (Bloom and Steinhart). A major stress is that, while an incarcerated mother is socially constructed in Indian culture to be like an omnipresent God, she loses control over the children in the parenting process. As a consequence, readjustment is required (Murray 2007). Incarcerated mothers may also worry about the quality and type of care their children are receiving as well as reunification with their children (Houck and Loper; Warren et al.). In prison, a woman has no control over her contact with her children (Halperin and Harris; Young and Smith). Incarcerated mothers also face major reintegration issues after release from prison (O'Brien). Stigma and feelings of isolation of the family members compound her difficulties. Inmate mothers are not only seen to offend against society, but also against their role as mothers (Cunningham).

Female criminality in India has been a neglected subject of study. The majority of the women prisoners are from a rural background and illiterate. Most of them belong to the marginalized, economically and socially backward sections of society (Bajpai and Bajpai). These women prisoners face triple subjugation due to poverty, caste and gender (Cherukuri). This further leads to women's hesitation to communicate their needs and grievances to either the prison staff or inspecting authorities except when they reply to specific queries. Thus, very few complaints are lodged by women to either the judiciary or human rights bodies. Even during the course of an inspection by a judge or higher prison authority, the inmates are made to line up, their heads generally covered with a dupatta (veil), eyes downcast, holding a card identifying their alleged crime; the dehumanizing process can hardly lead to a redressal of a grievance.

A study conducted by PRAYAS in state of Maharashtra (1994-97) on imprisoned mothers showed that (i) after being arrested, most women reported that they were not allowed to meet their children, and were at a loss about what immediate action to take for their children; ii) women prisoners reported acute anxiety about the welfare of their children and had strong apprehensions about the children not recognizing and respecting them after their release; (iii) there was overwhelming distress about the coping ability of their minor/dependent children in absence of a father or a caregiver.

In another study on women's mental health in the central prison Bangalore, depression was found to be common in women inmates. Emotional reactions ranged from denial, anger, withdrawal and finally acceptance of their situation (Murthy and Parthasarthy). A fatalistic attitude is generally adopted as a coping mechanism. Another study on children of women prisoners in Indian Jails (Chattoraj) revealed challenging conditions and deprivations faced by children lodged with their mothers in different prisons in India.

The following discourses are based on the first-hand experience of the author and narratives of female inmates (names changed) in three states of India. The metaphors may differ, but the common threads of worry and anxiety about their children bind these women together.

> Prema was arrested on the charge of murdering her husband. Her children were in the custody of her in-laws, and she had absolutely no contact with them. Obviously, the relations with the husband's family had broken down. There was no letter, nor anyone to inform her about the well-being of her small children aged seven, nine, and eleven years old. Equally worrisome was the prospect of permanently losing custody of the children.

> Rajni, convicted for murder, has been in prison for around two-and-a-half years. During that time, she had not seen her three children, who were living with her sister-in-law. During the meeting with the author, she just kept crying and requesting that an arrangement be devised to enable her to see her children. The worry about her 12-year-old daughter, in particular, was immense.

The incarcerated women's relationships with their children who remain outside has to be understood in conjunction with their other relationships outside the prison. Women who are convicted for dowry related crimes have more stable relationships with their outside families. As dowry offences involve at least two family members, the other members of the family may also be in prison. A strained relationship with caregivers (e.g., with in-laws) results in less contact between mothers and their children. One inmate responded that her children had not come even once in three years, as they were living with her in-laws. There is also a fear in some that their children may succumb to wayward habits leading to inter-generational crime and other maladjustments like drug abuse. Marital dissolution may also be one main consequence of imprisonment, one that affects both the mother and child.

Moreover, where both the husband and wife are in prison (as in Sheela's case), there is no family meeting and bonding because they are lodged in different jails. Their children are the "prison orphans"; they are under state care and rarely have contact with their parents. Because there are strict regulations directed at keeping male and female prisoners apart in Indian prisons, there is no provision for family meetings even when both parents are held in the same prison. In most prisons, the visiting area is unfriendly—iron grills separate the inmates from the visitors. Thus, hugging the child is impossible and audibility is poor. The Prison Superintendent has sole right to allow freer *"mulaqat"* (meeting) and thus much depends on his discretion.

Family contact serves as a formal coping mechanism for stress. However, visits from either the family to prison or from the prisoner to the family on temporary leave schemes (like parole or furlough), while not always possible, are the most direct way of maintaining family relationships. Prison regulations, distances to be travelled, competing demands on family members, their willingness to visit and requisite money for visiting can prevent or limit direct contact between children and their imprisoned parents. Undertrials also informally meet their family members during the course of the court hearings. The telephone contact in some states facilitates easier accessibility and problem solving, which helps to mitigate some of their stress.

JUDICIAL AND POLICY INTERVENTIONS
SPECIFICALLY FOR INCARCERATED MOTHERS

The prison laws in India have been more or less static and do not emphasize any rights of prisoners. Prison reform has been largely affected by the legislative gap largely filled by the Supreme Court in its various decisions on prison related issues. The concept of "life" and "liberty" under Article 21 of the Indian Constitution has now been widely interpreted by the Judiciary to ensure dignity to prisoners (Lalli). Further, various Committees on prison reforms have recommended some changes in prison policy and the system. Earlier, the All India Committee on Jail Reforms (1980-83) and later, the National Expert Committee on Women Prisoners (1987), had stressed certain aspects pertaining to women inmates such as separate prisons, medical examination of newly admitted women prisoners, child birth outside prisons, etc.

The Supreme Court of India in 2004 while deciding the case of *R. D. Upadhyay vs. State of Andhra Pradesh*, dealt with the gender-specific issues of pregnant and nursing women in prison and their children. The Honourable

Court laid the minimum standards for care of mother and child in terms of proper pre-natal and post-natal care for pregnant women. Local birth registration for children born during incarceration was initiated to avoid stigma (iii). The courts dealing with cases of women prisoners, whose children are in prison with them, were directed so as to prioritize such cases and decide them expeditiously. In compliance to the directions, crèches have opened up in all women prisons, special diets for lactating mothers and babies are offered, though the condition varies from state to state. Medical checkups for pregnant women, health education classes for mothers, and vaccines for children are being provided. The state of women prisoners and their young children in prisons today is still far from satisfactory. However, the recommendations made by earlier-cited Expert Committees and the Courts have been implemented half-heartedly. Medical facilities continue to be inadequate. Scarce resources, lack of will, and general apathy have also resulted in a woeful neglect of women in prison. The marginalization of such women prisoners happens not just because of their lesser numbers, but also because there has always been a sense of complacency on issues surrounding women prisoners, as has been the case with women in general.

POLICY AND ORGANISATIONAL INTERVENTIONS FOR INCARCERATED MOTHERS

In India, changes in the *Prison Act* and related legislation are long overdue. Flexibility is needed to respond to the specific needs of pregnant women, nursing mothers and women with children. These changes need to be in consonance with the United Nations Bangkok Rules, or Rules for the Treatment of Women Prisoners and Non-custodial Measures for Women Offenders. In brief, the following interventions are suggested:

> Better physical and medical care facilities, including-pre natal and post natal care, should be made available for women inmates with children. The rights of both mothers and babies need to be considered in relation to pregnancy, childbirth, breastfeeding and post-natal care in prison.

Specialized psychological support and counseling needs to be provided to take care of the mental health needs of women inmates. A more purposeful prison regime will also help them in successful societal reintegration. Social workers/welfare officers can provide support services for children who are not permitted to stay with their imprisoned mother and also ensure that the child's relationship with their mother is maintained. Family contact is pivotal for the prisoner's reintegration, hence it should be facilitated by all reasonable means.

The visiting area needs to be improved in all prisons. A liberal system of telephonic contact for mothers in prison should be permitted. Extended contact with children should be encouraged, where possible. New prisons can have family units where children above six years can stay over the weekend with their mothers. To counterbalance those women prisoners who are detained far from home, the state can provide a travel allowance. Probation and short detention suspensions for women with caring responsibilities for children will be most helpful. Whenever possible, they should be permitted to make arrangements for their children. Decisions regarding early conditional release (parole), should favourably take into account women prisoners' caring responsibilities, as well as their specific social reintegration needs. Amendments in Parole rules need to be made to allow convicted women parole in the last months of pregnancy and until at least one month post delivery. Rules should permit parole during critical periods—like a child's illness, school admission, examination time, and the arranging of a child's marriage.

Very few incarcerated women and those with children pose a risk to public safety. The provisions of the Tokyo Rules should guide the development of appropriate alternatives to women offenders. Avoiding custodial sentences and pre-trial detention where possible will prevent many of the negative outcomes for both parents and children. Long term convicts can be shifted to open jails to enable better contact with their children. While building responsibility it also ensures a smoother transition to normal life. A restorative justice processes for mothers with dependent children should be used. A gender responsive justice system needs to be developed to consider the totality of women's lives and their roles in crime. It should not punish them from one prison to another. A continuum of care and support services are needed to meet the re-entry and reintegration needs of incarcerated mothers.

CONCLUSION

Ultimately, unless they die in prison, the vast majority of Indian prisoners will re-enter society one day. Unfortunately in India, incarcerated mothers are not a priority for the government because they are typically poor, illiterate and powerless. As marginal stakeholders, they have little voice. The ambivalence of the state and society to issues of incarcerated mothers must give way to a clearer approach. Society has to recognise their vulnerabilities, and the damages that the incarceration of mothers can have to the mothers themselves, their children and the community at large. It is time that the Criminal Justice System became responsive to gender specific needs and issues. The need for alternatives to imprisonment, better health care (including mental health), better contact with the family, support systems that provide for her reintegration needs, should receive much more attention from policy makers and prison administrators. Restoring a sense of dignity to incarcerated mothers is possible provided they are treated as individuals of self-worth and dignity.

WORKS CITED

Ahuja, R. *Violence Against Women*. New Delhi: Rawat Publications, 1969. Print.

Bajpai, A. and P. K. Bajpai. *Female Criminality in India*. New Delhi: Rawat Publications, 2000. Print.

Bloom, B. and D. Steinhart. *Why Punish the Children? A Reappraisal of the Children of Incarcerated Mothers in America*. San Francisco: National Council on Crime and Delinquency, 1993. Print.

Chattoraj, B. N. "Children of Women Prisoners in Indian Jails." LNJN National Institute of Criminology and Forensic Sciences, Ministry of Home Affairs, Government of India, 2000. Print.

Cherukuri, S. *Women in Prison: An Insight into Captivity and Crime*. New Delhi: Cambridge University Press India Pvt. Ltd., 2008. Print.

Cunningham, A. "Forgotten Families: The Impacts of Imprisonment." *Family Matters* 59 (Winter 2001): 35-38. Print.

Government of India. *Prison Statistics*. National Crime Records Bureau, 2009. Print.

Government of India. *Crime in India*. National Crime Records Bureau, 2010. Print.

Government of India. *Report of all India Committee on Jail Reforms 1980-83*. Justice Mulla Committee, Ministry of Home Affairs, New Delhi, 1984. Print.

Government of India. *Report of National Expert Committees on Women Prisoners* Justice Krishna Iyer Committee, 1986-87. Print.

Halperin, R. and J. L. Harris. "Parenting Rights of Incarcerated Mothers with Children in Foster Care: A Policy Vacuum." *Feminist Studies* 30.2 (2004): 339-352. Print.

Houck, K. D. and A. B. Loper. "The Relationship of Parenting Stress to Adjustment Among Mothers in Prison." *American Journal of Orthopsychiatry* 72.4 (2002): 545-558. Print.

Lalli, U. *Human Rights in Indian Prisons*. A monograph. New Delhi: Institute of Social Sciences, 2009. Web.

Murray, J. "The Effects of Imprisonment on Families and Children of Prisoners." Ed. A. Liebling and S. Maruna. *The Effects of Imprisonment*. Portland: Willan, 2005. 452-3. Print.

Murray, J. "The Cycle of Punishment: Social Exclusion of Prisoners and Their Children." *Criminology and Criminal Justice* 7.1 (2007): 55-81. Print.

Murthy, S. and R. Parthasarthy. *Manual on Mental Health Care for Women in Custody.* 1998. NIMHANS,Bangalore and NCW,Delhi. Print.

O'Brien, P. *Making It In The "Free World": Women in Transition from Prison.* New York: SUNY Press, 2001. Print.

Prayas. *Forced Separation: Children of Imprisoned Mothers (An Exploration in Two Indian Cities).* Mumbai Prayas. Tata Institute of Social Sciences, Mumbai, 2002. Print.

R. D. Upadhyay vs. State of Andhra Pradesh and Others. AIR 2006 SC 1946. Print.

Rules for the Treatment of Women and Non-Custodial Measures for Women Offenders, the Bangkok Rules. United Nations General Assembly, 2010. Web.

Warren, J. I., S. Hurt, A. B. Loper, and P. Chauhan. "Exploring Prison Adjustment Among Female Inmates: Issues of Measurement and Prediction." *Criminal Justice and Behavior* 31 (2004): 624-645. Print.

"World Prison Brief." Prisonstudies.org. Web. 2.10.2011.

Young, D. S. and C. J. Smith. "When Moms Are Incarcerated: The Needs of Children, Mothers, and Caregivers" *Families in Society* 81 (2000): 130–141.

Care and Respect

Mothering and Relatedness in Multigenerational Prison Settings

MANUELA P. DA CUNHA AND RAFAELA GRANJA

IN PORTUGAL, as in many other countries, prisons are gendered institutions. Men and women are incarcerated in different institutions and separate prison buildings. Further, prisons are shaped by gender ideologies and enhance gender asymmetries (Cunha 1994, 2007; Cunha and Granja). Parenting is one of the aspects in which such disparities become most salient. When the choice to allow infant children to stay with the imprisoned parent is afforded by prison institutions, it is typically available only in female prisons.[1]

Parenting is generally a more critical issue for female inmates than male inmates. While male and female prisoners may both be parents, it is more likely that mothers were the primary caregivers of children prior to their incarceration (e.g. Greene, Haney and Hurtado; La Vigne, Brooks and Shollenberger). This is especially true because, in many cases, fathers were already also imprisoned or were absentee parents (Henriques; Greene, Haney and Hurtado); parenting is a source of increased concern and responsibility for mothers upon their imprisonment.[2]

Incarcerated mothers face many challenges when seeking to maintain their relationships with their children. Besides trying to ensure their children's presence and maintain a sense of permanent connection with them,[3] mothers separated from their offspring by incarceration struggle to maintain parental authority and remain actively engaged in their children's lives. It is difficult to make decisions about their children's future, provide them with advice and stay informed of their whereabouts and progress in school (Celinska and Siegel; Enos). Incarcerated mothers may also retain some aspects of their role as financial providers for their children by sending money to children's caregivers.

Separation from their children is often a constant source of incarcerated mothers' stress. This separation can generate feelings of being a "bad mother" (Mahan; Morash and Schram), even when children's traumatic experiences have less to do with their mothers' conduct *per se* than with the unstable and volatile context in which they live (Cunha and Granja; Verea). Reuniting with their children is generally at the top of most inmate mothers' aspirations and is an important hope even for those mothers who didn't live with their children prior to incarceration (Datesman and Cales; Kazura; Eigenberg and Berry; Ferraro and Moe).

As recent research has shown (Comfort; Shamai), rather than invariably damaging relationships, incarceration can in the short term have more complex effects. In some cases, it may open venues for strengthening or renewing mother-child bonds, away from pressures and problems outside. In some cases, incarceration may interrupt destructive cycles of substance abuse and domestic violence. Prison has a potential to be a turning point in some troubled parent-child relationships, inasmuch as incarceration some-times functions, however inadequately, as the only social agency available for poor populations.

Women's carceral institutions may emphasize disparities along lines of gender through a formal or informal focus on reproduction and domesticity to the detriment of other aspects of women's lives (Cunha; Verea 43). An inmate's own discursive construction of gender and the way motherhood is sometimes hyperbolized in identity management may contribute to further emphasis on gender disparities. Women separated from their children by incarceration sometimes try to overcome the contradiction between the discursive exaltation of maternal identity and the fact that the role of mother is dissociated from that of caregiver for most incarcerated mothers. More specifically, we have shown elsewhere how incarcerated mothers try to perform that identity by mothering *from* prison (Cunha and Granja).

In this chapter we will confine ourselves to aspects of motherhood and forms of relatedness as they emerge *within* prison in different situations. In recent decades, widespread phenomena of mass imprisonment in Euro-American societies (e.g. Comfort; Pattillo, Weiman and Western; Wacquant) have changed and complicated the social landscape of prison.

One of the effects of mass imprisonment has been the co-imprisonment of relatives of multiple generations (Cunha 2002).[4] In-prison relationships be-tween mothers and their offspring now include children as well as adults—an aspect that has received little attention in the literature (but see Cunha 2002, Cunha forthcoming) and which raises additional issues regarding confined mothering and motherhood.

This paper draws on fieldwork, conducted at different periods over the course of three decades, in two Portuguese carceral settings located in the main metropolitan areas or the country: *Estabelecimento Prisional de Tires* (hereafter Tires) and *Estabelecimento Prisional de Santa Cruz do Bispo* (hereafter

Santa Cruz). The first was created in 1954 in the outskirts of Lisbon and is still today the major female penal institution in the country; the second opened in 2005 near the northern city of Oporto.

Although these two penitentiaries are intended to serve a similar type of penal population,[5] the contrast between their different historical origin and regional location allow for a more controlled grasp of regularities and variations between them and for an overall perspective regarding the aspects we set to approach in this paper.

Fieldwork in Tires was conducted in two periods separated by a decade, of two and one year respectively (1987-1989; 1997). This fieldwork achieved unrestricted access to all prison facilities. Besides conducting seventy in-depth interviews,[6] the fieldwork allowed for the observation and participation in most prison activities and daily life (which included those of mothers with children behind bars), as well as for engaging in informal individual and group conversations with prisoners on a regular basis and under varied circumstances. The six-month fieldwork in Santa Cruz during 2011 consisted of ethnographic observations centered mainly on prison visitors (especially family members) and in-depth interviews with 20 incarcerated women.

Tires' imprisoned population, which in 1997 reached 823 prisoners, had evolved towards a striking social and penal homogeneity in the span of only a decade. In 1997, 76 percent of women were imprisoned for drug trafficking compared to 37 percent ten years earlier, and property offenders represented no more than 13 percent. The majority of those convicted (69 percent) were serving sentences of more than five years. Prisoners increasingly came from segments of the working class and reflected the most deprived of economic and educational capital.

From 1987 to 1997, the proportion of women who held jobs in the bottom tier of the service economy rose from 4 percent to 33 percent, and the proportion who had never attended school or gone beyond the fourth grade rose from 47 percent to 59 percent. In Santa Cruz this proportion climbed to 67 percent today. This prison has an average population of 265 inmates between convicts and detainees. Most were imprisoned for drug trafficking (62 percent) and most of those convicted for more than 1 year (91 percent) were serving sentences of more than six years.

Santa Cruz thus approximately reproduces the pattern in Tires', albeit more mitigated in some respects, including the fact that an important proportion of prisoners have relatives imprisoned in the same institution or in other prison facilities.[7] Circles of co-confined kin in the same institution can be quite large (reaching up to more than a dozen people) and may extend to three or four generations (when a great-grandson is born in prison to a prisoner whose daughter and grand-daughter are also behind bars).

CONTROLLING MOTHERHOOD, INSTITUTIONALIZED RELATEDNESS

When Tires opened in mid-twentieth century, during the Portuguese *Estado Novo* dictatorship (1933-1974), the program for the "moral regeneration" of delinquent women drew heavily on dominant gender ideologies (Cunha 1994). While they were considered "double deviants" in Portugal—both as members of society and of their gender—the purpose of rehabilitating them through domesticity and motherhood was perfectly aligned with a State ideology that presented women as the nation's ultimate moral base. It emphasized women's dedicated performance as wives and mothers as the only route for women's participation in the collective destiny (see Beleza dos Santos; Salazar).[8] In prison, one of the treatment program's ingredients consisted of an attempt to instil feelings of maternal responsibility in inmates and cultivate their mothering skills. Although granting permission to keep infant children in prison took the children's interests into account, it was primarily justified by the program's goal to educate the mothers. Aiming at the "social promotion of the delinquent woman," it was determined that "offspring, in the case of infants, should remain with the mothers so as to maintain and promote their sense of natural responsibilities" (Pinto 56). Prison regulations also explicitly stipulated that prisoners should be taught to attend to their infant children inside the institution and children should spend time with their mothers daily, as well (Correia 279).

The focus on domesticity and reproduction would linger, albeit attenuated, long after the democratic revolution in 1974 and the geography of gender would continue to determine the prison regime. Explicit gendered moral considerations have long since been expunged from official regulations, and the focus of such arrangements has shifted from the moral regeneration of the prisoners (leading them into proper motherhood) to accommodating the child's interest. Other-wise, they have remained stable over time in their general principles: namely, the age limit for children allowed to live in the institution with their mothers (three years-old, exceptionally five);[9] the provision of a day nursery, within the prison compound but physically separated from prison blocks, where children remain during mothers' working hours, and where they are attended by trained personnel; and a prison wing that houses prisoners with children behind bars together. These elements are common to both prisons considered here.

Gender considerations involving parenting and the mother role nevertheless did not disappear from prison daily life. They remained infused in informal institutional practices and interactions. Mothers may, for example, be assigned to assist day care staff in an attempt to improve their mothering skills or by way of discouraging them to leave their children in the nursery too prematurely. A Tires prison warden said, reproachfully:

There are some mothers who want to get rid of the children and be as little as possible with them. It's I who has to force them to stay with the children in their cells when they are still babies, otherwise they would put them in daycare.

Besides criticizing mothers for being too impatient or not caring enough for their children, prison guards also intervene directly. Prisoners confined to the mothers wing feel that they are the object of constant additional control. Attempts to socialize with prisoners from other wings (e.g. by making up errands to the prison shop) may be immediately curtailed by warnings that they must go back to attending to their children. Guards are more rigorous over the hygiene and tidiness of these prisoners' cells (*"we have to check and warn them all the time because kids take everything within reach to their mouths and there are irresponsible mothers"*). Guards also admonish mothers if they deem a child's hygiene is being neglected or his feeding inadequate; they may punish prisoners for shouting too much at their infants.[10]

The inmates in question deeply resent these interventions as they arguably challenge their self-representation as mothers. They are especially adamant in repudiating them as intrusions in a domain perceived as indisputably their own: *"Guards should stay out of this, these are my children, not theirs!"* In their eyes, the role of mother supersedes that of inmate and should remain out of range of guards' authority. Paradoxically, it is precisely in the name idealized notions of motherhood (and of the importance of being a "good mother") that co-inmates approve guards' interference: *"The guards have every right to interfere; they have to educate them to be good mothers."*

Prisoners are aware that their inmate and motherly conditions are somehow merged and some even suspect that their performance as mothers is assessed in the same way as their behaviour as prisoners—that is, with the potential to impact parole board deliberations. In any case, they sense all too well that the in-prison relationship with their offspring and the language of *care* itself are inescapably intertwined in the coercive management of the "total institution" (Goffman). They also realize that children themselves, as they become socialized in prison routines, internalize their mothers' subject position within the institution, in which mothers may also be *scolded* like children. Antónia, a 42-year-old inmate arrested for attempted murder, said: *"My son knew. If the door opened and I hadn't dressed* [in the prison uniform] *he reminded me right away: 'Mother, put it on, otherwise Mrs. Guard is going to scold you!'"*

In recent decades, with the co-imprisonment of mothers and adult daughters (and sometimes granddaughters), such encompassment by the institutional coercive framework has become more extensive. Notions of care are intertwined in a complex way with *respect*. There is a prevalent ideal regarding family conduct, the criteria that should regulate relationships between children, parents and grandparents, and appropriate levels of intimacy, responsibility, support, and moral obligation among family members (Cunha 2002; Cunha forthcoming). A 56-year-old prisoner and mother of six—who at the time shared her cell with her 25-year-old daughter and whose husband and another son were serving time in a male prison facility—expressed this close connection between care and respect:

> *I brought up my children honourably. I always fed them, never abandoned them, never put them in an institution. I was always a good mother and I never had a man to help me. Respect was what I gave them. They all respected me* ... [In the meantime, her adult daughter arrives in the cell]. *Come on Rosa, say hello. Sorry, nowadays they just want to fool around, but they respect me. Just because I'm in prison, does that mean they shouldn't respect me?*

She then went on to complain about her sons' lack of reciprocity. They didn't respect their parents and neglected to visit and support them in prison. Failure to fulfil familial and supportive obligations elicits depreciative comments that denounce respectful behaviour. For example, a prisoner convicted for drug trafficking greeted an elderly woman passing by with:

> *Her daughters were real cows to her.... They don't have any respect for her. No respect at all. It's not because someone is in jail that they should lose respect. She's also got her grandson here, poor thing. The grandmother's the only one of them worth anything because the mother is a bitch to that child. The grandmother comes between them, which is just as well.*

Respect implicitly demands a hierarchical aspect to it. Imprisonment destabilises this as daughters, mothers and grandmothers are reduced to a common condition—that of a prisoner. Tirades such as: *"You're as much a prisoner as I am, it's the guards who tell me what to do!"* were not uncommon from daughters exasperated by older relatives' control over their behaviour. The levelling effect of being imprisoned and the resulting equalization of once hierarchical familial positions dims that authority. *Respect* is nevertheless an ingredient of prison sociality between mothers and daughters, and guards sometimes use its language as a valuable tool in their work:

> *The mothers do a lot of controlling and that makes the work of the guards much easier. There's a prisoner here who is completely unbearable when her mother is not around. When her mother comes, she shows respect and*

behaves herself. She calms down straightaway. I myself have a word with other kin when I see things getting out of hand.

These complex forms of institutional control coexist with others that reproduce forms of parental surveillance behind bars. For example, one inmate reconciled with her young adult co-inmate daughter (they were not on speaking terms before) and "chaperoned" her daughter's boyfriend prison visits during the early stages of the romantic relationship.

In the face of the particular circumstances regarding penal confinement, moral obligations, notions of responsibility, dependency and emotional intimacy may vividly emerge in the prison scene. For example, one prisoner turned down parole because, on the day it was granted, she discovered that her imprisoned mother had a tumour. Co-imprisoned family members also support children, sharing food and providing several kinds of assistance. Relatives may be such close caregivers that they are deeply disturbed when children, to whom they have become emotionally attached, reach the age of leaving the institution. In order to avoid memories that had become too painful, Isabel, a 32-year-old woman imprisoned in Santa Cruz for drug trafficking and who was doing time together with her mother, two sisters, and a baby niece, asked to be relocated in another block when her niece left prison: "*I couldn't bear to see the children. I helped to raise my niece and it was as if I was seeing her. I felt bad, bad.*"

But contemporary scenarios involving the co-existence of several relatives in the same prison may generate other kinds of painful experiences, such as the one reported by Fátima, a 27-year-old prisoner arrested for drug trafficking who was divorcing her husband and who was separated from her children by incarceration. Fátima's sister-in-law usually came to visit her own mother who was imprisoned in the same institution. She was accompanied by Fátima's children, yet never brought them to see her.

> *I was a year without seeing my children.... She used to come to visit her mother, and didn't bring my children. She brought them, but she didn't call me. Once I had to shout because I couldn't stand it, I knew they were here and I couldn't go and see them in the parlor. Another time it was the chief guard who let me in and be with them for five minutes. Only five minutes! And they were my children....*

In the face of extended forms of *relatedness* (Carsten) involving children, which also exist in these women's daily life outside of prison, "mothering" appears as a very narrow category. It obscures relatedness, bondedness, caregiving—and gatekeeping—which have a reality of their own, independent of motherhood and that cannot therefore be considered as its mere ersatz or extension.

Such forms of relatedness may also occur between non-relatives, especially in the mothers' prison wing. Inmates' sociality in this wing has a distinct quality. Children are put at its forefront. Besides the fact that mothers' spare time is largely absorbed by childcare (feeding their children, bathing them, washing their clothes, playing with them, watching over them), all inmates have a more or less collective relationship with the kids in the wing. They give them affectionate nicknames, comment on their progress and achievements, protect them when the respective mothers snap at them (one even physically threatened the mother of a child to whom she had become particularly attached). They help feed them, take them to the playground or for a walk when the mother is remanded in the cell, and take charge of them when the child's mother goes to court. Prisoners allowed to *go on* [home] *leave* sometimes collect children of imprisoned relatives or friends and look after them in their homes during those periods. They offer advice to co-inmates on their children's health issues and sometimes urge them to take the children to the doctor without delay when a child appears ill or injured. They share food, clothing and children items. Inmate mothers who do not share are loathed more than informers.

Unlike in other wings, sociality is strongly mediated by the presence of children, both in instances of solidarity (*we help each other out because of the kids*) as well as of conflict. When a child is sick, all inmates may knock simultaneously on their door cells in order to alert the guards or to demand that the cell in question is opened.

RESIGNIFYING AND REIFYING MOTHERHOOD

Some mothers express ambivalence about keeping their infant children with them behind bars. They express concern about the effects of prison limitations and the environment on children: the noise and the inmate fighting, the oppressive prison bars, locks and keys, cell confinement, and the lack of exposure to the outside world.

> *I couldn't bear the sight of her confined in a tiny space, asking me to open the door. Then I said no: it is me who is supposed to suffer, not the kid. I had to send her away. I regretted keeping him here when I went out with him on temporary leave. He had never seen a street before; he was scared of the cars.*

Out of guilt, some of these mothers renounce keeping their children in prison; others, usually middle-class prisoners, decide on principle not to bring them from the start, deeming it would be harmful to the child and selfish on their part.[11] However, this is not always an option, especially for less better-off inmates, who are the ones most affected by the consequences of mass incarceration and by the co-imprisonment of relatives.[12] Like Ana, an inmate who has her baby daughter with her and left a one-year old child to the care of her mother, mothers may decide to keep children behind bars in order not to overburden relatives: "*If I could, I would send her away*" [but no else in the family could bear another burden].

Otherwise, as illustrated by the following short excerpts, mothers' narratives commonly emphasize a recurrent theme: their children's presence fulfils them, helps them cope and softens their prison experience (Cunha 1994: 156, Serra and Pires 420).

> *The best thing here is that they let us keep our children with us. Time passes more quickly. There's no time to get depressed, it makes me react. / I don't take sleeping pills. My tranquilizers are my children. / Those who don't have their kids here are mentally upset. / The company they keep makes up for all the chores and all the trouble in the world. / I only feel lonely at night, when they go to sleep and I start thinking. / This would be heavy without the children. When my son is in daycare I don't know what to do, I'm longing for him to come back. / I'm always looking forward to the week-ends, so that I can be with my daughter all day long. / If I could have all my children with me, I wouldn't mind to be in prison. / They provide an escape, they give us strength to hold on.*

These narratives almost always express a highly idealized maternal self-image that does not necessarily match the actual interactions between mothers and their offspring. Likewise, there are claims by co-inmates who proudly suggest that it was under their influence that mothers actually started to enjoy their children and learned how to care for them: "*Before she didn't care, now she even says 'Oh my Chico is so pretty, isn't he?'*" Prisoners who admitted that at some point or another they had "no patience" for their children or that their presence in such an environment could also be overbearing ("*the kids altogether, it's a racket. We can do nothing but run after them, stopping fights*") were rare exceptions. Rosy narratives may be even more prevalent in inmates' recollections whose children have already left prison, insofar as only the gratifying moments are remembered. Separation itself, whether during the prison sentence or upon imprisonment, allows for re-imagining mother-child relationships in a positive light.

Yet, as Cristina Palomar Verea (372) has also noted, by taking some of the burdens away from women's day-to-day lives the prison environment does allow for experiencing motherhood in new ways. Sheltered from the pressures of everyday survival, poverty and violence, with time available to dedicate to their children (who now also receive specialized medical and psychological attention), and with consistent exposure to expert educational and pedagogical discourses and programs, mothers may experience an unprecedented and intense bond with their children. This creates new subjectivities in which motherhood takes centre stage, and through which mothers also resignify previous experiences of motherhood. In such a context, motherhood becomes hyperbolized in narratives of personal identity, including the way it is perceived in retrospect or projected into the future.

FINAL REMARKS

Children and a mother's separation from her children is at the top of the "pains of imprisonment." These are pervasive themes of prison discussion. Motherhood is recurrently invoked by inmates as a motive and justification for the offence that led them to prison (*I did it for my children; I had to feed my kids*). Reference to motherhood is thus often a gendered "technique of neutralization" (Sykes and Matza). Furthermore, the discursive importance of the "good mother" may be instrumental in refusing a "deviant" identity and may be invoked as a synonym of a "good citizen" (Cunha 1994).

However, contextual variations caution us against presuming that motherhood predefines women's whole identity in incarceration situations.[13] As a gendered anchor of a "non-deviant" social identity, motherhood was more central during the 1980s. Since the 1990s, a new sense of collective identity and shared destiny have emerged; these have been based on prisoners' common provenance from the same destitute and ill reputed urban areas, as well as on kin, friendship, and neighbourhood ties, and on a shared position at the bottom of the class structure—which included, for the first time, an endured sense of collective stigma (see Cunha 2002).

Overshadowed by new categories of agency and identity within which prisoners came to react to their common marginalization, identity dimensions such as gender receded to the backstage of the prison social scene. This was also complicated by mass incarceration and the co-imprisonment of relatives. The sociography of relatedness, as well as the "ethics of care," once identified with women *qua* mothers, are not limited to mother-child dyads anymore, but involve wider circles of relationships; furthermore, as it simultaneously involves more than two generations, the ethics of care is enmeshed in a more (even if not altogether) gender-neutral ethics of respect, reciprocity, and moral obligation.

The prison environments discussed here focused on reproduction and on the mother-child bond (a notion also formatted by expert discourses and popular psychology)[14] and this promotes a highly idealized and essentialized notion of motherhood. This ideal construct of motherhood is disconnected from the harsh realities and actual experiences of these women's lives. In many cases, it is behind bars that these mothers find the time, structure or the resources necessary to focus on motherhood. By overstating the exclusivity of the mother-child relationship and by totally detaching it from the wider context of relatedness in which it is enmeshed both behind and beyond bars, this idealized construct of motherhood obscures the changing complexities of care and support in the age of mass incarceration; it veils how care and support are shared by a multitude of others.

The support of the following institutions is gratefully acknowledged: FCT (Project, "Care as Sustainability in Crisis Situations": PTDC/CS-ANT/117259/2010); Gr. "Representações sobre os impactos sócio-familiares da reclusão: visões femininas e masculinas," SFRH/BD/73214/2010/J5395389SQ03; Wenner-Gren Foundation for Anthropological Research (Gr. 6099).

[1]Although such possibility is not necessarily barred to inmate fathers by prison regulations such as the Portuguese's (which today may not even specify gender), logistical and practical conditions hardly allow for its implementation (e.g. there are generally no daycare centres in male institutions).

[2]See Wall and Lobo for the growing importance of single parents' households in Portugal.

[3]For example, through tattoos, photographs, letters and stories (Ferraro and Moe; Clark).

[4]In Portugal the co-imprisonment of kin, as well as the presence of multiple neighbours and previous acquaintances doing time in the same prison facilities, has to do with the systematic provenance of prison populations from a handful of poverty-stricken urban territories in the two main Portuguese metropolitan areas (Lisbon and Oporto). Since the 1990s, these neighbourhoods were associated with a booming petty drug economy and drew an intense attention from law enforcement agencies and the criminal justice system, which increased the probabilities of detention (for a mere detailed explanation see Cunha 2005, 2008).

[5]The latter (Santa Cruz) even came to absorb, upon its opening, part of the prisoners of the former (Tires), which was overcrowded then.

[6]Women were selected by combining a snowball progression that followed 'natural' networks and a systematic sampling that diversified inmates along lines of penal and social profile, as well as length and experience of confinement (Cunha 1994, 2002).

[7]In the case of Tires, according to a conservative estimate based on data registered in social-educational files, between one-half and two-thirds of the inmates in Tires had family members inside the same institution (sisters, cousins, aunts, nieces, mothers, grandmothers). This estimate does not include male partners and kin serving their own sentences in other facilities. In Santa Cruz, on the

other hand, there are records on the proportion of prisoners (40 percent) who have applied for visits in male institutions (brothers, sons, husbands/partners), which leaves inmate women relatives unaccounted for. Fieldwork, however, confirmed their existence along a similar pattern.

[8]This State ideology was at odds with social realities in that it could only be fulfilled, or afforded, by the elites. With the exception of these groups, women in Portugal—and more so among the poor—have always massively resorted to work and wage labour as a survival strategy, without this being considered in their social milieu as a transgression of a gender cultural script (Cole; Ferreira; Pujadas).

[9]For recent general regulations, see Regulamento General dos Estabelecimentos Prisionais, Decreto-Lei n.º 51/2011 at <http://dre.pt/pdf1s-dip/2011/04/07100/0218002225.pdf>.

For a comparison, in various countries, of modalities allowing children to stay with their mothers behind bars, as well as the effects of such measures, see e.g. Tomasevski; Verea.

[10]Guards also bring presents and toys to children, and sometimes buy them sweets, tell stories and cajole them into entering the cells when they are reluctant to do so.

[11]This opinion is also often expressed by male prison guards. Women guards tend to understand mothers' decision to keep the children with them.

[12]Before the 1990s, children of imprisoned mothers would typically be taken care of by relatives, friends or neighbors outside. However, phenomena of collective incarceration have caused the overload of these informal community networks of support. This is a combined effect of the increased length of prison sentences, which raises the amount of time children have to be looked after by others on the outside, and the imprisonment of many of those available to provide this temporary care (for a development of this point see Cunha, forthcoming). For example, a grandmother can thus find herself looking after several grandchildren, either simultaneously or consecutively, when sons and daughters-in-law are imprisoned. As a result, children enter an unpredictable circuit. Besides being separated and distributed among family and neighbors, brothers and sisters will move successively from uncles to grandparents, godparents and neighbors—and eventually into institutions when other children arrive or when expense becomes unbearable. State or charity institutions are a viable option. But support emanating from institutions is hardly conceptualized as "care" in prevailing cultural ideologies, however "caring" might be the concrete processes and interactions through which it takes place. Only support provided by persons is considered to be genuinely "caring," as institutions would, in this view have an impersonal, contract-oriented approach to human relationships (Cunha forthcoming).

[13]This point is developed in Cunha and Granja.
[14]See also Young (148-158) for a related point.

WORKS CITED

Beleza dos Santos, José. *Nova Organização Prisional Portuguesa*. Coimbra: Coimbra Editora, 1947. Print.

Carsten, Janet. *Cultures of Relatedness: New Approaches to the Study of Kinship*. Cambridge: Cambridge University Press, 2000. Print.

Celinska, K. and J. A. Siegel. "Mothers in Trouble: Coping With Actual or Pending Separation From Children Due to Incarceration." *The Prison Journal* 90.4 (2010): 447-474. Web. 15 October 2010.

Clark, Judith. "Impact of the Prison Environment on Mothers." *The Prison Journal* 75 (1995): 29-35. Print.

Cole, Sally. *Women of the Praia: Work and Lives in a Portuguese Coastal Community*. Princeton, NJ: Princeton University Press, 1991. Print.

Comfort, Megan. *Doing Time Together: Love and Family in the Shadow of the Prison*. London: The University of Chicago Press, 2008. Print.

Correia, A. Malça. *Tratamento Penitenciário*, Lisboa: Centro do Livro Brasileiro, 1981. Print.

Cunha, Manuela "A reclusão segundo o género: Os estudos prisionais, a reclusão de mulheres e a variação dos contextos da identidade." *AAVV, Educar o Outro: As Questões de Género, dos Direitos Humanos e da Educação nas Prisões Portuguesas*. Coimbra: Publicações Humanas, 2007. 80-89. Print.

Cunha, Manuela. "Closed Circuits: Kinship, Neighborhood and Imprisonment in Urban Portugal." *Ethnography* 9.3 (2008): 325-350. Print.

Cunha, Manuela. *Entre o Bairro e a Prisão: Tráfico e Trajectos*. Lisbon: Fim de Século, 2002. Print.

Cunha, Manuela. "From Neighborhood to Prison. Women and the War on Drugs in Portugal." *Global Lockdown: Race, Gender, and Prison-Industrial Complex*. Ed. Julia Sudbury. New York: Routledge, 2005. 155-165. Print.

Cunha, Manuela. *Malhas que a Reclusão Tece. Questões de Identidade numa Prisão Feminina*. Lisbon: Cadernos do Centro de Estudos Judiciários, 1994. Print.

Cunha, Manuela. "The Changing Scale of Imprisonment and the Transformation of Care: The Erosion of the "Welfare Society" by the "Penal State" in Contemporary Portugal." *Careful Encounters: Ethnographies of Support*. Ed. Marcus Fletcher and Frederika Fleischer. London: Palgrave MacMillan, forthcoming.

Cunha, Manuela and Rafaela Granja. "Gender Asymmetries, Parenthood and Confinement in Two Portuguese Prisons." Ed. Stéphanie Latte Abdallah and Coline Cardi. *Revue Champ Pénal, Special Issue Detained Motherhoods,*

Fatherhoods: Parenthood in Imprisonment and Conflict Situations (2013): forthcoming.

Datesman, S. K. and G. L. Cales. "'I'm Still the Same Mommy': Maintaining the Mother/Child Relationship in Prison." *The Prison Journal* 63.2 (1983): 142-154. Web. 1 August 2011.

Eigenberg, Helen M. and Phyllis E. Berry. "Role Strain and Incarcerated Mothers : Understanding the Process of Mothering." *Women & Criminal Justice* 15.1 (2003): 101-119. Print.

Enos, Sandra. *Mothering From the Inside: Parenting in a Women's Prison.* New York: SUNY Press, 2001. Print.

Ferraro, Kathleen J. and Angela M. Moe. "Mothering, Crime, And Incarceration." *Journal of Contemporary Ethnography* 32.1 (2003): 9-40. Web. 14 February 2011.

Ferreira, Virginia. "Padrões de Segregação das Mulheres no Emprego: Uma Análise do Caso Português no Quadro Europeu." *Portugal: Um Retrato Singular.* Ed. Boaventura de Sousa Santos. Porto: Afrontamento, 1993. 233-257. Print.

Goffman, Erving. *Asylums: Essays on the Social Situation of Mental and Other Inmates.* New York: Garden Books, 1999 [1961]. Print.

Greene, S., C. Haney and A. Hurtado. "Cycles of Pain: Risk Factors in the Lives of Incarcerated Mothers and Their Children." *The Prison Journal* 80.1 (2000): 3-23. Web. 9 August 2011.

Henriques, Zelma. "Imprisoned Mothers and Their Children." *Women & Criminal Justice* 8.1 (1996): 77-95. Print.

Kazura, Kerry. "Family Programming for Incarcerated Parents." *Journal of Offender Rehabilitation* 32.4 (2000): 67-83. Print.

La Vigne, Haley, Lisa E. Brooks and Tracey L. Shollenberger. "Women on the Outside: Understanding the Experiences of Female Prisoners Returning to Houston, Texas." *Justice Police Center Research Report.* Urban Institute Publications, 2009. Web. 10 January 2011.

Mahan, Susan. *Unfit Mothers.* Palo Alto: R&E Research Associates, 1982. Print.

Morash, Merry and Pamela Schram. *The Prison Experience: Special Issues of Women in Prison.* Prospect Heights, IL: Waveland Press Inc., 2002. Print.

Pattillo, Mary, David Weiman and Bruce Western. *Imprisoning America: The Social Effects of Mass Incarceration.* New York: Russel Sage Foundation, 2004. Print.

Pinto, J. Roberto. "O tratamento penitenciário de mulheres." *Boletim da Administração Penitenciária e dos Institutos de Criminologia* 25 (1969). Print.

Pujadas, Joan. "Processos Sociais e Construção de Identidades nas Periferias Urbanas: Os Casos de Lisboa e Catalunha." *Mediterrâneo* 4 (1994): 11-19. Print.

Salazar, António de Oliveira. *Como se Levanta um Estado*. Lisboa: Golden Books, 1977. Print.

Serra, Dinora and António Pires. "Maternidade atrás das grades: comportamento parental em contexto prisional." *Análise Psicológica* 2.22 (2004) : 413-425. Print.

Shamai, Michal. "'Motherhood Starts in Prison': The Experience of Motherhood Among Women in Prison." *Family Process* 47.3 (2008): 323-340. Print.

Sykes, Gresham and David Matza. "Techniques of Neutralization: A Theory of Delinquency." *American Sociological Review* 22.6 (1957): 664-670. Print.

Tomasevski, Katarina. *Children in Adult Prisons: An International Perspective*. Londres: Frances Pinter, 1986. Print.

Verea, Cristina Palomar. *Maternidad en Prisión*. Guadalajara: Universidade de Guadalajara, 2007. Print.

Young, Jock. *The Exclusive Society: Social Exclusion, Crime and Difference in Late Modernity*. London: Sage, 1999. Print.

Wall, Karin and Cristina Lobo. "Famílias Monoparentais Em Portugal." *Análise Social* 34.150 (1999): 123-145. Print.

Wacquant, Loïc. *Punishing the Poor: The Neoliberal Government of Social Insecurity*. Durham: Duke University Press, 2009. Print.

Incarcerated Indigenous Australian Mothers

Maintaining Patriarchal Colonization

RUTH MCCAUSLAND AND EILEEN BALDRY

INDIGENOUS WOMEN have been the fastest growing group of prisoners in Australia for the past decade. Indigenous women, making up only two percent of the Australian women's population now make up 30 percent of women in prison. Most Indigenous women prisoners have children and most of them have their children removed. Indigenous women have specific experiences based on the intersection of their race and gender (Aboriginal and Torres Strait Islander Social Justice Commissioner; Wirringa Baiya Aboriginal Women's Legal Centre). For example, Indigenous women experience high levels of family and community violence but are under-represented in formal reporting of such abuse, arguably due to their experience of racism in the criminal justice system (Wirringa Baiya Aboriginal Women's Legal Centre). Intersectional and institutional discrimination manifest in government policies and programs for women and for Indigenous peoples generally. These policies do not respond to the specific circumstances of Indigenous women who are, on the whole, invisible in the Australian political environment (Aboriginal and Torres Strait Islander Social Justice Commissioner).

In this chapter we argue that the contemporary over-representation of Indigenous women in prison cannot be understood in isolation from Australia's history of colonial, paternalistic control of them and their children, and the commensurate failure to allow them agency and participation in decision-making regarding matters affecting them, their families and communities. The historical characterisation and treatment of Aboriginal women has direct and real consequences today in the policy failure to support positive change in their lives. We also explore and reflect upon the views of and about incarcerated Indigenous mothers. Then, we analyze the policies and practices shaping their lives, choices and relationships. We argue that the over-representation of Indigenous women in prison is a contemporary manifestation of the two centuries old colonial patriarchal impetus to control Indigenous Australian women and their children.

HISTORY OF CHARACTERIZATION OF INDIGENOUS WOMEN

Aboriginal and Torres Strait Islander people's experience of the criminal justice system in Australia has been characterised by discrimination, over-regulation and unfair treatment (Royal Commission into Aboriginal Deaths in Custody). Historically, Indigenous Australians were criminalised for reasons directly related to their Indigeneity, including by laws that restricted movement on and between reserves and into towns, and to possession of alcohol (LRC of WA 94). Indigenous people were also subject to discriminatory laws, policies and practices that enabled the forcible removal of their children on the basis of their race and racist assumptions about their children's welfare (HREOC).

Indigenous women were particularly vulnerable to colonial force and violence: portrayed as "sexual objects, Aboriginal women were seen as fair and easy game for white men; as members of a colonised people, they were also subjected to a range of racist indignities" (Behrendt 2003: 360). Historian Ann McGrath describes the way that Indigenous women were presented in the early years of colonisation as "slaves" and "chattels" to their husbands, as "property, victims of male violence, of primitive rituals, of unrefined lust" (McGrath 32, 36-37). Portraying themselves as "heroic rescuers" of Indigenous women gave the British male "a heightened sense of masculinity" providing a means by which to assert "a superiority over the primitive" and demonstrate their "gentle treatment of women" (McGrath 37). This stands in stark contrast to the many accounts of exploitation and abuse of Indigenous women by white men. Many colonial representations portray Indigenous women alternatively as promiscuous or as helpless victims, seemingly to either justify their exploitation by white men, or to be in need of their protection.

Aileen Moreton-Robinson describes the way:

> White Australia has come to "know" the "Indigenous woman" from the gaze of many, including the diaries of explorers, the photographs of philanthropists, the testimony of white state officials, the sexual bravado of white men and the ethnographies of anthropologists. In this textual landscape Indigenous women are objects who lack agency. (1)

Drawing on the work of Linda Tuhiwai Smith, Moreton-Robinson highlights the way that the process of "en-gendering descriptions of the Other" has had very real and material consequences. The representations and objectification of Indigenous women during the nineteenth century, it is argued, has marginalized them both in their own and the colonizing societies (qtd. in Moreton-Robinson 1). Whether portrayed as the "wilful seductresses of white men', or as pathetic victims of Indigenous and white male violence, Indigenous women were still irretrievably "fallen" and "other"—a characterisation that was to have long echoes in Indigenous policy into the twentieth century, as was the associated stereotype of the traditional Indigenous family structure as inadequate (Goodall 79).

Such representations of Aboriginal women informed the laws, policies and practices that had a direct and often devastating impact on the lives of Aboriginal women, their families and communities. Records from nineteenth and twentieth century political and legislative debates and meetings of bodies such as the NSW Aborigines Protection Board bear evidence of the negative terms of official characterisation of Indigenous women (Goodall 76). The traditional values and skills which Indigenous women brought to the work of mothering were maligned, according to Heather Goodall, as "dangerous and corrupting and needed intensive training to be undone"; and then, when their "primitive" habits had been erased, officials depicted Aboriginal women as needing to be taught to work effectively in both the paid labour force and in the domestic work areas of mothering, childcare and homemaking (76). She describes the way that questions of sexual stereotyping and regulation of sexual activity, of policy in relation to Aboriginal mothers and children, and of the nature of Aboriginal women's engagement in the labour force as domestic servants, are inextricably entwined (76). Adding further trauma to this ongoing treatment of Indigenous women, they were locked up in disproportionate numbers in women's "factories" and in mental asylums and punished further by having their children removed (Baldry). Indigenous women in particular bore the brunt of the "white man's burden" in Australia.

The legislative power to summarily remove children from their families and place them into state or church-run institutions or with non-Indigenous families had a devastating impact on all Indigenous communities, though its implementation was particularly gendered. Goodall notes that in the 1910s and 1920s the policy of child removal in NSW was aimed not at just any young child, but was quite explicitly directed at removing girls reaching puberty from Indigenous communities. The Aborigines Protection Board used the popular images of Indigenous women and Indigenous families as "places of uncontrolled sexual activity and vice" as a means to gain control over Indigenous girls (81). While there can be no doubt that Indigenous men also suffered deeply from the loss of children, it was on women's behaviour that the protection and welfare authorities predominantly focused (93). Grandmothers and aunties were as vulnerable as mothers in the Indigenous social context where the raising of children was seen as a collective family responsibility (92).

When, in the 1950s, assimilation policies were deemed to have not had the desired effect of subsuming Indigenous people into white mainstream society, the Aborigines Welfare Board began to locate the cause of this "failure" in Indigenous people themselves:

Statements blaming Aborigines for failing to assimilate and for actually creating the racial prejudice they faced became a regular inclusion in AWB reports. Much of the cause was said to rest on, or to be manifested in, bad Aboriginal housekeeping and home making. In these 1950s statements, there were strong echoes of the Protection Board's earlier accusations that Aboriginal mothers were negligent and corrupting parents who therefore "deserved" to have their children taken away from them. (Goodall 96)

In the range of disempowering and demeaning depictions of Indigenous Australian women historically, the image of captivity is one of the most powerful. Indigenous women were "captives of the male gaze, captives of patriarchal histories, with often captive bodies, and captive imaginations for mythologising" (McGrath 46). This is a salient image given the contemporary over-representation of Indigenous women in prison.

CONTEMPORARY LEGAL AND POLICY CONTEXT

Overall, directly discriminatory legislation against Indigenous Australians had been repealed by the late 1960s. A formal Commonwealth Government policy of self-determination for Indigenous Australian people was adopted in the 1970s. Nonetheless there has been general antipathy—even hostility—on the part of institutions, governments and the broader non-Indigenous community to measures to support human rights for Indigenous people. This includes both those human rights to which all Australians are entitled and to distinct Indigenous rights such as to culture and land (HREOC; Behrendt 2003). Indigenous Australians still bear the colonizing legacy of negative and stereo-typical representations and treatment. In fact, the reproduction of colonizing mindsets continues and shapes non-Indigenous and Indigenous Australians' attitudes to and views about Aboriginal peoples (Smith; Sherwood 270-272). Indirect race discrimination, where Indigenous people are disproportionately and negatively affected by laws, policies and practices that are not overtly dis-criminatory, continue to be reproduced and to have an impact on Indigenous peoples' socio-economic status, access to education, employment and housing, and interaction with the criminal justice system.

Aboriginal women in particular are denied power under and before the law as a result of their race, their gender and often in addition, their low so-cio-economic status (qtd. in NSW LRCpar 6.29). The challenges of Indigenous women's access to justice have been elicited through evidence submitted to various government inquiries and fall across Indigenous and non-Indigenous specific service providers (Davis 21). The Australian Law Reform Commission identified Indigenous women as the most legally disadvantaged group in Australia. Kate Kerley and Chris Cunneen have argued that criminal law, from policing to sentencing, treats Aboriginal women more harshly than any other group, and that particular conceptions of gender and Aboriginality have the effect of creating more punitive interventions in relation to Aboriginal women (83). The NSW Law Reform Commission report into the sentencing of Indigenous women offenders noted that "the enormous pressures arising from the combined effects of poverty, violence, sole parenthood, alcohol and substance abuse, and gender and race discrimination give some indication of the vulnerability of Aboriginal women to contact with the criminal justice system"; and that "until the law recognises the socially and economically oppressed position of Aboriginal and Torres Strait Islander women, it will continue to treat them unequally and, therefore unjustly" (qtd. in NSW LRC par 6.29).

Despite the findings of various government inquiries, the systemic discrimination against Indigenous women in the legal and criminal justice systems remains pervasive. Aboriginal women academics, lawyers, service providers and community representatives have been consistently outspoken for decades about the interconnectedness of past discriminatory laws, policies, practices and the current circumstances faced by Indigenous women, with seemingly little effect. Almost 20 years ago, Sharon Payne argued:

> the issues facing Aboriginal women in the criminal justice system are a double indemnity; a reflection of the wider issues of dispossession, alienation, poverty, and discrimination which feature customarily in the everyday life of Aboriginal people, as well as the socio-economic position of women generally within a male dominated "western" society. These issues will never be fully resolved while Aboriginal women occupy, whether by ignorance or design, their current position in Australian society. (73)

Almost ten years ago, the Aboriginal and Torres Strait Islander Social Justice Commissioner found:

> Indigenous women face an unacceptably high risk of incarceration in prisons across Australia. The rising rate of over-representation of Indigenous women is occurring in the context of intolerably high levels of family violence, over-policing for selected offences, ill-health, unemployment and poverty (135–136).

Still, the rate of Indigenous women's imprisonment in 2011 was 357 per 100,000 of adult Indigenous females compared with 16 per 100,000 for non-Indigenous females (Australian Bureau of Statistics 58). A recent Commonwealth Government parliamentary committee found the escalation of the number of Indigenous women in detention "disturbing":

> Indigenous women are critical to the future strength of Indigenous families and communities. They play an important role in the care of children, providing the future generation with a stable upbringing. Continued growth in the number of Indigenous women being imprisoned will have a long lasting and negative impact on the wellbeing of Indigenous families and communities. (Standing Committee on Aboriginal and Torres Strait Islander Affairs)

A 2010 report confirms that Indigenous women generally serve shorter sentences than their non-Indigenous counterparts, which suggests that Indigenous women are being imprisoned for more minor offences, especially public order offences (Bartels ix). The data on juveniles indicate over-policing of young Indigenous females and under-utilisation of diversionary mechanisms (Bartels 18). According to the most recent data, acts intended to cause injury, (ie violence not causing injury or not causing serious injury) although still a small proportion of Indigenous women's offending, accounted for a greater proportion of offences for which Indigenous women were imprisoned, compared with non-Indigenous women. This pattern is indicative of higher rates of and in response to domestic violence and other forms of abuse against Indigenous women (x). The intergenerational impact of the incarceration of Indigenous women is significant, with children often increasingly vulnerable to abuse, neglect and homelessness as a result of their mother's incarceration.

In the most significant study on Indigenous women in prison in Australia to date, *Speak Out Speak Strong* (Lawrie), most of the Indigenous women who were interviewed (representing half of the Indigenous women prisoners at the time) were single mothers with a number of children; were responsible for children other than their own; had a prior conviction as an adult; were using alcohol or drugs at the time of their last offence with a strong connection between their alcohol or drug use and offending behaviour; and had long and serious histories of abuse (25-51). A little over half the Aboriginal women in custody had come from a family that had been affected by the stolen generation (53). Along with other research (Aboriginal and Torres Strait Islander Women's Social Justice Commissioner 16) domestic violence was identified as one of the most serious forms of abuse these women faced when in the community (51). Finding stable, suitable, supported housing to allow them to live with their children upon release was their key concern but in their experience, the most difficult problem to resolve (27).

Confirming Rowena Lawrie's findings, the most severely disadvantaged amongst all participants in Eileen Baldry, Desmond McDonnell, Peter Maplestone, and Manu Peeters' NSW and Victorian post-release study were Indigenous women. These women experienced the highest rates of re-incarceration and homelessness in the sample. They came from, and after prison returned to, a very small cluster of highly disadvantaged suburbs or towns, and moved frequently within these same disadvantaged areas. A lack of suitable housing was found to be a fundamental problem and a predictor of return to prison. It was also associated with multiple short prison episodes and having minimal social or material goods prior to incarceration. Cycling in and out of prison was almost the norm, and did not prepare the women for nor create pathways to successful community living (27). It is theorised by the researchers (28) that these women are subject to serial institutionalisation that throws them frequently from highly structured living (in prison) to chaotic living in the community. This has the effect of depleting the social, cultural and physical resources and resilience of those individuals, their children and their communities, and compounding exclusion from stable, functional family life (Baldry and McCausland 290-291).

THE INVISIBILITY OF INDIGENOUS WOMEN

Indigenous academic Megan Davis argues that Indigenous women's experiences in Australia provide an important case study of the "blind spot" in democratic governance; for Indigenous women, the state's blindness is dual—not only is the democratic form patriarchal; it is also discriminatory (20). This continues to manifest in government policies and programs that do not respond to the specific circumstances, needs or priorities of Indigenous women, and a failure to allow Indigenous women agency and participation in decision-making regarding matters affecting them, their families and communities. In writing about Indigenous women's standpoint, Aileen Moreton-Robinson reflects on the everyday lived experience of being an Indigenous woman, stating:

> The intersecting oppressions of race and gender and the subsequent power relations that flow from these into the social, political, historical and material conditions of our lives is shared, consciously or unconsciously.... As Indigenous women, our lives are framed by the omnipresence of patriarchal white sovereignty and its continual denial of our sovereignty. (1)

The report of the Australian inquiry into the forcible separation of Indigenous children from their families, *Bringing them home*, found that the trauma associated with the forcible removal of children had taken a devastating toll on their mothers as well as on their extended families (Human Rights and Equal Opportunity Commission). Link-Up (NSW), an Indigenous organisation that assists people to reunite with their families, advised the Inquiry that Aboriginal women were experiencing such "pain, grief and anguish" about losing their children that they were unable to speak to the inquiry and continued:

> We end up feeling helpless in front of our mothers' pain. We see how hurt they have been. We see that they judge themselves harshly, never forgiving themselves for losing their children—no matter that they were part of ongoing systematic removal of Aboriginal children....
> (qtd. in Human Rights and Equal Opportunity Commission)

Link-Up documented the shame and sense of failure Aboriginal mothers felt not being able to raise their children. This internalization by Indigenous women of culpability for the forcible removal of their children is one of the most insidious manifestations of racism in Australia's history. Indigenous women were subjected to sexual stereotyping and coercionist policies as a means of vindicating the colonial project, and then blamed for its effects. The intergenerational impacts have been particularly cruel. Evidence to the *Bringing Them Home* Inquiry provided distressing information about Aboriginal children who were stolen going on to have children of their own who they did not know how to parent:

> we ... were not parented by other people and as adults and as women we go on to have children and that those skills and experiences that our extended family would have instilled in us are not there - that puts us at great risk of having our children removed under the current policies and practices that exist today (qtd. in HREOC).

The disruption of Indigenous family structures and the denigration and undermining of Indigenous mothering has been affected in concert with the institutionalization of generations of Indigenous children. Although the laws mandating the forcible removal of Indigenous children from their families in order to erase their Indigeneity and disrupt their kinship and cultural ties have been repealed, their intergenerational legacy remains.

This is in stark evidence in the all too common experience of incarceration of Indigenous women. A recent study of Indigenous women in prison in NSW who have children, asked the women about their experiences and their hopes and needs (Baldry 14). The overwhelming theme in the women's interviews was the importance of their children in their lives, and the desire to help to provide them with safety, security and love:

I look at my babies and I want them to be safe.

And I've just had a rough ride…. But I put my kids first before myself.

The women reported feelings of deep loss and of "missing out" on their children's lives (Baldry 15). Their capacity to protect and nurture their children is severely undermined by episodes in prison, however short. The interviews highlighted the significant challenges around custody of and access to children for women who have been incarcerated (Baldry 15).

[Once released] I'll be living with my oldest son, and my baby daughter is with my cousin, and she's only two streets away, and they said I can only see her once a month until it goes back to court.

Indigenous children are often cared for by extended family members, although the burden on the mostly female carers to take responsibility for numerous children for indefinite periods of time and to navigate the complex child protection and custody regulations and processes often proves prohibitive. It is reportedly not uncommon for children of Indigenous women prisoners to be made wards of the state without direct consultation with, or the knowledge of their mothers (Baldry 15). Women are often overwhelmed by barriers created by the legal requirements to regaining custody of their children.

For all the women interviewed, separation from families and loss of culture, kinship and heritage has had an ongoing impact (Baldry 16).

I was never raised with my Aboriginal family. I was adopted although my Aboriginal family lived in the same community. I've still got issues there, you know.

Alcohol and other drug abuse was identified as a significant barrier to gaining and maintaining custody of children, along with stable housing, education and employment opportunities (Baldry 15).

I just suppressed my emotions, my depression and my sadness and went to alcohol and smoking marijuana. They were my scapegoat. Everything… it's a horrible burden.

Appropriate counseling was generally inaccessible for the women due to barriers of culture, geography or timing (Baldry 15).

Eileen Baldry's interviews with Indigenous women in prison found that the impact of sexual and physical abuse—whether childhood or ongoing—and domestic violence were consistent painful experiences (16). The women identified that their offending behaviour was often a response to pain and anger arising from personal, generational and cultural trauma, and they felt that they had not been afforded safe spaces or places in which to begin to address the impacts of this trauma.

The evidence of Aboriginal mothers' significantly greater vulnerability to imprisonment, removal of their children, intergenerational trauma and ongoing violence and discrimination speaks to the ongoing impacts of a society that maintains, at its heart a colonial attitude to Indigenous peoples.

MAINTAINING PATRIARCHAL COLONIZATION

From the earliest days of colonization, Indigenous women have been stereotyped as both helpless victims and uncontrollable perpetrators. Both characterizations have been used to mandate the intervention of white authorities into the most personal aspects of Indigenous women's lives, with devastating effects. Indeed such characterizations have often been conflated as if to justify such intervention; the regulation and institutionalization of Indigenous women have been argued as necessary for their own protection as well as for the protection of white society. Indigenous women have been rendered marginal, invisible and culpable.

In seeking to understand contemporary penal culture and its severity and excess in relation to Indigenous people and women, Baldry and Cunneen (forthcoming 4) argue that an analysis of colonial patriarchy assists in explaining why it is that certain social groups such as Indigenous women are identified as high risk, dangerous and marginalized. Legal institutions both civil and particularly criminal were fundamental to defining and enforcing patriarchal colonial relations. The law defined who was and was not Aboriginal and delimited a range of economic (who could work and for what wages), social (who needed to be institutionalized, who could live in which area, who could marry) and citizenship rights (who could vote, who was entitled to social security), and enforced these through civil and criminal penalties (13). British colonial law constituted the white mythology that governed a gendered and colonial order; that placed Indigenous men and particularly Indigenous women in a particular relationship to the colonial state and colonial civil society (13). They also argue that these patriarchal colonial understandings and constructions of Aboriginality and gender have permeated, from the beginning, the development of institutional forms of control of Indigenous Australians and Indigenous women in particular, including that of penality (13).

This very particular relationship between past and current colonial States and Territories through the criminal justice system and Indigenous Australian women and their children, as discussed in this paper, has no clearer manifestation than in the extraordinarily high rates of Indigenous children in out of home care (OHC) with 32 percent of children in OHC representing a risk of 9.7 times the likelihood of being in OHC for Indigenous compared with non-Indigenous children although rates vary substantially between the States and Territories (Berlyn et al. 3). In juvenile detention across Australia Indigenous young people are 24 times more likely to be incarcerated than non-Indigenous children (Richards 4). Although the policy of taking Aboriginal children from their parents was formally discontinued in the 1960s, Indigenous children are still being removed via other means, continuing the transgenerational trauma and control of Indigenous mothers and their children.

CONCLUSION

The current over-representation of Indigenous women in prison, many of them mothers, cannot be understood or adequately responded to in isolation from the generations of stereotyping and regulation of Indigenous women's behaviour. There has been an institutionalized undermining of Indigenous women's relationships with their children, and the impact on Indigenous communities in Australia has been devastating. Patriarchal colonization remains present in the lives of Indigenous women through the individualization of blame for dysfunction and disadvantage.

WORKS CITED

Aboriginal and Torres Strait Islander Social Justice Commissioner. *Social Justice Report*. Sydney: Human Rights and Equal Opportunity Commission, 2005. Print.

Australian Bureau of Statistics. "Prisoners in Australia 2011." Australian Bureau of Statistics, 2011. Web. 1 Dec 2011.

Australian Law Reform Commission (ALRC). *Equality Before the Law: Justice for Women. Report No. 69*. Sydney: Australian Law Reform Commission, 1994. Print.

Baldry, Eileen. "Home Safely: Aboriginal Women Post-Release and their Children." *Indigenous Law Bulletin* 7.15 (2009): 14-17. Print.

Baldry, Eileen and Chris Cunneen. "Contemporary Penality in the Shadow of Colonial Patriarchy." *Fifth Australian and New Zealand Critical Criminology*

Conference Proceedings, 1-15, JCU, Cairns. Print.

Baldry, Eileen, Desmond McDonnell, Peter Maplestone, and Manu Peeters. "Ex-Prisoners, Accommodation and the State: Post-Release in Australia." *Australian and New Zealand Journal of Criminology* 39 (2006): 30–34. Print.

Baldry, Eileen and Ruth McCausland. "Mother Seeking Safe Home: Aboriginal Women Post-Release." *Current Issues in Criminal Justice* 21 (2009): 288–301. Print.

Bartels, Lorana. "Indigenous Women's Offending Patterns: A Literature Review." *Australian Institute of Criminology Reports, Research and Public Policy Series* 107. Canberra: Australian Institute of Criminology, 2010. Print.

Behrendt, Larissa. "Aboriginal Women and Crime." *Encyclopaedia of Women and Crime.* Ed. Nicole Hahn Rafter. Phoenix: Oryx Press, 2000. 1-2.

Behrendt, Larissa. *Achieving Social Justice.* Sydney: The Federation Press, 2003. Print.

Berlyn, Claire, Leah Bromfield and Alister Lamont. *Child Protection and Aboriginal and Torres Strait Islander Children.* Melbourne: Australian Institute of Family Studies, 2011. Print.

Davis, Megan. "The Challenges of Indigenous Women in Liberal Democracies." *Indigenous Law Bulletin* 7.1 (November 2007): 20-22. Print.

Goodall, Heather. "'Assimilation Begins in the Home': The State and Aboriginal Women's Work as Mothers in New South Wales, 1900s to 1960s." *Labour History* 69 (November 1995): 75-101. Print.

House of Representatives Standing Committee on Aboriginal and Torres Strait Islander Affairs. *Doing Time—Time for Doing.* Canberra: Parliament of Australia, 2011. Print.

Human Rights and Equal Opportunity Commission (HREOC). *Bringing them Home: The Report of the National Inquiry into the Separation of Aboriginal and Torres Strait Islander Children from their Families.* Sydney: HREOC, 1997. Print.

Kerley, Kate and Chris Cunneen. "Deaths in Custody in Australia: The Untold Story of Aboriginal and Torres Strait Islander Women." *Canadian Journal of Women and the Law* 8.1 (1995): 531–552. Print.

Law Reform Commission (LRC) of WA. *Aboriginal Customary Laws: The Interaction of Western Australian Law with Aboriginal Law and Culture, Final Report. Project 94.* Perth: Law Reform Commission of WA, 2006. Print.

Lawrie, Rowena. *Speak Out, Speak Strong.* Sydney: Aboriginal Justice Advisory Committee, 2003. Print.

McGrath, Ann. "'Modern Stone-Age Slavery': Images of Aboriginal Labour and Sexuality." *Labour History* 69 (1995): 30-51. Print.

Moreton-Robinson, Aileen. *Talkin' Up to the White Woman: Aboriginal Women and Feminism.* St Lucia: UQ Press, 2000. Print.

NSW Law Reform Commission (LRC). "Report 96—Sentencing: Aboriginal offenders, Chapter 6. Female Offenders." *NSW Law Reform Commission*, 2000. Web. 2 Nov 2011.

Payne, Sharon. "Aboriginal Women and the Law." *Aboriginal Perspectives on Criminal Justice*. Ed. Chris Cuneen. Sydney: Institute of Criminology, Sydney University Law School 1992. Print.

Royal Commission into Aboriginal Deaths in Custody. *National Report.* Canberra: AGPS, 1991. Print.

Richards, Kelly. *Trends in Juvenile Justice in Australia.* Canberra: Australian Institute of Criminology, 2011. Print.

Sherwood, Juanita. *Do No Harm: Decolonising Aboriginal Health Research.* Sydney: UNSWorks, 2010. Web. 2 Nov 2011.

Smith, Linda Tuhiwai. *Decolonizing Methodologies: Research and Indigenous Peoples*. London: Zed, 1999. Print.

Standing Committee on Aboriginal and Torres Strait Islander Affairs. *Doing Time—Time For Doing: Indigenous Youth in the Criminal Justice System.* Canberra: Parliament of Australia. 2011. Web. 1 Dec. 2011.

Wirringa Baiya Aboriginal Women's Legal Centre. *Discrimination: Have You Got All Day? Indigenous Women, Discrimination and Complaints Processes in NSW*. Sydney: Public Interest Advocacy Centre, 2001. Print.

PART II
Lived Experiences of Incarcerated Mothers

Voice of the Mothers

ALISON WITH BRENDA, SARAH, MARTINA, TANYA, DEVON, JENNIFER,
BETTY, RENEE, PATRICIA, MO, KELLY AND LINNEA

FOR 13 YEARS I worked in women's prisons as a Recreation Therapist and serve here to weave together the voices of the mothers. I, too, am a mother. This story is dear to my heart. The opportunity to observe, encourage and offer support to women in this program was a profound learning journey and privilege.

The stories came into being in three prisons: Burnaby Correctional Centre for Women (BCCW) a blended provincial and federal prison, closed in 2004. BCCW had a minimum security annex called the Open Living Unit (OLU) where Renee and others had their children. The closure resulted in the opening of Alouette Correctional Centre for Women (ACCW) for women serving provincial sentences of less than two years and Fraser Valley Institution (FVI) for federally sentenced women serving two years to life.

ACCW mothers and babies were housed on a dedicated unit, in the same building as healthcare and immediately beside the staff centre called the "bubble." It was equipped with cameras, a quiet nursery, frequent staff attendance for "count" and general monitoring. Prison is a sad environment, at times confrontational and always permeated with the energy from historical trauma. But almost all women have an instinct to care for babies and this changed everything.

The stories tell that systems are in place for the Mother-Child Program to operate successfully: to be safe and effective. From 2005-2007 it took the conviction of two women Brenda and Sarah to make it happen for twelve mothers and babies and all the other women alongside. The Mother-Child Program ended at ACCW in 2007 and was officially announced "Closed" in 2008 by British Columbia Corrections, without giving any legitimate reason. One statement mentioned safety but there was no explanation or incident to support this. The women have contributed freely to the present essay because of their commitment to supporting this program for future mothers and infants.

My overarching memory and the piece I will keep is the courage of these mothers. Once on a healing journey, they approach their histories and futures with dedication in the face of multiple and frequently redundant barriers placed in their way by the "systems" they have to navigate and negotiate. Our job as staff is to help women find hope and their own healing track. Babies are often the starting blocks for this healing.

BRENDA: WARDEN OF ACCW 2003-2007

In 2004 after renovations we opened ACCW in Maple Ridge, B.C., a minimum/medium security facility for provincial sentenced women. Women-centred programs had been developed and staff mostly from BCCW received training specifically for working with women offenders.

While meeting with the key players around the healthcare component for the new facility. Sarah, director of Fir Square unit, approached me and requested we consider having babies born to moms in custody return with their mothers to ACCW to facilitate breast feeding, nurturing, and bonding. Research they had completed on the unit strongly supported that the babies did much better if not removed from their mothers after birth. They wanted to promote these positive outcomes with our co-operation.

With the support of the Corrections Branch Headquarters, ACCW healthcare, correctional managers, line staff and other provincial personnel it was decided we could facilitate the return of mothers and babies "pairs" to custody when recommended by Fir Square and with the final authority of the Ministry of Children and Family (MCFD).

I believe twelve mothers returned to ACCW with their babies and stayed at the facility for varying periods until their discharge. The longest stay was one year. The babies' health and development was monitored by the Ministry of Health community nurses, ACCW healthcare, and MCFD social workers. Release planning frequently included placement at a supportive residence that took mothers and their infants, helping the women make the transition to the community.

Involvement in this initiative had a profound effect on me, on the mothers involved, staff and other women offenders; also the people in the ministries and community agencies involved. I was struck by how initially other agencies and ministries were so cautious regarding the proposal of the newborn babies returning to the facility. It took many meetings for everyone to feel comfortable to work with us and B.C. Women's Hospital on this initiative. There seemed to be a general feeling that the right of the child to be with the mother was overshadowed by believing this privilege should not be afforded to the incarcerated mothers.

It is generally accepted around the world that nursing infants and small children should remain with their incarcerated mothers: this practice is rarely seen in Canada. As the initiative continued and more mothers came back to ACCW with their babies, I could see the attitudes shift from cautious and guarded to comfortable and supportive. Community agencies were willing to provide a variety of supportive services within the facility to both mother and child.

Mothers directly involved expressed great joy and were grateful they could continue to nurture their babies at the facility. They were willing to participate in all we asked of them to ensure the safety and health of their babies: they seemed to be filled with hope for their future. A number of mothers involved were First Nations and the history of infants being removed from Aboriginal women is something of concern to all. It was meaningful to contribute in a small way to a more positive outcome for this group that is so over-represented in our correctional facilities.

Other women at the facility had to deal with the reminder of the pain they had suffered by being sentenced away from their children: seeing the infants triggered their feelings of loss. But a general feeling of hope permeated the entire population and the atmosphere at the facility was more positive in many ways.

Seeing other ministries and agencies support this initiative impacted many women who had very little trust in government agencies due to previous negative interactions. Seeing the agencies working together to have the babies stay with their mothers gave them a different perspective. Some voiced a new interest to work with agencies to initiate contact with children they had lost and to work to improve their lives to make a better future for their children.

Seeing the mothers and babies thrive at the facility and be released to the community together continued to reinforce my feeling that this initiative was not only the child's right but the right thing to do for the child.

SARAH: MANAGER/ CLINICAL PRACTICE LEADER
OF FIR SQUARE UNIT

Fir Square is a dedicated 12-bed unit for pregnant substance using women and their infants at B.C. Women's Hospital. It opened in 2003 in response to the need for both medical detox and stabilization, and to keep women and babies together at the bedside after birth so that the natural bonding could take place, along with breast feeding. We conducted research after we started rooming in for the babies of substance using mothers, and discovered that there had been a 40 percent reduction in the need to treat opiate exposed babies for withdrawal. There was also a 40 percent increase in the number of babies going home with their mothers.

We worked with ACCW to provide medical stabilization for pregnant women in custody. Staff from the prison attended discharge planning meetings on Fir Square, with the mother, social workers, physicians, addictions counsellors, and myself. I had discussions with Brenda about the possibility of a woman going back to the facility with her baby.

During one of these discharge planning meetings, the Ministry social worker stated that she wanted the client to go into treatment with her baby. However, the only treatment facility where this was possible can only take infants over three months old. The social worker did not want to separate the mother from her baby; this is when Brenda decided it was time to start the mother-baby program. Within a very short time they had purchased all the supplies, and took the first mother back to ACCW with her baby.

Fir Square philosophy of care is based on the tenets of harm reduction and woman centered care. For women to keep their infants and parent while at ACCW completely fit this philosophy, and was a unique and wonderful opportunity.

I visited ACCW and witnessed happy healthy babies, content mothers, and many inmates (as well as staff) enthralled to have a baby in their midst. It somehow changed the atmosphere. Mothers told me what a wonderful opportunity it was for them, and how difficult and different it would have been without their infants with them. I had always thought that a correctional institute was there to help people re-enter the world, give them skills and teach them how to deal with the past traumatic issues in their lives in a more positive coping style. This program did just that, and it was a travesty when it was closed down, closing the door on hope for many women.

Martina:

I think I am one of the few blue-uniform people who thinks the program was fantastic. The babies had such a calming effect on the women—when L brought baby to the kitchen the smiles were so great to see…. I miss that so much. I found it terrible to take the girls to deliver babies and the social services come and take them away and we bring the inmates back to jail. How traumatic for the mother, and the baby. Not sure who is punished more.

Tanya:

I was two months pregnant when I arrived at ACCW in 2005 with a 20-month sentence. Due to the possibility of losing my child, the months to come would bring me stress and emotional instability.

At the end of July, the Prison management recommended that I leave ACCW on an Unescorted Temporary Absence to attend a four to six week program at B.C. Women's Hospital. During my stay on Fir Unit, I completed many programs including: parenting, alcohol and drug program, relationship counselling, psychologist appointments, one-to-one with the Chaplain, methadone withdrawal, acupuncture therapy (for detoxification) and infant respiratory management. A meeting was held regarding future planning and placement of my newborn. The Warden and other managers met with me and an MCFD social worker and all agreed to wanting me to remain with my son. They informed me they would be willing to start the Infant and Mother Health-Initiative at ACCW to accommodate both my son and me in prison! I felt the weight of stress lift from me immediately!

I returned to ACCW and was greeted by many women, staff and inmates, who expressed their happiness for us. My little boy brought an abundance of positive energy to the institution: when women saw us coming, their mothering instincts immediately kicked in, their demeanour changed, their voices lowered and the conversations revolved around family and children.

Prior to this program, a woman would go to the nearest hospital, give birth and return to jail within three days—leaving the baby, in most cases, to go to foster care. This was a traumatizing event for both mother and child. The setting at ACCW was more geared towards healing and rehabilitation, as opposed to the usual warehousing and institutionalization that has happened in the past. The warden and managers were very committed to doing what was best to assist women to return to their communities, and to sustain their change to being law-abiding and contributing members of society.

Alison:

I recently visited with Tanya, about to produce another beautiful baby. She is thriving with full custody of her boys and no MCFD involvement in their lives.

Devon:

Having my son at ACCW probably saved my life. He was my reason for getting out of bed every day. Alder was not like a unit at all, but like a home. It wasn't just a positive experience for me and my son, but for all the women on the unit. When it was time for me to leave, it was a very emotional goodbye. I was scared to go out on my own and I knew I would miss the support I had there. Had I not been able to keep my son with me, I doubt that I would be doing everything that I am today. Everything I do, I'm doing it so that I can make a better life for him.

Since leaving ACCW, I have gone on to accomplish a Diploma in Residential Care, an Associate's of Arts Degree in Psychology, I was the valedictorian of my college graduating class, and am currently working towards a Bachelor of Science Degree in Psychiatric Nursing. It's unlikely I would've done any of these things had it not been for my son, and wanting to give him the best life that I can. None of these things would have been possible were it not for the Mother Baby Program at ACCW.

Jennifer:

Finally after being on the run for eight months, I got caught and had to redo my community sentence order. The judge decided I would do it in jail. I was sick and throwing up, thought it was an ulcer due to the stress I was under worrying about getting caught or something. I ended up getting a pregnancy test and found out I was almost two months pregnant, I couldn't believe it. I was shocked and grateful that I got arrested when I did, considering all the drugs I was putting into my body. I had all these emotions running through me I was so happy and scared at the same time but mostly relieved. I was safe and clean and knew things were going to be different from here on out. I felt as though I had a reason to get my life back on track and things were going to be different for me.

After a month they moved me to ACCW. I remember having been there in 2005 when they had just started the baby program. During my time at ACCW I got ultrasounds monthly and went to a pregnancy program a few times too. Every time I had something happen they took me to the hospital which was good because Sierra ended up being two months early. It was scary but I knew we were going to be okay. I stayed at B.C. woman's hospital on Fir Unit a few weeks before Sierra was born. When she came on June 18 she was three pounds seven ounces, so tiny. She was in an incubator for over a month and I got to stay right by her side the whole time.

Alison:

At ACCW it was possible to make a solid argument for an idea that would encourage and support healing: it would be heard. Mothers today have videos of their newborns. It is part of the deep maternal pride that nurturing and bonding are built with and may well serve as a memory to keep a mother strong. It was approved for me to make a small video of our precious premature bundle. The DVD was not allowed in the prison but was shown to Jenn and now is safely in the delightful home she has created for herself and Sierra.

Jennifer and Sierra:

I had to wait for Sierra to gain enough weight to take her out of the hospital. She had to be big enough to fit in a car seat. When I got to bring Sierra back to finish the rest of my sentence I couldn't wait for the ladies to meet her as we all thought I would have had her after I was done my sentence. When I got to ACCW and the gates opened I saw people waiting for us. When I got to my unit, my room was all made up for us there was a crib, baby blankets, toys, etc. Sierra had other little friends on the unit so she wasn't the only child. There was support too. I was so happy to have her with me I couldn't imagine what my life would be like without her.

Getting the chance to bring her to ACCW with me changed my life completely. It's really upsetting to know that now they don't have the program anymore. It's so heartbreaking to know that if you're in jail and pregnant that you will go directly to the hospital to have your baby and then back to jail without your baby to finish your sentence. It makes me realize everyday how lucky me and my daughter were.

I remember when we were there that the nurses were right next door so if I had any problems or questions I could just go over to health care which was very helpful and comforting. My daughter got her first shots there and we were both well looked after. Now me and my daughter are living in Vancouver together and she's four years old. She's happy, healthy and she's the best thing that ever happened to me and if I never had the chance to keep her with me I have no idea what would have happened to her or myself and I am so grateful for having this....

Betty:

As an environmental activist I was no stranger to prison..... There is a built-in urge for grandmothers to pick up babies. And rock them. Twice I got into trouble over this. In May, 2009 *Reader's Digest* published an article entitled "Babies Behind Bars," which featured Jennifer, mother of Sierra, and described their stay at ACCW while I was there. Jennifer, in her early twenties, mentions the night she was at her wit's end trying to calm a crying baby that seemed determined not to be calmed. Jennifer and her new baby hadn't been in the prison long and were placed in the room next to mine. That night I could hear Jennifer crying in acute distress at being unable to calm her baby. I got up, knocked on her door, picked up the crying baby from her crib with Jennifer's consent, stepped into the common room that held the magic rocking chair and sat down with the baby. After rubbing Sierra's little tummy for a moment and burping her as I rocked her gently all the time, she stopped crying and began to drift off to sleep—just as the guards walked through the door making their rounds.

Ah, I was in deep trouble. I was severely lectured, even though Jennifer explained I was only trying to help. The guards were not impressed. This was my second offense and it could very well mean my transfer to another unit. I was even prepared for this but a funny thing happened. Or didn't happen. I didn't hear any more about the incident. The guards either forgot, or ... and then I remembered. They were mothers, too.

Patricia:

Suffering and loss was nothing new to me as I experienced abuse, neglect, and family addiction throughout the course of my life and lost both my father and only sibling to alcohol and drug related incidents at the age of 14. In 2008 I was 30 years old and three months pregnant. I received a sentence of two years in federal jail. My negative choices faced me with the imminent reality that my innocent child would suffer the same grim adversity because of my wrong doings. The program to keep mothers and babies together had been suspended. Guilt accompanied the thought like no grief I have ever felt before.

The day at the hospital when I had to kiss her goodbye was the most excruciating agony; the most hopeless, miserable and empty experience of my life. At a time that was supposed to be wonderful and amazing I stood and watched in horror as my whole world walked out the door. I had let my little girl down and she needed me. She needed my love, my nurturing, my smell, my voice, and of course my milk. All of these things we had shared together for 40 weeks, were all taken away. I asked why was she being punished for something that I did? I pleaded that my daughter be allowed my breast milk. Tears would run down my face while I pumped milk for my newborn. Crying over spilled milk took on a whole new meaning for me.

Alison:

I was supposed to be Patricia's birthing coach but I was teaching and got there 15 minutes too late… Perfectly though, the correctional officer assigned for hospital duty that day filled in the spot and has been forever changed from a disbeliever in this program to an advocate who feels very attached to this mother-child pair and is always glad to hear about their success. She is a mother too, of course.

Patricia:

I was released from Fraser Valley Institution on parole five weeks following her birth and attended a treatment facility for women and their children. My daughter was returned to me there. She has been with me since that time. With my hard work and determination I now have a beautiful three year old daughter who is looking forward to meeting her baby brother, due to be born in the near future. With the expectation of another baby I have had many emotions, anxiety and deep grief re-surface surrounding the removal of my daughter at birth. The trauma of it all was so extreme that I stuffed it somewhere in order to survive.

I still have nightmares that I am in jail without my daughter and I relive the emotions all over again. I truly don't know how I made it through that time in my life. My thoughts are with all of the women and babies in prison going through what I went through. There really are no words that can describe that kind of pain and cruelty.

Renee:

I was sentenced to 18 months in jail at BCCW in 2003. I had four children, aged eight, six, three, and six months. I am not a drug addict or a gambler, but was diagnosed with mental health issues once I received treatment in custody. Upon my incarceration I cut off all contact with my family including my children.... I started seeing a psychologist and a psychiatrist who put me on medication which helped me begin feeling more stable.

I heard about the OLU and how some women had been able to have their young children live with them there. I immediately began to show interest and ask about the program. Within ten days I had moved to the OLU, and had a full time job in the prison flower shop. I applied to have an open/unsupervised visit with my children. Upon seeing them, I was instantly aware of the empty void I was feeling... and needed/craved that connection that only a mother/child could have... I applied to begin overnights with my children.... Since my boys were over two years of age, they did not qualify, but my eight-year-old daughter and my eight-month-old baby girl both were considered candidates for the program. My eight-year-old spent a total of six overnight visits with me in my room and came to work with me on Saturdays in the flower shop. My baby began to stay with me on a regular basis about two weeks after I had been moved. I had approved inmate babysitters to help me with her when I was working or attending therapy or meetings.

The mother/baby program was the most rewarding, fascinating program I participated in while in custody. The respect and care I got from staff was rewarding and validating, and the other women living in the OLU at the time were all shown and showed lots of patience, caring and understanding. There was an atmosphere of joy and safe surroundings while Paris was with us... every woman showed nurturing and love, and as women a common interest and concern for the baby.

Another woman had her son on a few weekends, and we bonded over caring for our children and were able to see each other as more than the bank robber or—the junkie. Above all else, we were mothers ... wanting to pursue the mother/child relationship no matter the circumstances.

Alison:

Renee has full custody of all four of her children and neither Renee, or her friend have returned to prison for many years.

Mo:

When I was high for all those years, I learned to live in denial and try to forget that I had children.... Having babies in the prison slapped me in the face. But at the same time it was a start for me to heal and deal with my issues as a person, as a mother.... At night I would lie in my room awake wondering what my own children looked like or where they were.

Alison:

We tried everything we could to help Mo find her children; we connected with a social worker: nothing was successful. It was after release that Mo was able to locate her three children through Facebook! They are all back in her life now and Mo continues to study and change her life every day while working to educate others through documentaries she has produced and presentations she gives.

Kelly:

Babies in Prison: A Way Home to My Daughter—I am still in awe when I think about the profound effect that the babies in prison had on my life. As I sit here I am reflecting on the past four years and how it has evolved. I attribute much to the opportunity to live on the mother/baby unit at ACCW. It was certainly not the cool unit but a place where I could face the emotions tied to my own mothering and move through a process of cleansing and healing, by living day to day with the babies ... to face my own pain day after day, until finally the demons in my head had calmed their evil voices.... this opportunity to be with the babies peeled a layer of my hardened heart; slowly some of the rough edges started to smooth away. As I softened, becoming more loving and thoughtful towards others, I had to face the sorrow that I felt for abandoning my own family. Prison is an interesting place to have to do this work. It is very introspective and it requires courage and an outlet for expression. Mine was journaling and beading. On the unit, the babies came first and we learned to respect the babies and the mothers. Any woman that interfered with the 'code' that we had set for Alder was asked to leave.

It wasn't just Alder that experienced change from the presence of babies; the prison as a whole was different. There was less violence, less bullying and swearing. The environment in the prison was less intimidating and more welcoming for the first time offenders. I had been incarcerated back in 2005 when the first mother and child arrived at ACCW. Now two years later, several mothers and their children had gone through the program. The prison, the staff, the inmates, and administration had all experienced the wonder of the babies. The change in the prison over the past two years was evident.

Alison:

To live on this unit a woman had to apply to the administration and a process would be undertaken to assure that the applicant would not cause any harm to a baby or a mother.

Linnea:

In 2007 I wrote, "I've just come from delivering a mom and toddler from ACCW to Peardonville, where mom is going on her parole. Her baby was born while she was at ACCW and he is just over a year now. As we drove through the gates, in our jammed to the roof car, she was very emotional. The staff handling her discharge had given out individual hugs to both mom and son. The well wishes being called out to her as we drove through the grounds were from both inmates and staff. Some of the relationships that she has formed she hopes will last for the rest of her life. Her son had a safe environment to be nurtured for that critical first year of his life. She is leaving with some pretty realistic plans for her life. She is fortunate in having solid support on the outside."

Her plans changed with time, but four years later she and her son are happy and moving on with life. She has excelled at higher education and is still studying while working in her field of choice. She has also risen to the challenge of coping with a chronic disease that her son developed. I enjoy hearing of their progress in our ongoing contact.

Betty:

Women are programmed to respond to children, particularly babies. If they weren't, the human race would never have survived. Women in prison are no different. And this is the connection. The babies in the unit and indeed, for the entire prison, connected us as women, as mothers. It was a very healthy thing. The Government in charge of provincial prisoners, acting in their desire for punishment rather than rehabilitation, has cut the mother-baby program entirely. The mother-child bond is the strongest bond in nature. To deliberately sever this bond for whatever reason is to commit a crime against nature and society.

Alison:

Women have taught me that more than physical and possibly even sexual abuse, the lack of maternal love is the most profoundly damaging: how can we possibly contribute to another generation living this pain? Mothers are all different—some would not choose to take part in and some are unsuitable for this program. However, we, the mothers, believe that the opportunity for maternal magic to heal and for hope, must be available and possible.

"It Was Easier to Say I Didn't Have Kids"

Mothering, Incarceration and Relationships with Social and Criminal Justice Policies

OLIVIA SCOBIE AND AMBER GAZSO

MOTHERING IS A SIGNIFICANT challenge for any woman who attempts to raise a child but particularly for mothers who experience low income and must rely on support from the government or family and friends. For low-income mothers who commit crime, the challenges of caring for children are even greater. In this paper, we explore how previously incarcerated mothers perceive the combined influence of state, criminal and social policies on their attempts to reconnect, as mothers, with their children. Three transitions emerged in our analysis of in-depth interviews with nine mothers—becoming mothers and committing crime; incarceration; release—during which mothers struggled to access formal and informal support and manage their mothering identity.[1]

Though we were interested in mothers' post-release experiences, we found that mothers in our study encountered the negative economic effects of neoliberal inspired social policies and programs early in life, had to navigate difficult policies and programs during their imprisonment, and then typically faced substantial social, financial and logistical barriers when attempting to re-establish their family lives. Mothers' relationships with social and criminal justice policies and programs before, during, and after incarceration had the effect of fracturing their mothering identities.

SITUATING MOTHERS' CRIME: PRE AND POST-RELEASE

Women account for approximately nine percent of the provincial prison population and five percent of the federal prison population in Canada (Trevethan et al.). The majority of incarcerated women are single mothers in their early thirties, unemployed, and with less than a high school education (Finn et al.); two thirds of women in federal prisons are mothers (Elizabeth Fry Society of Peterborough); 23 percent of the provincial female prison population and 20 percent of the federal female prison population are Aboriginal (Balfour and Comack 68).

From the perspective of feminist political economy, the link between poverty and the crime committed by mothers is contextualized by the neo-liberal retrenchment of the welfare state and changes to the criminal justice system. Neo-liberalism is an economic doctrine and ideology that has shaped policy reform from especially the 1990s onward in line with goals of smaller government, targeted spending, and free market competition. Assumptions that citizens are responsible, self-sufficient, and efficient additionally underpin neo-liberalism. In practice, neo-liberal reform has translated into a rolling back of social policies and programs from the 1990s onward. Dramatic cutbacks were made to social assistance, subsidized childcare, and housing, cutbacks that coincided with decreased public sector employment (Tuominen). The result has been that government transfer programs, such as social assistance and child benefits, do not provide monthly incomes above Statistics Canada's Low Income Cut Offs (National Council of Welfare). Considering prisons for women, neo-liberal restructuring has involved the devolution of state responsibility for crime prevention and control and the roll-out of new responsibilization strategies tied to government and community partnerships (Hannah-Moffat 514).

Existing research establishes explicit connections between neo-liberal restructuring and women's crime. Julia Sudbury (69) observes that since women still maintain positions as primary caregivers even as their economic stability has declined, some choose to compensate for challenging financial circumstances by engaging in criminal acts. Madonna Mainment argues that neoliberal economic policies crafted by the state heighten market inequalities, which then contribute to gender, race and class marginalization and may lead citizens to participate in the market in illegal ways. Indeed, changes to social assistance have contributed to women's poverty but neoliberal ideology has placed the responsibility for climbing out of poverty on those suffering from it (Golden 12). However, should women choose crime as their escape from economic oppression, they are punished and their crime is viewed as an individual problem. And, once incarcerated, women face a newer neo-liberal message of self-governance that is behind much in-house programming: that they must self-govern; they are responsible for not just their crime but also their rehabilitation and/or empowerment (Hannah-Moffat, 519)

The effects of poverty and racialization that contribute to some women's criminality create further obstacles to their successful re-entry into society. Perhaps the most significant challenge that mothers face when exiting the prison system is establishing an adequate income (McGowan et al. 20) that provides for housing and other needs like child care. Although many newly released mothers do survive off of state support (Travis and Waul 324), monthly social assistance benefits are hardly sufficient. For mothers who desire paid labour, many do not feel that they are adequately prepared to return to the workforce (Carlson 79). As well, having a criminal record makes it difficult to find work in traditionally feminized roles such are childcare or health care (Golden 117). Women are more likely to work in dead end, low paying jobs. These economic challenges exacerbate previously incarcerated mothers' efforts at re-gaining custody of their children. Mothers cannot always meet the government's requirements of adequate housing and income (Halperin and Harris 341). Pre- and post-incarceration, the majority of mothers experience a social context where their economic oppression, consequent of neo-liberal reforms, is normalized.

Mothers in prison are subject to social and moral regulation of their mothering identities just like other mothers. Many women from North American culture have internalized an identity of *intensive mothering*, defined as mothering that is child centered, emotionally consuming, and self-sacrificing (Hays). This lens establishes clear societal guidelines about what constitutes a "good" and "bad" mother. Mothers who put their children ahead of themselves are "good" mothers (Hays), who would therefore never leave their family, regardless of their emotional or physical well being (Buskens). In contrast, mothers who leave their children are quickly labelled as "bad." Once imprisoned, mothers have to confront this stigma alongside their new identity as "criminal."

Upon release, mothers continue to struggle with their maternal identity. Mothers may worry that they will not be able to provide for their children and find it difficult to become reacquainted with them (Harm and Phillips 11). Mothers who suffer from addiction face the additional challenge of maintaining sobriety. It can be difficult to reestablish relationships with their children after suffering significant stress and lowered self esteem due to imprisonment. Many mothers describe returning to their families as the best *and* most challenging part of release (Harm and Phillips 10), as the mother/child relationship has frequently been altered.

METHODS

We conducted in-depth interviews with previously incarcerated mothers in order to understand how they perceive the combined influence of state, criminal and social policies on their attempts to reconnect with their children. Purposive and snowball sampling was used to recruit mothers who served time in the provincial correctional systems in both British Columbia and Ontario. In each province, one agency that supported female prisoners before and after incarceration assisted in the distribution of written and electronic advertisements of the research study. Women interviewed recommended other women eligible for the study.

To be eligible to participate, mothers must have had a biological child prior to their incarceration, or to have given birth during their time in prison. During their incarceration, each mother also must have participated in at least one prison program designed to offer personal support, have been released from prison for at least six months and be in contact with at least one of their children. In total, the sample was made up of nine Canadian mothers. Five mothers disclosed that they identified as Aboriginal. Six women were from B.C. and three were from Ontario.

Our analysis of the interviews was informed by the qualitative traditions of narrative analysis (Sandelowski) to allow the mothers to shape their own narratives. We coded the interview transcriptions according to topics generated by the mothers' answers across collective interviews. What surfaced was a series of dominant themes embedded in key life course transitions. For example, each mother had a unique experience with accessing social assistance but every woman spoke about this as a challenge after their release. During coding, it became clear that the re-entry process of newly released mothers was greatly influenced by their life experiences before and incarceration.

FINDINGS

Becoming Mothers and Committing Crime

During the early years of child rearing, the nine mothers had two very different experiences of mothering. Joyful mothers were mothers who had their children before their prison sentence, including the two who had children in prison. The remaining three mothers were identified as disconnected mothers during their children's early years.[2] As will become apparent, these categories are fluid and transitional. Mothers identified as both joyful and disconnected at different times in their lives.

During their children's infancy, joyful mothers reported that they thoroughly enjoyed caring for their children and maintained a strong effort at emulating a nuclear family, which they claimed would bring them a sense of security that they felt was missing from their own childhoods. They interpreted their mothering experiences as rewarding and recounted having felt grounded during this time in their lives. They enjoyed the routine in their day, could easily express love to their children, and worked hard to provide a "normal" household. These mothers were attached to a partner, and although they lived on meager incomes, aligned themselves with the ideals of the nuclear family and took pride in domestic work such as cooking, cleaning, and childcare. Mindy describes this time in her life: "I loved it. I'm totally domesticated. Like, I loved just being at home with my kids and cooking and cleaning and—like that was my life."

Many mothers that experienced joyfulness with their infants and young children expressed a desire to create households that were superior to their own experiences of early family life. Their own experiences as children, however, meant that they did not feel secure in their parenting abilities. So, to be a "good" mother, not just a happy mother, they actively sought out informal and formal support. They received help from friends and family and all of them received social assistance. Despite their awareness of their need to self-regulate to maintain their receipt benefits, they perceived this was offset by their participation in free young child drop-in centres which offered a wide variety of government sponsored programs such as nutritional advice, parenting classes, young mother support groups, and music and play lessons. The mothers also largely reflected on the substantial role of playgroups in shaping their mothering communities and claimed that these programs provided them with the tools to mother in the way that they desired.

Disconnected mothers reported a drastically different experience of motherhood. They shared that they felt that they had not been adequately taught how to mother and could not live up to societal expectations of mothering, including dominant ideas that mothering is performed in nuclear families. This group expressed the same desires to be a great mom, but lacked the supportive infrastructure from which the joyful mothers benefited; they were largely lone parents or their children's fathers made infrequent contact with them. They described feeling isolated and inundated by the demands of motherhood, feelings compounded by their perception of the wider public stigma associated with lone parenthood. Because of these feelings of exclusion, they did not make reference to having extensive nor consistent access to formal support from the state, such as community programs, social assistance, or subsidized childcare. Additionally, the mothers that identified as being disconnected from their children did not have a close network of friends/family. Instead they reported feeling consistently overwhelmed by the demands of their children, living in a perpetual state of exhaustion. These mothers missed the freedom that they had prior to becoming mothers, and longed to escape to a life with reduced personal and financial burdens. During a period of feeling disconnected, Dale explains her experience, "I think the biggest thing that I always noticed is that I lost who 'Dale' was and all I became was mom."

Disconnected mothers also reported feeling ill-equipped to care for their children physically and emotionally. They claimed that they did not adequately bond with their children due to their own childhood experiences that had lacked sufficient love and attention, and that they had not yet learned how to internalize or express affection at the time their first child was born. They suggested that this led to a lack of connection with their children and thus hindered their mothering enjoyment. Unlike joyful mothers, they were either unaware of or did not seek out supports in their communities. Julia explains "It was totally different than it has been now.... It was—it was distant... I was not, uh, not maternally connected to her."

Incarceration

Once the mothers had been arrested and provincially sentenced, many began to participate in prison programs with varying degrees of success. It was noted that the prison in B.C. offered a diverse range of programs to the inmates and focused much more on healing and rehabilitation. The goal of this prison was to support and empower the inmates, and the mothers recalled being granted opportunities to have a voice and take on leadership roles. Laurie explains:

> [Jail] is very ... you know, it's fun! I mean, we have BBQ's, sports days, you know, uh, I was inmate coordinator.... I think it was a huge impact in there at the time. I mean they listened to us right ... we were a person, right. Our needs were actually—you could ask.... I mean there are the times the staff didn't even know what was going on. But it gave women ownership of their lives, right? (Laurie, two children, B.C., self-identified Aboriginal)

One of the programs offered to support women in the B.C. prison is the *Mother and Baby* program, used by Gina and Marisa who were pregnant at the beginning of their incarceration. In this particular program, pregnant women and mothers of children under three are allowed to live inside the minimum security prison with their children. Gina and Marisa claimed that this opportunity allowed them to bond with their babies, become motivated to work to maintain their sobriety, and inspired them to advance their education. Other mothers who had been incarcerated in B.C. also reflected on how the *Mother and Baby* program influenced their mothering identity in a positive way. The mothers who recalled raising their own infants as a joyful experience enjoyed the reminder of these memories while spending time with the mothers and their young children inside the prison. They claimed that supporting new mothers was a strong motivational tool for them to work on their sobriety so they could reconnect with their own children upon release.

With the exception of Gina and Marissa, none of the women interviewed had regular contact with their children during the time in which they were incarcerated. All nine mothers struggled to stay connected due to the geographic distance between where the prison was located and where their children resided, the cost of long distance phone calls or their children's caregivers' choice to avoid or limit their contact. For mothers with these experiences, finding their children upon release was exceptionally difficult. Laurie was so upset by how the lack of contact with her children disrupted her mothering identity that she refused to discuss them with her fellow inmates. She recalled, "It got to the point where I didn't even tell people I had children. It was easier to say I didn't have kids than to explain where my kids were."

Among the mothers originally identified as joyful, their stories of incarceration seem to suggest that they lost this mothering identity. In many ways, they too became disconnected mothers. We speculate that this was because they were not able to maintain regular contact with their children while incarcerated. With the exception of the two mothers who had children in prison, the mothers spoke very little about what it meant to be a mother during incarceration even despite our questioning. Instead, mothers chose to speak of incarceration as a time to focus on their needs, as opposed to caring for children, and to create strategies for self-improvement (e.g. developing social, personal, and educational skills) that would especially benefit their re-entry into society. This was most noticeable for the mothers from B.C. and can perhaps be attributed to the model of self-governance that accompanies prisons subject to neo-liberal restructuring.

Release

The amount of formal and informal support the mothers had after their release significantly impacted the process of reintegration into their families and communities. The mothers all claimed that formal support from government benefits, criminal justice transitional programs and community programs made their recovery possible. Yet, at the same time, they struggled to navigate a system laden with obstacles.

Mothers' efforts at securing housing were very different, depending on their province of residence. Mothers from B.C. reported meeting with a release counselor who assisted them in finding housing and applying for social assistance prior to their release date. As a result, all mothers from B.C. who struggled with addiction were relocated to addiction treatment centers almost immediately upon release.[3] The five mothers in B.C. who resided in a treatment facility immediately after incarceration found that the challenge in finding housing occurred at the end of their treatment. Interestingly, these mothers reported that there were a greater number of housing options for women fleeing abusive domestic relationships or sex workers in danger than for women exiting the prison system. In contrast, Ontario mothers made no mention of having release counselors, and instead reported that they were expected to make housing arrangements on their own. These mothers found assistance in filing their paperwork from support agencies such as The Elizabeth Fry Association or services specifically geared to support Aboriginal women. Two mothers resided in shelters for several nights directly after their release, which was problematic while attempting to maintain sobriety. These mothers reported feeling uncertain about what to do with their days and did not find it easy to apply for subsidized housing or social assistance because they did not have readily available access to the technology necessary to facilitate this, such as telephones or computers with Internet access. This led to short relapses in their recovery because these were often the same friends or family with whom they had engaged in substance abuse with prior to their incarceration. Eventually, each mother was able to find housing, although the time this took ranged from four weeks to six months. The more quickly the mothers were able to establish housing and acquire a monthly income, the sooner they were able to set new goals for themselves—specifically finding work, advancing their education, or regaining access to their children.

The five mothers with preschool or school-aged children upon release expressed a desire to exit social assistance and enter the labour market. These mothers reported barriers to finding paid work. Most notably, having a criminal record limited the type of work opportunities that were available to them. They were typically qualified only for low-waged, precarious employment due to their minimal education and years out of the labour market during which they were incarcerated, raising children, or struggling with addiction. Many mothers also reported that they felt fearful of being judged by potential employers and this concern prevented them from actively applying for jobs.

> 'Cause I did not feel that I was, I don't know, like, my self-esteem was low and stuff like that, and like, I still have barriers when it comes to work. Um, like, just a month ago I was searching for a job... and I get into a panic when I go looking for jobs because nine times out of ten they are going to ask you for criminal record check. (Mindy, four children, B.C., self-identified as Aboriginal)

Regaining access to children post-incarceration was a significant challenge for five of the nine mothers. The ages of children significantly impacted the ease or difficulty with which mothers were able to re-establish their maternal relationships. The younger the child was when the mother was released, the more difficult it was to renew the mother-child relationship. Three mothers had children still in the public school system or younger and found that their children did not wish to return to living with them full-time because they had grown accustomed to living with their non-maternal caregiver. However, the mothers did not express feelings of disappointment over their children's choice. They had frequent visitation and likened the experience of mothering to sharing custody of a child after a divorce or separation. They claimed that living separately allowed them to maintain a closer relationship because the time they did spend together was especially devoted to their children and was not confounded by the other stresses that corresponded with their post-incarceration daily routines. Marie stated, "I think that I'm closer than a lot of the moms I know that are divorced or separated."

With the exception of the two mothers who had their children during their incarceration, all of the mothers felt disconnected from their children during their incarceration. Yet, we observe that re-entry into society seemed to positively impact the women's perceptions of their mothering identities. Regardless of whether a mother had identified as joyful or disconnected during her children's early years, six mothers noted a marked improvement in their relationships with the children with whom they were able to reconnect. Although they tended to suspend their mothering identities while incarcerated, it was exactly because of the personal growth and healing that they had achieved through the prison programs in which they had participated, specifically emotions management or rehabilitative centers, that they believed they could be "good" mothers post-incarceration. In this way, the self-governance imposed on mothers in prison can have a much later, positive impact on mothering identity upon release.

DISCUSSION

Previously incarcerated mothers' stories illustrate how neo-liberal infused social and criminal justice policies impacted their lives and influenced their mothering identities. Although each mother's path to incarceration was unique, their histories of trauma, abuse, poverty and addiction created circumstances whereby they could not fully rely on family or friends and felt they had to rely on other formal supports. However, some state supports failed to deliver the resources needed by mothers largely because of the changes to them brought about by neoliberal restructuring. When incarcerated, mothers also differently experienced the influence of neo-liberal oriented policies and programs depending on the province in which they were incarcerated. After the release of The Arbor Report, the Canadian government promised to make an effort to shift away from male centered, punishment based approaches (Horri, Parkes and Pate). Some scholars argue this is a goal that has not yet been reached and that inadequate funding is making this objective challenging to implement (Micucci and Monster). Our research suggests that although the Canadian government committed to women's centered prisons at the federal level, at the provincial level these guidelines have been better implemented in some female prisons, such as those in B.C., than others, such as those in Ontario. As well, we find that previously incarcerated mothers experience a mix of punitive or rehabilitative support, depending on the prison location and to what extent neo-liberalism has influenced the scope of programming available.

We learn from mothers in our study that their relationships with social and criminal justice policies and programs before, during, and after incarceration had the effect of fracturing their mothering identities. Earlier life events, such as time spent in their nuclear family of origin (pre-separation of their parents), influenced each woman's sense of identity as a mother prior to incarceration. As well, their experiences of being marginalized mothers—mothers who had to rely on formal support like social assistance in order to make ends meet—played a role in their perceptions of themselves as joyful or disconnected mothers.

Once incarcerated, the focus of correctional programming impeded their identities as mothers. The mothers who recalled joyful memories of active mothering appeared to be embarrassed by their minimal relationship with their children, suggesting that they repressed their mothering identities. The disconnected mothers did not express the same feelings of regret and embarrassment, but they also experienced the repression of their mothering identities. With a focus on the self but exclusive of mothering, the majority of prison programs provided mothers with few avenues to explore what it meant to mother while incarcerated and after release. The two mothers that participated in the *Mother and Baby* program in B.C. had a slightly different experience, as they became mothers in prison. For these women, the time that they spent in rehabilitation did not only focus on recreating themselves, but on transitioning to motherhood.

Finally, upon release, mothers had to re-imagine what mothering meant to them in the midst of legal and structural barriers that impeded their re-connection with their children. For example, of the few mothers with pre-school children upon release, they shared an interest in continuing their mothering work at home until their children were at least old enough to attend a full day school program. However, expectations of their labour force participation within social assistance policies did not make it easy for lone parents to remain a full time caregiver. Many mothers were pressured into finding a job despite the lack of full time work that paid a living wage and coincided with day care hours. Other mothers who expressed their desire to return to work or school found that their criminal record administrative policies excluded them from many occupations and educational programs.

CONCLUSION

Previously incarcerated mothers perceive that neo-liberal infused policies and institutions have shaped their mothering experiences in often inequitable and troubling ways and these processes occur not only during or after their prison sentence, but begin early in their life history. Incarceration itself is a distinct life course event that can disrupt a woman's sense of herself as a mother and what it means to be a mother. Mothering identities can be suspended, either through the influence of correctional programming or the need to depend on caregivers for children. Upon release, the act of re-claiming a mothering identity is also made difficult by accessing some formal supports largely under the influence of neo-liberalism. For example, social assistance provided only a semblance of relief; monthly benefit incomes maintained mothers' experiences of poverty. In our view, our conceptions and discussions of crime committed by mothers must be reframed to account for these challenging experiences in our current neo-liberal social climate. Only then will we have an adequate foundation of knowledge from which we might begin to develop formal state supports that can improve the lives of this marginalized group.

[1]Whereas formal supports refer to organized, government funded supports (i.e. social assistance or rehabilitative services in prisons), informal supports refer to supports offered from family, friends or community organizations, including living with peers or free childcare from extended family (Armi, Guilley and D'Epinay).

[2]Our use of these categories should not be read as perpetuating the stereotypical dichotomy of "good" and "bad" mothers. Instead, these categories are based on the language that the interviewed mothers used when describing their identities as mothers.

[3]Those mothers were perceived as single, with no dependants. Even though they had children, this perception of their eligibility was important to their receiving a space, as some programs are designed for mothers with dependants, while others do not accommodate children.

WORKS CITED

Armi, Franca, Edith Guilley and Christian J. Lalive D'Epinay. "The Interface Between Formal and Informal Support in Advanced Old Age: A Ten-Year Study." *International Journal of Ageing and Later Life* 3.1 (2008): 5-19. Print.

Balfour, Gillian, and Elizabeth Comack. *Criminalizing Women: Gender and (In)justice in Neo-Liberal Times.* Halifax: Fernwood, 2006. Print.

Buskens, Petra. "From Perfect Housewife to Fishnet Stockings and Not Quite Back Again: One Mother's Story of Leaving Home." *Mother Outlaws: Theories and Practices of Empowered Mothering.* Ed. Andrea O'Reilly. Toronto: Women's Press, 2004. 105-119. Print.

Carlson, Joseph. R. "Evaluating the Effectiveness of a Live-in Nursery Within a Women's Prison." *Journal of Offender Rehabilitation* 27.1/2 (1998): 73-85. Print.

Elizabeth Fry Society of Peterborough. "Just the Facts." 2009. Web. 29 Oct. 2011.

Finn, Anne, et al. "Female Inmates, Aboriginal Inmates, and Inmates Serving Life Sentences: A One Day Snapshot." *Juristat Canadian Centre for Justice Statistics* 19.5 (1999): 1-15. Print.

Golden, Renny. *War on the Family: Mothers in Prison and the Families They Leave Behind.* New York: Routledge, 2005. Print.

Halperin, Ronnie, and Jennifer L. Harris. "Parental Rights of Incarcerated Mothers with Children in Foster Care: A Policy Vacuum." *Feminist Studies* 30.2 (2004): 339-352. Print.

Hannah-Moffat, Kelly. "Prisons that Empower: Neo-liberal Governance in Canadian Prisons." *British Journal of Criminology* 40(2000): 510-531. Print.

Harm, Nancy J. and Susan D. Phillips. "You Can't Go Home Again." *Journal of Offender Rehabilitation* 32.3 (2000): 2-21. Print.

Hays, Sharon. *The Cultural Contradictions of Motherhood.* New Haven: Yale University Press, 1996. Print.

Horii, Gayle, Debra Parkes, and Kim Pate. "Are Women's Rights Worth the Paper They're Written On? Collaborating to Enforce the Human Rights of Criminalized Women." *Criminalizing Women.* Ed. G. Balfour and E. Comack. Halifax: Fernwood. 2006. 302-322. Print.

Mainment, Madonna R. "We're Not All That Criminal." *Women and Therapy* 29.3 (2007): 35-56. Print.

McGowan, Brenda G., Karen L. Blumenthal, and National Council on Crime and Delinquency. *Why Punish the Children? A Study of Children of Women Prisoners.* Hackensack, NJ: National Council on Crime and Delinquency, 1978. Print.

Micucci, Anthony and Miranda Monster. "It's About Time to Hear Their Stories: Impediments to Rehabilitation at a Canadian Provincial Correctional Facility for Women." *Journal of Criminal Justice* 32.6 (2004): 515-530. Print.

National Council of Welfare. 2011. Web. 14 Dec. 2011.

Sandelowski, Margarete. "Telling Stories: Narrative Approaches in Qualitative Research." *Journal of Nursing Scholarship* 23.3 (1991): 161-166. Print.

Sudbury, Julia. "Celling Black Bodies: Black Women in the Global Prison Industrial Complex." *Feminist Review* 70 (2002): 57-74. Print.

Travis, Jeremy and Michelle Waul. *Prisoners Once Removed: The Impact of Incarceration and Reentry on Children, Families, and Communities.* Washington, DC: Urban Institute Press, 2003. Print.

Trevethan, Shelly, John-Patrick Moore and Christopher J. Rastin. "A Profile of Aboriginal Offenders in Federal Facilities and Serving Time in the Community." Correctional Service of Canada, 2009. Web. 29 Oct. 2011.

Tuominen, Mary. "Caring for Profit: The Social, Economic, and Political Significance of For-Profit Child Care." *The Social Service Review* 65.3 (1991): 450-467. Print.

Mothering Through Adversity

Voices of Incarcerated Women

CHRISTINE A. WALSH AND MEREDITH CROUGH

W OMEN'S UNDERSTANDINGS of motherhood and self as mothers are continually defined, interpreted and redefined through internal negotiation and social interaction. Mothers who experience incarceration stand at the margins of socially constructed rubrics of motherhood. Incarcerated mothers' interpretations of mothering, challenges and strengths and ultimately their stories, too often go unacknowledged, further perpetuating their marginality. Discourse, both public and academic, surrounding incarcerated mothers is sparse, and often characterized by a lack of hope. In this article we offer a discussion of motherhood in the context of our action research project on incarceration and reintegration into the community.

REVIEW OF LITERATURE

Profile of Incarcerated Mothers

Up to 80 percent of institutionalized women in Canada are mothers (Berry, Johnson, Severson and Postmus 293; CAEFS 2), most of whom have been primary caregivers prior to their arrest (CSC; Enos 2). Women's circumstances prior to, and often between, periods of incarceration provide context to understand their involvement with the justice system and mothering identities. For instance, the majority of female offenders receive sentences for economically motivated crimes related to poverty, mental health concerns and addictions (Ferraro and Moe 12; CCJS 10; Pollock 6). Mothers who become incarcerated not only struggle with these layers of criminalized marginality as individuals, but also as children's caregivers.

Motherhood and Identity

Mothers in conflict with the law are marginalized not only because they violate society's legal bounds, but also because they step outside of society's definition of a "good mother." The mainstream picture of mothering identity involves a strict rubric, typically embedded within patriarchal, racial and class based assumptions regarding gender roles and family structure (Ferraro and Moe 14). Social discourse suggests that "mothers should be the central caregiver of their children, and a mother should spend great amounts of time, energy and material resources on her child. A good mother should always put her children's needs before her own. Women are also expected to be dedicated breadwinners, but children should always come before paid work" (Aiello 4). Herein lies the presumption that a woman has the ability to choose to spend the majority of her time with children, and that she possesses adequate resources, education and employment to provide for her children.

Despite their existence outside the social norm, incarcerated mothers experience motherhood as a powerful facet of identity (Gat 27). In particular, exercising at least some control over who cares for their children, determining how to explain her incarceration to her children and maintaining emotional contact if she deems it appropriate are major avenues for incarcerated mothers to sustain mothering identity and positive self-concept (Berry and Eigenberg 105-06; Frye and Dawe 106-07; Hunter 24; Jensen and DuDeck-Biondo 135; McGee and Gilbert 339; Poehlmann 351; Turek and Loper 37).

Impacts of Incarceration on Mothering

Incarceration disturbs the development of a mothering identity, replacing it with a criminalized identity (Enos 109). Prisons and jails fall into Erving Goffman's characterization of the total institution (Baldwin 20); in particular, the mortification process is germane to the issue of incarcerated mothers. Goffman describes mortification as a process wherein the institution separates the inmate from outside identity by restricting or curtailing the inmate's ability to participate in extra-institutional roles (277). Correctional institutions heavily regulate motherhood and incorporate it into the punitive system. For instance, visitation (which is not available to all incarcerated mothers) is restricted due to institutional factors, including excessively long distances between prison and the community(ies) where her children live, lack of or inappropriate space for visitation, constant monitoring and humiliating practices such as strip searching (Jensen and DuDeck-Biondo 124; Marlow 139; Snyder, Carlo and Coats Mullins 40). Separation from children consistently ranks as the most painful and problematic stress of incarceration for mothers (Luke 934) associated with increased levels of anxiety, depression and guilt (Arditti and Few 104; Jensen and DuDeck-Biondo 126; Poehlmann 354). The resulting elevated levels of parenting stress women experience due to incarceration often leads to increased aggression and rehabilitation difficulty (Tuerk and Loper 24).

Community Reintegration and Motherhood

Following release from incarceration, women's processes of redefining themselves as mothers are vital to successful reentry and personal healing (Brown and Bloom 314; Eljdupovic-Guzina 1). Release involves returning to existing mother-child relationships, or becoming more actively involved in them (Gat 25). Other women make the difficult decision to fully relinquish custody or some who have lost custody of their children and wish to regain it must face the intricacies of the legal system (Hunter 70). Mothers on parole or probation must repair relationships within the restrictions of the justice system including competing with demands of those related to obtaining employment and housing, attending counseling and checking in with correctional officers (Hayes 65). Beyond these issues, mothers must resist internalizing the self-destructive label of "bad mother" that the legal system, social services, the media and society at large ascribe to her (Hunter 27). Additionally, mothers may feel trapped and lose confidence as the people who raised their children during incarceration struggle to relinquish the caregiver role (Hayes 66).

METHODS

We collected stories on motherhood with a group of women in Calgary, Alberta, with lived experience of incarceration, who are now living in the community. Our examination of motherhood was a facet of a larger participatory action research study aimed at developing solutions to reduce the cycle of homelessness and incarceration among women. This methodology emphasizes the agency of the community members participating in research, the value of their contributions as partners in research (Conrad 14; Finley 685), fostering mutual understanding between social groups, and empowering marginalized communities (O'Neill 6; Springgay and Carpenter 11).

We used snowball sampling to recruit participants with lived experience of incarceration. Over the course of a year we met weekly with women, four of whom contributed to a three hour facilitated focus group discussion of motherhood for incarcerated women. A separate individual interview was conducted with one woman who was unable to attend the focus group. We created a field guide to lead the discussion that was vetted by the participants. Though the women described the conversation difficult, as the issue is deeply personal and not one they feel comfortable discussing, the women in this study instigated this conversation, indicating their desire to share their stories of motherhood in a safe setting. Jen, Stacie, Toni and Yvonne chose to use their real names; Marcy is a pseudonym. One woman resided in the transitional home where the discussions occurred, others were continuing to reintegrate into the community on their own. Two women were White and two were Aboriginal; three participants identified as heterosexual and one as a lesbian.

We analyzed the data using qualitative coding, grouping the data into themes and sub-themes as identified from the women's words on motherhood and incarceration (Neuman and Robson 336-7). One researcher performed the initial coding, and another checked it over for consistency. As we identified themes and supporting quotes and began the interpretation we held two subsequent meetings with the women for the purposes of member checking (Neuman and Robson 306). We identified four major themes: mothering prior to incarceration; mothering during incarceration; mothering after incarceration, and hope through mothering and incarceration, each of which are briefly described with supporting quotes.

DISCUSSION

Mothering Prior to Incarceration

The women in the study shared common histories of economic, social and psychological marginalization. Women struggle not only to provide for their own welfare, but also for the welfare of family members and children. Marcy spoke of her challenge to maintain an adequate standard of living for her family and her frustration when she was unable to do so, "I went to the doors [social assistance], and no one would help me."

Emotional, physical and sexual abuse was a common experience. Toni described her history of childhood trauma, noting that it impacted her parenting.

> I never grew up with parents. All I knew was the street. All I knew was running away, and running away from my pain and not knowing how to deal with any of this stuff and not knowing how to be a proper parent.

For three women, addictions masked their psychological wounds. Yvonne recounted seeking solace in her addiction, and how it interfered with her ability to mother,

> I started getting sad and lonely and lost and crying and then I'm with somebody and then boom, you know, I'd be gone, and I'd forget about it. So you know, I think that's probably one reason why I stayed high the whole time, cause I couldn't be there [with her family].

For some, breaking society's legal bonds became a viable means of mothering. Marcy recalls not earning enough to pay the rent and pay the daycare, "I had three kids, and no way of putting food on the table, never mind anything else."

Jen, who became a single mother after her husband died of a drug overdose, took over her husband's work as a drug dealer to provide for her two sons. "I was selling crack to support my family." Toni felt that her socioeconomic circumstances and personal issues would not allow her to mother her children; she chose to be a mother by giving her children up for adoption. "I figure the Creator gave me something ... so I said, well, I'll have them and then give them to someone that can give them a proper life.... So I've done the best I could for my children." Though women acknowledged the "wrong" in their actions in legal and social terms, they expressed a sense of self-respect in doing what they felt was necessary to give the best to their children within extremely challenging circumstances.

For these mothers, hardship marked life leading to periods of incarceration. Toni, an ex sex-worker, reflected on the pain she experienced after she gave up her first child.

> I'm not worth anything. I can't be a mother to this child; I can't be a mother to my other child.... All that I'm worth is the corner [the street where she would sell sex].... And my second Mothers Day I got so drunk. I went out and I got so drunk I ended up going with this guy that I wouldn't have went with and he kicked the shit out of me. He left me for dead out in a field.... I didn't care 'cause I lost my baby.

Struggles with guilt and negative impacts on mothering continued for the women during incarceration.

Mothering during Incarceration

Women expressed frustration with institutional barriers to mothering in prison including legal structures regarding custody issues and prison regulations limiting contact. The women explained that when first incarcerated it often took up to ten weeks before they are able to re-establish contact with their children. Arranging and obtaining visitation time was also noted as problematic. As Stacie suggested, "I think the hardest thing that ever was, was being in prison and having those prison obligations forced on me and then try and maintain a relationship with my daughter."

Women preserved their mothering identities and their sense of involvement with their children by exercising some level of control over their child's living and care situation during their incarceration. Jen, whose children were in temporary custody of her in-laws, maintained her mothering role through telephone contact. "I never stopped being their mom.... I wasn't there physically but the boys still knew that I was there and that there were expectations and that they still needed to behave themselves." Yvonne sought support from family to co-parent her children, "I went to jail and then figured, you're going to be here for a couple months, so I did the smart thing.... I phoned the reserve and got a permanent guardianship order and so she [her mother] came up to [the institution] to see me with a permanent guardianship order." Stacie decided that she could best meet her daughter's needs by giving custody to her partner.

> *When I knew my ex-wife was gonna take her I was happy. I was relieved. It was just one thing in my life that I didn't have to worry about, another responsibility that I would have been obligated to and I was ok with that.... And even today I'm okay with that ... as long as she was healthy and taken care of with structure and morals and values and teachings and love I was okay. I wanted her to have everything that I didn't, and that was everything.*

Forced separation during periods of incarceration not only affected practical aspects of the women's mothering, but also their identities and sense of self. Marcy described watching her children leave her after their first visit as the most painful event of her imprisonment.

> *I was calm until they [the guards] came out and said, "It's time for them to go".... And they hung on so hard that my mom and dad had to pull them off me. Then they were on that side, and I'm over here, standing by myself and I can't even hug them.... And I guess I looked at it, like you know what, they can strip search you when you're here, they can make you bend over, they can do all kind of nasty things, but nothing's gonna hurt me as much as I did that day, 'cause that killed me.*

The women's stories portrayed recurring feelings of guilt and self-doubt regarding their mothering and its impact on their children. When asked how she thought of herself as a mother while incarcerated, Marcy explained, "Like shit. Like shit. I remember thinking, like how do you be, how do you be a mom?" Exiting prison did not necessarily eliminate these concerns.

Mothering after Incarceration

Renegotiating their mothering roles was strongly connected with the journeys of restoration post-incarceration. Arranging custody was a primary challenge for the women after release. Jen described the demanding parole restrictions with which she had to comply in order to regain custody of her sons from foster care. Those who chose to resume active positions in their children's lives shared the challenges and importance of determining how to re-exercise authority as mothers. Yvonne, who continues to co-parent with her mother, shared how she was attempting to reinstate her maternal authority, while reassuring her mother's continued role in her grandchildren's lives:

> ...*She [her mother], and I get so mad sometimes 'cause whatever they want to do, they can. She doesn't want them to get mad at her or, but I keep telling her that they're going to be a part of her life, and they always will be. And I think she's scared too that I'm going to go back there [jail] you know, go back to that [street life].*

Women actively mothering expressed a sense of accomplishment over the growth in their relationships with their children. As Yvonne expressed, "I have been doing so many things that I would never do before … it was like wow, so cool, you know. So just getting memories; making memories." Jen was able to reestablish a stable routine for her sons, that fostered their independence, "they're not so clingy and it's not like mom's leaving again." These milestones are major points of celebration for the women as they journey towards their goals for mothering.

The women in the study spoke about their experiences of empowerment in mothering after incarceration. They expressed that in their personal journeys through marginalization and interactions with the justice system they gained unique wisdom to share with their children. Stacie, who currently does not have contact with her child, looks forward to one day passing on wisdom as her key focus of her identity and influence as a mother.

> *When I have the opportunity [I want] to teach her what I know and show her where she comes from and be her friend, her guide, her teacher. I got a lot of love to give, a lot of knowledge to share.... So to say what it [being a mother] means to me, I just think that when you're healthy you should pass those on.*

The women agreed of the importance of creating a legacy of strength for their children through seeking healing for themselves and for their children while owning up to their past failures. As Jen affirmed that to have lived through incarceration as mothers, "speaks to our strength and our devotion and our love for them, and I like to think that at some point in their lives they will see that … you know it would be nice to leave that legacy."

During their transition into the community, restoring self-esteem and positive identity was key to successful reintegration. Toni managed to reclaim her mothering identity; a positive part of herself that she once thought was lost:

> *I would never have that chance again, I screwed it up you know, no way in hell am I ever going to get my babies back. But I worked and she's home,*

she's eight, she's home with me now. And you know what, through all that she's still my baby, she still loves me. I'm mom. I'm mom. And that's my biggest accomplishment.

Hope

Contrary to the tone and emphasis of much literature surrounding the issue of motherhood and incarceration, the women in our study told stories of hope, strength and restoration. Similar to research with Canadian incarcerated women (Eljdupovic-Guzina 1) participants expressed that their children offered powerful motivation to build healthy lives outside of prison, and that the process of maintaining their mothering identities through and after incarceration helped them to develop a personal sense of agency and inspired them to pursue their own healing. Stacie expressed that simply being aware of her daughter's existence reinforces her positive development as a person.

> *For the first time in my whole life I felt love, I had a reason to live... she saved my life.... Knowing that one day she's gonna want to be in my life is a lot of the reason that I do all kinds of good things now.*

The women expressed deep guilt for mistakes they made in the past. However, at this stage in their lives they are taking active control of their lives, for themselves and for their children. Jen described coming to the realization that she could not, and would not allow regrets and guilt to hold her back from being the mother/person she wants to be:

> *I had a lot of time to think and a lot of time to cry, some time to kick myself in the ass. But you know, I think that I had come to a point in my life where I had kicked my ass for so long that I was just tired of kicking it. I just needed to accept what I had done and do my time and get on with it.*

Marcy expressed a feeling of growing strength in her ability to show her children how to take responsibility for themselves by her own example:

> *I'm proud of the fact that they know I screwed up.... I have shown them, by example that you own up to your mistakes, you pay that consequence, and you learn from it.... Now I find that when they do something wrong, or they do screw up, they're the first to admit it. They never would have done that before. I am proud of that.*

Throughout their time before, during and after incarceration the women struggled with maintaining a strong mothering identity. While acknowledging that their mothering does not fit into an idealized, socially prescribed standard, women have negotiated motherhood within their own circumstances to fulfill goals that are common to all mothers such as encouraging growth, responsibility and understanding for self and others. As Jen explains:

> *All the shit and all the bad things we've done in our lives and how they've affected our kids, for them to see us suck up, own it, deal with the consequences and move forward, I think we're teaching our kids more about resilience... more than we ever could before we went to jail.*

In accepting and learning from their past the women are taking agency in their lives and identities as mothers. They are claiming hope and healing for their children and for themselves.

HONORING WOMEN'S STORIES AND ENCOURAGING EMPOWERMENT

Women shared their multiple layers of marginality including their gendered status, poverty, and for some, histories of abuse, addiction they experienced (Arditti, Burton and Neeves-Botelho 144; Berry et al. 293-294). As Bob Mullaly suggests, these elements of social and personal oppression constitute threats not only to physical survival, but also to identity development as well as mental and emotional wellness (61). As the women's stories highlight, women undergoing marginalization are likely to internalize their oppression and react in self and socially destructive ways (Mullaly 65). For others, managing motherhood in the context of economic marginality directly contributed to criminal activity, as a means for provide as a mother. This not only puts women in conflict with the law, but also with society's unforgiving demands on and definitions of mothering (Ferraro and Moe 14).

As the women confirmed, motherhood and all of its related activities and emotions are a key to their identity (Gat 27). Incarceration challenged the women's ability to maintain this identity, requiring persistence and stamina as they determined how to mother, and who they were as mothers in prison. As J. B. Miller observes, women build themselves in the context of relationship, suggesting that breaks in relationship can be detrimental to the development of positive self concept (83). Self-defeating cycles of guilt and shame impacted the women in the study and jeopardized their positive personal and mothering identities. However, in agreement with the literature, women in the study noted that though incarceration made this difficult, being aware of and able to choose who cared for their children provided them some sense of peace, stability and agency (Luther and Gregson 87). Managing and enacting motherhood through periods of addictions, criminal behaviour or incarceration varied for the women in the study: some gave up custody permanently, others negotiated temporary arrangements during the time they were unable to parent. Though choices differed, the desire to give the best to their children was shared, and the same as the aspirations of most mothers, incarcerated or not.

In mothering, post incarceration, the women identified congruent and overlapping goals of personal and relational restoration. Although efforts to reestablish themselves as mothers in the community ranged from fighting for and obtaining custody, to maintaining physical distance for their children, the women were uniform in enacting their mothering identities in ways that constructed a healthy environment and provided a sense of normalcy for their children and themselves (Hunter 130). Overall, the women expressed empowerment and happiness in their revitalized positions in their relationships with their children. In particular they took pride in the wisdom they have earned and are now able to share. They described the power of their mother-child relationship to influence positive identity development through giving but also gaining strength (Miller 41).

The strongest message the women gave through their stories of mothering through incarceration is hope. Hope in the face of multiple degrees of socio-economic and political marginalization, histories of abuse and addiction, criminalization and incarceration. Hope even in the face of crushing guilt, shame and self-doubt. In negotiating and reclaiming identity as mothers they are discovering and exercising the agency necessary to resist and overcome oppression and foster hope. In this project, women, in their own words, demonstrate the power and resilience of mothers in conflict with the law. It is our hope that these women's stories can encourage, empower, and inspire service providers, members of the justice system, policy makers, and mothers with lived experience of incarceration to oppose oppression and find healing on individual and structural levels.

WORKS CITED

Aiello, Brittnie. "'I Always Thought I Was a Good Mother': Intensive Mothering in a Women's Jail." *Conference Papers – American Sociological Association* 1 (2009). Web. 1 June 2011.

Arditti, Joyce A. and April L. Few. "Mothers' Reentry into Family Life Following Incarceration." *Criminal Justice Policy Review* 17.1 (2006): 103-123. Web. 1 June 2011.

Arditti, Joyce, Linda Burton and Sara Neeves-Botelho. "Maternal Distress and Parenting in the Context of Cumulative Disadvantage." *Family Process*

49.2 (2010): 142-164. Web. 1 June 2011.

Baldwin, Joshua Thomas. *We've Come a Long Way Baby...Or Have We? The Phenomenon of Community Re-Integration for Incarcerated Women.* Unpublished dissertation, University of Alabama, 2009. Ann-Arbor: ProQuest/UMI (Publication no. 3356451). Web. 15 June 2011.

Berry, Phyllis and Helen Eigenberg. "Role Strain and Incarcerated Mothers: Understanding the Process of Mothering." *Women and Criminal Justice* 15.1 (2003): 101-119. Web. 5 June 2011.

Berry, Marianne, Toni Johnson, Margaret Severson, and Judy L. Postmus. "Wives and Mothers at Risk: The Role of Marital and Maternal Status in Criminal Activity and Incarceration." *Families in Society: The Journal of Contemporary Social Services* 90.3 (2009): 293-300. Web. 1 June 2011.

Brown, Marilyn and Barbara Bloom. "Reentry and Renegotiating Motherhood Maternal Identity and Success on Parole" *Crime & Delinquency* 55 (2009): 313-336. Web. 10 June 2011.

Canadian Association of Elizabeth Fry Societies (CAEFS). *Fact Sheet: Criminalized and Imprisoned Women.* Ottawa: CAEFS, 2011. Web 2 July 2011.

Canadian Center for Justice Statistics (CCJS). *Female Offenders in Canada.* Ottawa: CCJS, 2008. Web. 1 July 2011.

Conrad, Diane. "Exploring Risky Youth Experiences: Popular Theater as Participatory, Performative Research Method." *International Journal of Qualitative Methods.* 3.1 (2004): 12-25. Web. 1 June 2011.

Correctional Service of Canada (CSC). *Understanding Violence by Women: A Review of the Literature.* Ottawa: CSC, 2007. Web. 2 July 2011.

Eljdupovic-Guzina, Gordana. *Mothering During Incarceration: Connecting the Past and the Present Experiences.* Unpublished dissertation, Carleton University, 2003. Ann Arbor: ProQuest/UMI (Publication no. 0-612-71935-0). Web. 15 June 2011.

Enos, Sandra. *Managing Motherhood in Prison: Examining the Enactment of Motherhood in a Special Setting.* Unpublished dissertation, University of Connecticut, 1998. Ann-Arbor: ProQuest/UMI (Publication no. 9831873). Web. 15 June 2011.

Ferraro, Kathleen J. and Angela M. Moe. "Mothering, Crime and Incarceration." *Journal of Contemporary Ethnography* 32.1 (2003): 9-40. Web. 1 June 2011.

Finley, Susan. "Arts-Based Inquiry: Performing Revolutionary Pedagogy." *The Sage Handbook of Qualitative Research.* 3rd ed. Ed. Norman K. Denzin and Yvonne S. Lincoln. Thousand Oaks, CA: Sage Publications, Inc, 2005. 681-694. Print.

Frye, Sally, and Sharon Dawe. "Interventions for Women Prisoners and their Children in the Post-release Period." *Clinical Psychologist* 12.3 (2008): 99-108. Web. June 5 2011.

Gat, Irit. *Incarcerated Mothers: Effects of the Mother/Offspring Life Development Program (mold) on Recidivism, Prosocial Moral Development, Empathy, Hope, and Parent-child Attachment.* Unpublished dissertation, University of Nebraska-Lincoln, 2001. Ann Arbor: ProQuest/UMI (Publication no. 9976990). Web. 15 June 2011.

Goffman, Erving. "The Process of Mortification." *Humanistic Sociology.* Eds. Claude C. Bowman. New York: Meredith Corporation, 1973. 277-83. Print.

Hayes, Margaret. "The Lived Experience of Mothering After Prison: The Preliminary Study." *Journal of Forensic Nursing* 4.2 (2008): 61-67. Web. 10 June 2011.

Hunter, Vicki L. *Transitions in Mothering: The Social Construction of Motherhood Among Women Recently Released from Prison.* Unpublished dissertation, Kent State University, 2005. Ann Arbor: ProQuest/UMI (Publication no. 3209661). Web. 15 June 2011.

Jensen, Vickie and Jill DuDeck-Biondo. "Mothers in Jail: Gender, Social Control and the Construction of Parenthood Behind Bars." *Sociology of Crime, Law and Deviance.* Ed. Stacy Lee Burns. Vol 6: Ethnographies of Law and Social Control. Amsterdam: Elsevier JAI, 2005. 6121-142. Print.

Luke, Katherine. P. "Mitigating the Ill Effects of Maternal Incarceration on Women in Prison and Their Children." *Child Welfare* 81.6 (2002): 929-48. Web. 1 June 2011.

Luther, Kate and Joanna Gregson. "Restricted Motherhood: Parenting in a Prison Nursery." *International Journal of Sociology of the Family* 37.1 (2011): 85-103. Web. June 5 2011.

Marlow, Lana G. (2004). *Mothers in Prison, Women's Autobiography, and Activism (Texas).* Unpublished dissertation, University of Texas at Austin, 2004. Ann-Arbor: ProQuest/UMI (Publication no. 3145403). Web. 15 June 2011.

McGee, Zina T. and Adrianne N. Gilbert. "Treatment Programs for Incarcerated Women and Mother-Child Communication Levels." *Criminal Justice Studies* 23.4 (2010): 337-345. Web. 5 June 2011.

Miller, J. B. *Toward a New Psychology of Women.* Boston: Beacon Press, 1973. Print.

Mullaly, Bob. *Challenging Oppression: A Critical Social Work Approach.* Don Mills, ON: Oxford University Press, 2002. Print.

Neuman, W. Lawrence and Karen Robson. *Basics of Social Research: Qualitative and Quantitative Approaches.* Toronto: Pearson Education Canada, 2009. Print.

O'Neill, Maggie. "Transnational Refugees: The Transformative Role of Art?" *Forum: Qualitative Social Research* 9.2 (2008): 1-23. Web. 1 June 2011.

Poehlmann, Julie. "Incarcerated Mothers' Contact With Children, Perceived Family Relationships, and Depressive Symptoms." *Journal of Family Psychology* 19.3 (2005): 350-57. Web. 5 June 2011.

Pollock, Shoshana. *Locked In, Locked Out: Imprisoning Women in the Shrinking and Punitive Welfare State.* Waterloo: Wilfred Laurier University, 2008. Print.

Snyder, Zoann K., Teresa. A. Carlo, and Megan. M. Coats Mullins. "Parenting from Prison: An Examination of a Children Visitation Program at a Women's Correctional Facility." *Marriage and Family Review* 32.3/4 (2001): 33-61. Web. 5 June 2011.

Springgay Stephanie and Stephen B. Carpenter II. "Unframing" Arts-based Research: New Directions and Conversations." *Journal of Curriculum Pedagogy* 4.1 (2007): 9-15. Web. 1 June 2011.

Tuerk, Elena, and Ann Loper. "Contact Between Incarcerated Mothers and Their Children: Assessing Parenting Stress." *Journal of Offender Rehabilitation* 43.1 (2006): 23-43. Web. 5 June 2011.

"I Wanted to Be, I Tried to Be, I Will Be a Good Mother"

Incarcerated Mothers' Construal of the Mother-Role

GORDANA ELJDUPOVIC

MANY YEARS AGO during a visit to a women's prison, I talked with a woman who spoke of her four children with great pride. She told me she could not wait to get out and reconnect with them, as they had all been very young when she became incarcerated. I remember telling her that having two young children of my own, I could not imagine how exhausting it had been for her to cope with four little ones. She replied, "Oh, no, it wasn't a problem at all. I was never tired. Back then, I was on crack. We always had so much fun." She was not joking or being sarcastic; she was relating an honest memory.

This conversation lead me to explore assumptions about motherhood, and how our own personal experiences often provide the basis upon which we judge others' experiences, thus imposing the "shoulds" and "coulds" of mothering. According to Sara Ruddick, "to be a 'mother' is to take upon oneself the responsibility of child care, making its work a regular and substantial part of one's working life" (17). Many of these aspects are stripped from incarcerated mothers' identities, yet they continue to self-identify as mothers and continue to mother their children in varying fashions, sometimes through years of physical separation. Some incarcerated mothers never were primary care-providers for their children prior to incarceration, nor do they plan to re-connect with them upon release. For others, however, knowing their children are out there sustains them emotionally and provides hope. Some correctional facilities recognize the importance of this relationship and have designed parenting programs to help incarcerated parents build and maintain positive relationships with their children. Many incarcerated parents welcome these programs and request them. And yet, the assumptions implicit in these programs about normative parenting practices remain unstated, and are often at odds with the realities of parenting in a context of incarceration and disadvantage.

It is well documented that most incarcerated women come from marginalized backgrounds: poverty, lack of education, and a lack of opportunities are the rule rather than the exception . Further, an overwhelming number of incarcerated women report having experienced some type of childhood abuse (Boritch; Chesney-Lind and Pasko; Comack; CSC; Eljdupovic-Guzina; Maidment; Shaw et al.; Sommers; Tapia). For women in prison, then, few of their early life histories exposed them to the mainstream notion of a "good mother."

This study explored mothering before and during incarceration as experienced from "within," by incarcerated women themselves. Fifteen women who were mothers, and incarcerated in two Canadian federal institutions, were interviewed. Interview methodology was chosen as an explicitly feminist tool; interviews have been described as potentially transformative, a way to shape "new frameworks and theories based on women's lives and women's formulations" (Anderson and Jack 18). As Jeanne Marecek, Michelle Fine and Louise Kidder wrote of qualitative inquiry, it requires "attention to context, meanings, and power relations in data collection *and* analysis" (38). The analyses subsequently performed on the data were located in an interpretive framework that addressed the "what," as well as the "how" and "why" of the women's experiences (Denzin). The data were organized into "conceptual categories" or themes from a "grounded" baseline, and these categories were continually linked with new emergent categories (Neuman) to create a theory of incarcerated mothering, based on the lived experience of incarcerated mothers.

In order to reflect how women's experiences of mothering evolved over time and through the changing circumstances of their lives, the following sections are organized according to both chronology and theme, documenting the stages of pregnancy, incarceration, and plans for post-incarceration. Themes that emerged from the data were coded to reflect not only emotional responses to mothering and incarceration, but also with an eye to how the changes in responses were linked to changes in the women's material conditions, such as during the transition to prison. Quotes from the interviews are presented in order to depict and convey interviewees' points of view as much as possible, because "when researchers restrict participants to speaking only in our terms, we lose access to theirs" (Marecek, Fine and Kidder 33).

PREGNANCY AND "ROMANTICIZED" MOTHERING

When asked about mothering before incarceration, the immediate response of most women was to reflect on how they felt upon first learning they were pregnant. Their accounts reflected Iris Marion Young's observation that, "In the experience of the pregnant mother, this weight and materiality often produce a sense of power, solidity and validity… the pregnant woman can gain a certain sense of self-respect" (53).

The majority of women described feelings of joy and happiness. For some, it was about the bodily experience of carrying a child. As Mia said, "I was glowing, my eyes were sparkling, I love being pregnant, there's a little life inside you." For others, it was associated with pride or a sense of self-worth. As Helga stated: "…I made something. She's so cute …. I've got something to show off to everyone." Becoming a mother was welcomed by some as a way to help them "shape up" or mature. In Wilma's words, "…it made me grow up fast…. I was kind of out of control." The joy of being pregnant was often associated with the mother's desire to make up for what she missed in her own childhood. Some women were determined to create a better world for their child. As Vera recalled, "I didn't want it [her childhood experience] happening to my kid; I didn't want her to grow up the way I was raised." The hope that they could create a better world for their children was voiced both by women who were happy to learn of their pregnancy, as well as by those who expressed some trepidation over becoming mothers.

Descriptions of their pregnancies also reflected, for some women, an imagined new world or "other life" opening up, bringing with it "…a privileged relation to this other life, not unlike that which I have to my dreams and thoughts, which I can tell someone but which cannot be an object for both of us in the same way" (Young 49). This "privileged relationship" to their unborn children, as-yet unconnected to day-to-day mothering, allowed women to project their dreams and secret hopes, as well as the idea of their future mother-role, onto their children.

And then the baby was born!

A SHIFT FROM "ROMANTICIZED" TO "REALISTIC" MOTHERING

At first, I thought: is this really true? And then afterwards, I thought, this is a drag. I had nobody to talk to…. (Tessa)

All I ever wanted to be is a mom … then things got hard. (Nika)

A number of women introduced temporal qualifiers, pinpointing a specific time when a marked shift in their mothering experiences emerged and when, in contrast to the imaginings of pregnancy, they started to feel differently about mothering. This point was after the baby was born. With the onset of the day-to-day chores and obligations associated with caring for a child, women recounted losing their initial romanticized view. The realm of possibilities they encountered in this stage was quite different from the pregnancy stage when they projected, but had not yet lived, day-to-day mothering. A profound sense of loneliness, isolation and lack of social support dominated women's accounts. As Tessa recalled, "I was a scared and lonely parent, I always kept her [daughter] close with me... I kept distance from meeting people because I was always afraid something would happen to me, or my child." This woman was a single mother, young, with minimum resources and no family support. Throughout her life, Tessa reported learning that she could only expect bad things from people. For that reason, in her attempt to be a good mother and as a means of protecting her child, she stayed away from everyone. She went for long, endless walks. She carried her baby in a Snuggly, wearing an extra large old man's coat she purchased in a thrift shop that allowed her to keep herself and the baby warm. But one can walk through a Canadian winter for just so long. Avoiding people at the very time when she most needed resources and support, when she was uncertain of how to cope with this new stage of her life, only deepened her sense of loneliness and increased her stress. Eventually, she returned to a more familiar life style, to her old friends and drugs.

Given that most of the women grew up in difficult or abusive environments, a lack of social support at this stage of their lives was not new. However, the isolation that came with new motherhood, combined with a powerful desire to "do it differently," was particularly accentuated during the period when women were raising their children. Sue's account highlighted the lack of basic essential material resources from her community:

> ...Money was always hard and so was food and stuff... I tried hard to make ends meet.... Having to do it by myself was hard.... No resources, no lady you can go and chat to. No programs.

It is important to keep in mind that the stressors associated with poverty and isolation were not just occasionally faced, but rather, they permeated every aspect of women's daily lives. Money and food were an issue for Sue every day. Women's strong determination during pregnancy that everything would be different for their children was rapidly eroding as each day went by. The effects of these stressors were cumulative and gradually rendered women weaker, with less emotional and physical energy. A vast majority of them struggled with substance abuse and abusive relationships, which perpetuated the stressors.

The extent to which women's circumstances shaped their mothering experiences is equally well illustrated in the case of two respondents whose circumstances were quite different from most of the other women. These two women were never substance abusers and both were incarcerated for fraud. Ironically, it is because of the fraud that they were able to secure financially stable and comfortable life styles before incarceration, including having a live in nanny in one case. Hence, their material circumstances were not drastically altered upon having a child, and consequently, they did not recount a marked shift in how they thought about mothering, as did Sue and many other women.

As the gap between respondents' aspirations for motherhood and the reality of mothering became more apparent, disappointment emerged. Most were not able to be the mothers they had wanted to be. Due to poverty and other stressors, they were often tired, insecure, and scared. And yet, they continued to care for their children. Many of the women's narratives explicitly addressed how they were able to sustain mothering through hardship.

MAKING SENSE OUT OF HARDSHIP AND
FADING MEMORIES OF THE MAINSTREAM MAMA DREAM

In some descriptions of their day-to-day childrearing prior to incarceration, women spontaneously drew a distinction between how they perceived their mothering "then," at the time, versus how they perceived it "now," during incarceration. As Vera said, "Up until now I thought I was a good parent. Now I see I've done a lot of wrong things." Vera's idea that only "then"—pre-incarceration—could she believe she was doing the right thing is of particular interest and requires further exploration. What existed "then" that led her to see herself as a good mother, and why is it missing "now"?

In Vera's case, and that of many others', substance abuse was a primary reason for this shifting idea of what constituted good and bad parenting. Substance abuse was a dominant theme in the interviews: 11 of 15 interviewees struggled with substances. As suggested in the opening quote of this chapter, many narratives indicated that women made sense of their mothering experiences in different ways during periods of substance abuse.

Some women spoke about their attempts to hide their substance abuse from their children by making reference to the idea of "parallel lives." It was this effort at hiding that led them to perceive they were doing the right thing and being a good mother. Sustaining a parallel life was difficult, and some women invested great energy in ensuring their children did not notice anything unusual. Some women were proud that their children were always well looked-after in spite of the substance abuse. As Kelly stressed, "They were well taken care of ... Because I wanted to go out and drink, I'd take them to a motel room ... I'd bring along a cousin to look after them ... they'd get everything [they wanted]...."

While these accounts primarily describe the logistics of balancing parallel lives (substance abuse and mothering), the following description reflects a mother's inner dialogue about how she re-framed her role in order to keep viewing her mothering in a positive light:

When I started to use again, in my mind I was still doing the same [mothering], but ...I was in the bathroom all the time [taking drugs], I had a lot of baths but I never got wet; if I partied the whole night, I'd put on pajamas in the morning, so he [son] thinks I just got up....

This pattern of seeing and understanding one's behaviour in different ways based on changing circumstances was not only related to the issue of substance abuse. The same pattern of shifting from one point of reference to another to construct or salvage a self-evaluation of adequate mothering emerged in narratives associated with living with abusive partners and exposing their children to abusive environments.

Abusive relationships were often interlinked with economic dependence. Mia's partner was physically and verbally abusive; he controlled her and limited her freedom; but, in her words, "he was a good provider." Thea's partner repeatedly beat her and humiliated her, "but ... he gave us a roof over our heads." It is well documented that women become more vulnerable to abusive relationships when they are poor, have children to support, and lack financial independence (Adelberg and Curie; Boritch; Ferraro; Maidment). Participants' accounts show they were cognizant of having to balance their "options." Providing food and shelter while experiencing abuse made them feel like better mothers than not having the essentials for their children. From the outside point of view, this hardly makes a difference, but from the inside, it mattered enormously.

For some women, a reassuring point of comparison was with their own mothers. No matter how poorly they mothered their children, they still felt they were better than their own mothers. Vera recalled:

My mom gave us [her and the siblings] up ... sold me to her boyfriends.... I slept in a box for a few years, with clothes piled on it and stuff because I knew ... or I thought, people wouldn't know where I was and my Mom wouldn't be able to get me hurt no more.... So, I'd hide in boxes ... cut a hole and had blanket in there... and folded clothes on top ... wherever we went I always had one. It was a safe place ... they never found me when I was there.

Before incarceration, Vera's main source of income was selling drugs. In spite of this, she was proud that she could always afford a two-bedroom apartment so her son could have his own room, bed, desk and computer. From an outsider perspective, relying on the discourse of middle-class parenting, this could hardly be considered adequate. However, compared to the way she was mothered, Vera was a good mother.

The way that negative experiences of being mothered led many women to desire or need to mother their children differently is noteworthy. As mentioned above, the determination to do everything differently for their children despite their own materially limited circumstances was one of the main themes from the interviews. However, it was precisely these limited circumstances that undermined their mothering and added multiple barriers to the role they had projected during pregnancy. They oscillated between their 'inherited' model of mothering that they tried to reject, and the romanticized, mainstream model, which the conditions of their everyday lives made impossible to achieve.

INCARCERATION EXPERIENCES AND PROJECTIONS FOR THE FUTURE

... Jail is not bad at all, all your basic needs are met, I'd stay here forever if I had my daughter here. (Nika)

Studies on incarcerated women point out that women tend to perceive incarceration as either shelter or the very opposite, as utter loss of control over their lives (Arbour; Arditti and Few; Garcia Coll et al.; Heney; Maidment). The interviewees in this study showed that sometimes, the same women may have both experiences, but at different points in time. For instance, Wilma introduced a temporal qualifier in describing incarceration as shelter: "Now it is not like shelter, but it was initially—it was a relief to be in because of the pressures on the outside." Nearly all the women interviewed perceived prison as shelter for at least part of their period of incarceration. For many, being incarcerated did not mean losing control of their lives, but as an opportunity to re-establish control over their circumstances. Interviewees acknowledged that initially they needed to "work through their issues," to get clean from drugs and to have some quiet and peaceful time to think about their lives. However, once this was accomplished, they wanted their children back.

Thea emphasized this view, saying, "I need my daughter in my life more than anything, now that I'm straight." She felt that if her daughter were with her, mothering her would help her maintain sobriety and make up for missed opportunities to interact with her daughter. Many women derived strength from the fact that they had children on the outside. It represented their only source of pride. As Mia said, "Out of all the rotten things and terrible things, the bad life I had, that is one thing nobody can cut me down for ... I have beautiful children ... something to be proud of ... Gives me hope to straighten up." These narratives resembled in some aspects the hopeful projections voiced when recounting expectations during pregnancy. For instance, some believed then that the child would help them "straighten up their lives."

179

But women also expressed the need to "fix themselves first" before resuming the mother role upon release. As Mila stated, "Sure I could walk out these gates and walk right up and hug him [her son], but I know that I need more help staying straight first. I'm no damned good to him if I go back to drugs." She had a clear projection of the future; once she takes care of her addiction, she and her son can have a good life. Like most of the other interviewees, the central theme in her account was the need to work on her psychological issues and substance abuse, with an assumption that once that is overcome, mothering will be just fine.

ACTION, INSTEAD OF A CONCLUSION

In examining the accounts of incarcerated women, this study treated their experiences with mothering as an ongoing process, rather than as a 'snap shot.' This allowed the researcher to identify the expectations and beliefs that the women developed—and were encouraged to develop—during incarceration; among them were beliefs that better served a mainstream normative view of mothering, rather than the realities of these women's lives. For instance, a number of interviewees believed that once they "straightened up" (once "I" changes), everything else would be "just fine" with regard to their mothering. These expectations reflect a deeply embedded assumption that any problem with mothering points to a problem located within the mother, that something is wrong with her personally. If she were only 'fixed,' then the natural and problem-free process of mothering could begin. This point of view is reflected by the dominant discourse on mothering, which perceives any mother, including the incarcerated mother, as separate and independent from her context.

Interviews revealed that although women could pinpoint and articulate how their socio-economic circumstances and the disadvantaged context imposed limitations on their mothering, they did not perceive their 'inability' to be good mothers as reflecting these circumstances. Rather, they internalized these experiences as their personal failures. The romanticized projections of mothering developed during pregnancy started to fade as their material realities and hardship unfolded after children were born. The initial boost to self-worth associated with becoming a mother began to be intertwined with a sense of inadequacy, disappointment, and guilt.

The romanticized view of mothering identified during pregnancy recurred during incarceration. In some cases, the accounts of mothering during incarceration and pregnancy had identical wording: "the kid will help me straighten out; I will do everything differently." Pride and hopeful plans for future interaction with their children dominated women's narratives in both instances. While mothers, or their babies, are on the 'inside,' as is the case with incarceration and pregnancy, a greater space is created for mothers to imagine and idealize their future relationship with their child. Mothers' main contact with the child is, at that point, limited to their inner dialogues with the baby, and their dreams and projections of the future. What is common in these two situations, and what allows this space for projections to emerge, is the absence of the day-to-day mother-work.

Given that upon release, women return to the same or worse circumstances, it is likely that they will again encounter obstacles and difficulties. When women experience prison confinement as shelter, it speaks of the extent to which their lives on the outside are unsupportable and oppressive. Due to the lack of social support, one might expect them to fall back into their old patterns, as Thea did:

> *Things are not as easy as you think they're going to be. When I got out, I set myself up for a fall.... I worked hard on myself [during incarceration], went out there and boom, I couldn't handle that lifestyle, I didn't know it.... Once I got out there I was bored, lonely. Because this new life, I knew nothing about. I didn't know where to begin, how to act, whatever. I've had this life for so long. And I didn't have to act, I didn't have to be anybody, just myself. I could swallow alcohol and drugs.*

One may question why Thea would resort to her old ways when during incarceration she clearly voiced a desire to change. This writer suggests, through this qualitative study, that an answer to this question can only emerge once her experiences and hopes have been analyzed from "within."

During particularly difficult periods, many women appeared to develop new criteria and points of reference from which to evaluate themselves as mothers. The ideas embedded in "parallel lives" or "at least we had a roof over our heads" can become acceptable from an insider perspective; they are unacceptable, however, from the outsider perspective, including when the women's own points of view distance them from those difficult circumstances (such as when they were incarcerated). So in fact, their accounts on mothering were subject to changing circumstances across time, demonstrating, as Norman Denzin articulated, how the structures of an experience can be altered and shaped as it is lived.

Women's self-evaluation as mothers shifted according to the conditions under which they constructed their accounts: in the "sheltered" space of prison, they applied the mainstream standards and ideals of motherhood, and it was this situation's affordance (i.e., the absence of daily care for children) that enabled them to switch to assumptions reflecting the dominant discourse. Perhaps this is the reason—this context-dependent change in beliefs about good mothering—that in the literature on incarcerated mothers, not only researchers but sometimes mothers themselves claim they were "bad parents" prior to incarceration and request parenting programs (Adelberg and Currie; Garcia Coll et al.; Thompson and Harm).

Such claims, however, can lead to implications and tangible practices that may not be warranted. For example, if the women and the "establishment" both agree they were bad mothers before incarceration, the institution of parenting programs during incarceration becomes justified on the grounds that the women need to "improve their skills." This not only locates the problem entirely within the individual woman, but neglects the fact that once circumstances change and daily stressors again accumulate, the mothering experience will change and the normative assumptions of what makes a good mother may need replacing. Switching back to a "real-life" context may render the assumptions and values held during incarceration irrelevant. An awareness of the contextual nature of assumptions around mothering needs to be developed and addressed when preparing women for re-entry into society. Analysis of their pre-incarceration living environment clearly indicated a significant need for socio-economic resources and social support. If change is to be achieved, it is these material circumstances that need to change and be supported by societal structures; expecting only "I" (the woman) to change is insufficient and unjustified.

A note of caution: I began this paper describing an encounter that led me to explore assumptions about the needs of incarcerated mothers, which resulted in afore-described study. However, others' experiences could lead to different questions or conclusions. While research on the impact of maternal incarceration describes devastating experiences for both women and their children, we must be aware that incarcerated mothers are not a homogenous group and do not all share the same desires and needs. As with some mothers outside the prison system, there are some incarcerated women who would maintain separation from their children regardless of incarceration. Such separation may not necessarily (nor inevitably) be the result of meagre socio-economic resources, deprived childhoods, or mental health challenges that impair their judgment to make the "right," socially expected decision. Some women simply choose not to take on the mother role. For this reason, when working with and advocating for incarcerated mothers, it is important to be attuned to the nuanced and varied range of needs and desires they may have regarding their children. We should not assume that all women want to mother their children; some may make choices very different than those who wish to engage in mainstream-like mothering practices during incarceration. If we did, such "assistance" might be nothing more than a continued institutional imposition of mainstream norms and values, instead of facilitating emergence of their own norms and values.

WORKS CITED

Adelberg, Ellen and Claudia Currie. "In Their Own Words: Seven Women's Stories." *In Conflict with the Law: Women and the Canadian Justice System.* Ed. Ellen Adelberg and Claudi Currie. Vancouver: Press Gang Publishers, 1993. 117-153. Print.

Anderson, Kathryn and Dana Jack. "Learning to Listen: Interview Techniques and Analyses." *Women's Words: The Feminist Practice of Oral History.* Ed. Sherna Berger Gluck and Daphne Patai. New York: Routledge, 1991. 11-26. Print.

Arbour, Louise. *Commission of Inquiry into Certain Events at the Prison for Women in Kingston.* Ottawa: Public Works and Government Services Canada, 1996. Print.

Arditti, Joyce and April Few. "Maternal Distress and Women's Re-entry into Family and Community Life." *Family Process* 47 (2008): 302-321. Print.

Boritch, Helen. *Fallen Women: Female Crime and Criminal Justice in Canada.* Toronto: International Thomson Publishing Company, 1997. Print.

Chesney-Lind, Meda and Lisa Pasko. *The Female Offender: Girls, Women and Crime.* Thousand Oaks: Sage Publications, Inc. 2004. Print.

Comack, Elizabeth. "Coping, Resisting, and Surviving: Connecting Women's Law Violations to their History of Abuse." *In Her Own Words: Women Offenders' Views on Crime and Victimization.* Ed. Leanna Fiftal Alarid and Paul Cromwell. Los Angeles: Roxbury, 2006. 33-45. Print.

Correctional Service of Canada (CSC). *Creating Choices: Report of the Task Force on Federally Sentenced Women.* Ottawa: Correctional Service of Canada. 1990. Print.

Denzin, Norman D. *Interpretative Interactionism.* Newbury Park: Sage Publications, 1989. Print.

Eljdupovic-Guzina, Gordana. *Parenting Roles and Experiences of Abuse in Women Offenders: Review of the Offender Intake Assessments.* Ottawa: Correctional Services of Canada, 1999. Print.

Ferraro, Kathleen. *Neither Angels nor Demons.* Boston: Northeastern University Press, 2006. Print.

Garcia Coll, Cynthia et al. "Incarcerated Mothers: Crimes and Punishments." *Mothering Against the Odds: Diverse Voices of Contemporary Mothers.* Ed. Cynthia Garcia Coll, Janet L. Surrey and Kathy Weingarten. New York: Guilford Press, 1998. 255 - 275. Print.

Heney, Jenn. *Dying on the Inside: Suicide and Suicidal Feelings Among Federally Incarcerated Women.* Unpublished doctoral dissertation, Carleton University, Ottawa. 1996. Print.

Maidment, Madonna. R. *Doing Time on the Outside.* Toronto: University of Toronto Press, 2006. Print.

Marecek, Jeanne, Michelle Fine and Louise Kidder. "Working Between Worlds: Qualitative Methods and Social Psychology." *Journal of Social Issues* 54.4 (1998): 631-644. Print.

Neuman, William L. *Social Research Methods: Qualitative and Quantitative Approaches.* 6th ed. Boston: Pearson Press, 2006. Print.

Ruddick, Sara. *Maternal Thinking: Toward a Politics of Peace.* Boston: Beacon Press, 1995. Print.

Shaw, Margaret et al. *Survey of Federally Sentenced Women: Report to the Task Force on Federally Sentenced Women on the Prison Survey.* Ottawa: Ministry of the Solicitor General, User Report No. 1991-4.

Sommers, Evelyn K. *Voices from Within: Women Who Have Broken the Law.* Toronto: University of Toronto Press, 1995. Print.

Tapia, Ruby C. "Certain Failures, Representing the Experiences of Incarcerated Women in the United States." *Interrupted Life: Experiences of Incarcerated Women in the United States.* Ed. Rickie Solinger et al. Berkley: University of California Press, 2010. Print.

Thompson, Patricia and Nancy Harm. "Parenting From Prison: Helping Children and Mothers." *Issues in Comprehensive Pediatric Nursing* 23 (2000): 61-81. Print.

Young, Iris Marion. *On Female Body Experiences: "Throwing Like a Girl" and Other Essays.* Oxford: Oxford University Press, 2005. Print.

Incarcerated Motherhood

Like Getting Hit in the Heart with a Dagger

KAREN SHAIN, LAUREN LIU AND SARA DEWATH

L EGAL SERVICES FOR PRISONERS WITH CHILDREN (LSPC) fights for the civil and human rights of people in prison, those returning home and communities impacted by incarceration in California. We have represented women in the state prisons in numerous class action lawsuits, fighting for access to decent pregnancy care, implementation of mother-infant programs, and constitutionally adequate medical care. Since LSPC was founded in 1978, the number of women in state prisons has increased from approximately 1,000 to over 11,000 in 2008 (California Department of Corrections and Rehabilitation). It is estimated that at least two-thirds of incarcerated women have children—and that at least 14,000 children in California had a mother in prison in 2008 (Simmons and Danker-Feldman).

Shante, Barbara, Brenda and Maribel are incarcerated women who agreed to meet with us several times to explain how the treatment of incarcerated mothers violates their human rights as well as the rights of their children.

What follows are excerpts from interviews that the three authors conducted over the course of summer 2011.

PREGNANCY

Shante describes herself as a "one-half Puerto Rican, one-half black, healthy-sized woman. I'm very funny, generous, kind and positive. It has taken me a long time to be this person and I work on it every day." The mother of three daughters, she gave birth to her youngest while in jail.

"I was pregnant while I was in county jail. It was not a good situation. I was always hungry and I had a terrible labor. I had walking pneumonia while I was pregnant and didn't have regular prenatal care. At San Joaquin County Jail, pregnant women slept on a two-inch mattress on top of a hard metal bunk bed. We got one pillow, which was very hard and didn't help when it came to

Shante and Sincere

getting into a comfortable position. We did receive an extra blanket, which was good because it gets cold in that jail.

"While I was pregnant, I was sent to court often. Most of the courtrooms are on the same floor as the jail so I wasn't shackled when I went to court. But twice I was sent to a courtroom on a different floor. I was shackled around my belly and cuffed around my feet. I was eight months pregnant then.

"[When I went into labour,] the umbilical cord was wrapped around her neck. I was shackled to the bed during labor but not during delivery, and I can't remember whether or not I was shackled when I was in recovery. I gave birth at 4:00 p.m. on Friday afternoon. I was back in county jail at noon the next day. I saw her twice for 30 minutes each time. I was promised a third visit with her on Saturday morning but by the time they brought her to me I was already dressed and handcuffed to go back to jail so I could only bend over and kiss her good-bye. I can't begin to explain the loss that I felt. It was so deep. I was crying, the nurse was crying, everyone was crying except my guards. They made everyone stand to the side while I went past them with shackles around my feet and my hands. Everyone was staring at me. They made everyone get off the elevator so I could get on. I was angry about this because I hadn't even been convicted of a crime at that time![1] I named the baby Sincere so she'd know I sincerely loved her (G.)."

Barbara is the mother of four, the youngest of whom is now 13 and was born in jail. "While I was in jail, I had not yet been convicted of a crime. I spent my entire pregnancy in jail—there was no prenatal education, so I would check up on magazines from the hospital—and hygiene was difficult because I was issued only one pair of panties. As part of my prenatal care I was given pills, but they made me sick, so I submitted a court order to get Stuart prenatals. My mother bought these pills for me, and the jail issued them to me. It took about a month to get the pills—and most people in here wouldn't have known they could get a court order to change the pills, but I did because I am very assertive. The only snacks available to pregnant women were oranges and bologna—but I only ate the oranges.

"While I was at Riverside County Jail, I gave birth to a baby girl. I was handcuffed during labor, but not completely shackled because I kept refusing and finally they only handcuffed me.[2] I was not going to be shackled and let staff make it unsafe for the baby and me. Even though I was dilated and the baby was doing fine, they insisted that I needed to have a C-section, that the rash I had from the unhygienic conditions they forced me into was herpes; they were just abrasions from chaffing. I told them to take a sample and to test it. They did, but they coerced me into a C-section and never returned the results of the test even though I asked for it.

"After giving birth the jail staff took my baby girl away from me before I had a chance to hold her. During my recovery, I wasn't given any post-natal care, no pain medications, nothing. I didn't see my daughter until almost two days later, and by that time, even though I wasn't convicted and I had family in California, the jail staff contacted Child Protective Services (CPS) to take my baby. When I heard what they were planning, I needed to call my mom to pick up my baby so CPS wouldn't take her into their custody.

"Just getting to make the phone call was difficult. After several requests the first watch officer finally allowed me to make the call. I called my mom to get to the hospital at the jail immediately to come and pick up the baby because nobody had contacted my mother about the baby's birth—however, CPS was nevertheless contacted. Then, another officer took me to hold my baby for the first time, but I was only allowed to hold her in my arms for 15 minutes. My mom and sister drove through the night to come pick up my baby so that CPS wouldn't take her away—she was released into my mother's guardianship. (P.)"

The stories that Shante and Barbara tell are remarkably similar—unsanitary and dangerous prenatal care, uncertainty about family being able to bring the baby home, shackling and handcuffing during labor. Their stories are not unique.

In 2005, the state of California banned shackling of pregnant incarcerated women during labor, delivery and recovery. The new law went into effect on January 1, 2006 (Lieber). By 2010, 1/3 of all county jails still had no protocols in place (Shain, Strickman, Kjaergaard and Smith). That same year, a coalition of organizations (LSPC, Center for Young Women's Development, ACLU of Northern California and Time for Change Foundation) sponsored legislation to ban shackling during all phases of pregnancy. That bill has gone through

Brenda, her mother, and daughter Dalilah

the California legislature twice—and each time passed unanimously. Both times the governor vetoed it (Skinner, *Assembly Bill No. 568, Assembly Bill No. 1900*).[3]

SEPARATION

Shante and Barbara described the pain they felt when they had to leave their newborn infants upon return to prison. The separation is no less painful when a mother leaves an older child and goes to prison.

Brenda's daughter Dalilah was two years old when Brenda was arrested. "At the Orange County Jail, I saw her every week and the first time Dalilah visited me, I didn't want to see her and for her to see me like this. This was a month or two after I was incarcerated. I was 21 and I never felt that much pain. It felt like getting hit in the heart with a dagger. I was behind the glass and when Dalilah and my mom came in, she put her little hand up to the glass and ran around. She was looking for a door to get through the glass that was between us. It is sad to say you have to get your child used to seeing you like this.

"I came to VSPW in 2009. When I held her for the first time that year in July, I couldn't let go. I had gone three years without holding her. I got to sit down and talk to her and teach her how to draw. Dalilah's dad doesn't bring her to visit but my mom does. But because they live in southern California, the visits are not that often. It depends because it's an eight-hour drive from Orange County and my mom has to go to work and Dalilah has to go to school. It varies during the year how many times she visits me—no less than three times a year. I am grateful that I have a supportive family that encourages my daughter to visit. I would love for her to visit more like every weekend while I am here in prison. When she came to visit me for the first time, she was nervous. She

Maribel's graduation

just needs a lot of attention. I remember when she visited me on Mother's Day, she said, 'I'm Jenny's baby but you're my number 1 mommy.' It hurts. I thought I would be ready to hear her talk about the other woman but I wasn't.

"I send Dalilah stuff like drawings and puzzles in the mail. I feel like I would hold a lot of grudge and hatred if my mom left me. Now, I struggle talking to her because she has a fear of telling me things that she isn't supposed to talk about. For example, I found out from a friend that her dad's girlfriend is pregnant. When I asked Dalilah about it, she covered her mouth and said, 'I don't want to talk about it.' I tried to encourage her to talk about it and said how exciting it would be to be a big sister, and then she became excited too. I think it is building that trust. She tells my mom all the time that she doesn't tell me things that she thinks might hurt my feelings.

"It is hard and sad to watch your kid grow up on paper, over the phone. For people who don't even get that, it's hard. It's depressing. It's every horrible thing in the dictionary. It's hard when you have to tell your child, 'I have to hang up the phone now' when my time is up. It's hard to not have communication and not being there taking her to her first day of class, meeting with teachers, when she lost her teeth (B.)."

Maribel has one son, Kevin, who was a year old when she went to jail. "When Kevin found out the real reason I wasn't at home and was incarcerated instead, it was very shocking. He was eight years old. A social worker was at my older sister's house and my son heard a conversation about me being in prison. He asked me, 'Mommy, is it true you're in prison?' I told him, 'Yes it is true,' to which he replied, 'Oh. So when are going to be home?' I would tell him, 'Someday.' All these years everyone had told Kevin I was going to school so I could get a better job after. When he asked me, I first felt angry because

Maribel and her mother

all these years I asked Leopoldo (Kevin's father) to let Kevin visit so I can talk to him. I wanted to tell him and make him understand but I didn't get the chance and then the anger changed to hurt. How is this going to affect Kevin? I had no opportunity to explain.

"When I was in county jail, I would call every day but when I got here, I called twice a week on Wednesdays and Saturdays. Then the phone calls went to once a week and then once every other week over the course of 2007-2008 before Kevin was brought to Mexico. The last time we talked, he was going to be nine. I haven't talked to him for three years. When he was born, I took him everywhere and we did everything together. Since I've been here, we've talked on the phone. But as years have gone by, he would be short with me like he didn't want to talk. I think it all changed when he found out I was here like he didn't understand why I was in prison. I believe that made him think I was a bad person because growing up with his dad, his dad made him think if you go to prison, then you have done bad things and therefore, you are bad too (H.)."

Shante has three daughters: Sincere, who was born while Shante was in jail, and two older daughters who now live with their dad out of state. "I am very afraid that all three of my daughters will reject me. I abandoned them, even if I didn't mean to. They have every right to feel mad because I haven't been there for them. I try to deal with this in a positive way by thinking how I felt when I was 15 or 16. I'd want my mother to love me. I keep a journal for them—they each have their own journal. I think about my girls every day. The two oldest, I have written them a birthday card every year and place them in their journal. I write down things I would have liked to tell them. I date everything when I write down what I'm thinking about them. I ask them

190

questions and tell them how much I miss them. I ask them questions about their lives. I just want them to see how much I loved them and missed them while I was away. I am sure that someday I will be back in touch with them and I will have a journal to give to each of them. I draw cards for Sincere and I send her things. I have made her a belt and a bracelet since I've been here and I send them to her."

RELATIONSHIPS WITH FAMILY MEMBERS

Although many go into foster care, most children of incarcerated mothers live with family members (Simmons and Danker-Feldman). This is usually the best solution, but many stressful issues arise. For the children, there is the question of loyalty. For the mothers, there is the question of guilt. For everyone, there is a great deal of adjustment.

Shante: "I am glad Sincere is well taken care of, but I do have my differences with my mother-in-law. One of them is about Sincere's name. For the first several years, Sincere was called 'Missy' because she was missing her mom and dad. She didn't even know her own name! But the last time I talked with her (last December) she knew her name (she was four years old then).

"Sincere has been to the prison to visit me two times since I've been here. I have a hard time getting my mother-in-law to answer my calls or letters. I did talk with Sincere on December 24th. I have a recent picture of her. She's gotten so big!"

Brenda: "I want to know the good things and not just the bad things. [Dalilah's dad] is okay with communicating to me about Dalilah but he just doesn't give me enough info. The last thing I want is for things to be awkward. I'm trying to program myself to be okay. When new women come in and talk about their child, I have to put on my ear phones because I never got to do those things they are describing like take her to school, etc."

Barbara's case gained a great deal of notoriety. Because of this, her older children read and heard about the crime in the newspapers. "Since being incarcerated, my kids have tried to hold onto the image of their mother be-cause society and some of my family tried to distort my image, and my son, in particular, has had difficulty with feeling torn between his loyalty to me and to his grandma. What is available to the public doesn't reflect the situation accurately and doesn't reflect who I am—my children know who I am. My son is angry because he misses me and witnessed the custody battle for my youngest daughter. My mother has had a difficult time communicating with me and allowing my kids to see me, especially when they were younger. I think it is difficult for her because she's depressed and overwhelmed, [but] she does the best she can.

"When I was in jail, I talked to my kids on the phone every day or every other day, we didn't really write letters, and my kids visited about three times per week. During those phone calls, I would give all 15 minutes to one child so that we could talk about school, peer pressure, sex, how to deal with difficult people, and church—typical parenting stuff. Things changed when I went to prison. In prison, I don't talk to my kids on the phone or receive any letters. I do get visits twice a year, but since 2005 I haven't seen all of my children at once. Before 2005, I would see all four kids. Between 2005 and 2007 I saw one or two kids at a time, but not my youngest because I was in the middle of a custody battle with her father. From 2007 to 2011, I only saw one child at a time if I was lucky, but I didn't see my youngest, due to the custody battle, until Mother's Day 2011.

"Because my family still lives in Riverside, my kids visit maybe once or twice a year. Right now it has been a one-way street of communication. Before my dad died in 2007, I was able to communicate with my family through him, but since then—nothing. One time, my sister's son came to visit me, at Riverside County Jail, when he was six or seven years old."

REUNIFICATION

Reunification brings its own set of issues. Some mothers, like Barbara, don't have the hope of reunification while their children are young. Others go home to families that have changed dramatically. The women we spoke with spend a great deal of time thinking and planning for their return.

Brenda: "The counselor wants me to do a substance abuse program rather than live at home after I get out because it's hard to transition back. I feel like I will be abandoning my daughter. I would have a hard time going to a program when I have the chance to go home and pick her up from school. I don't know how to make the decision because it is a six month program. I know I have to get settled and get financially stable."

Shante: "My estimated release date is June of 2015—Sincere will be 9 years old then. I don't know how I will be able to relate to her when I am out. It is unrealistic to think of dragging her away from her grandmother. But I hope to have a relationship with her. I also hope to get support from my family."

Maribel's situation has gotten very complicated. Her husband went to prison at the same time Maribel did. When he got out, he was deported and took their son Kevin to Mexico. Maribel doesn't know where they are. "I hope that by the time I get out in 2014, the Mexican police will be cooperative and that the system will get better by then. I want to report him as missing in Mexico. The Mexican Consulate had helped him [Kevin's father] through the process to get custody of Kevin. [My mother] was summoned to the court and to bring

Kevin's stuff so it could be brought to the border. We knew that once [Kevin's father] got custody, it would be impossible for us to see him. I found out about the custody when I received paperwork. Nobody knows where they are and I don't have family over there that I am close to."

ALTERNATIVE CUSTODY/REALIGNMENT

In mid-2011, the U.S. Supreme Court confirmed a lower court decision that requires the California Department of Corrections and Rehabilitation (CDCR) to reduce its prisoner population by 30,000 people in the next two years ("Supreme Court stands firm"). In response to this, Governor Brown proposed that most people (those whose crimes are considered "non-violent, non-serious and non-sex offenses") no longer be sent to state prison, but instead be held in local county jails. This program is called Criminal Justice Realignment. California has 58 counties; all of them have county jails, many of which are already seriously overcrowded. The legislature urged counties to consider alternatives to incarceration (e.g., drug treatment or home confinement) but there is no financial incentive for this and most counties are planning to build more jail cells to accommodate the new population.

In 2010, California State Senator Carol Liu proposed that parents who had sole custody of their children or were pregnant when they were first arrested, have two years or less left on their sentences, and have never had a "violent, serious or sex offense" be released to their homes or to drug treatment or other programs in their home counties (Liu). CDCR determined that there were at least 500 women who qualified for the Alternative Custody Program (ACP). However, because these women are required to participate in some kind of programmed activities, e.g., parenting or anger management classes, while in ACP and there are so few available in the state, very few women will in fact be released under this plan. As of the writing of this chapter, only ten women have actually been released through the ACP. By the end of 2011, CDCR expects that 20 women will be released (KPCC Radio).

Together, realignment and ACP have the potential to make real changes in the lives of incarcerated mothers and their families. Because California has only three large women's prisons, most women are incarcerated far away from their homes. The two largest prisons are in Chowchilla, which is about five hours away from downtown Los Angeles, even though 60 percent of women in California's state prisons are from the state's five southernmost counties. If women are able to stay near their families, regular contact with their children could be easier. And for people like Barbara, who is facing the rest of her life in prison, less crowding and more programming for those left behind would be far preferable to the current overcrowding.

However, if mothers are held in overcrowded county jails without any ability to learn skills and get an education, if the medical care in the county jails doesn't improve and these same women continue to receive substandard medical care, and if county jails continue the practice of requiring families to visit on telephones behind glass walls, the situation for mothers and their families will not improve. And if people who are left behind in the large prisons are depicted as "the worst of the worst" who don't deserve access to decent programs or significant contact with the outside world, life for women like Barbara will only become more difficult.

Alternative Custody and realignment present a huge opportunity for California to begin to wean itself from its dependence on incarceration. CDCR budgets $52,000 per year to hold a woman in a state prison and $18,000 to hold her in Alternative Custody (Herndon). One requirement is more effective, humane programs that are designed to reduce recidivism and support families. In at least one California prison, the women themselves—in the face of extraordinary obstacles—have created such a program.

MOTHERS' ALLIANCE

In 2010, we were approached by members of the Mothers' Alliance at Valley State Prison for Women (VSPW), one of the largest women's prisons in the world. They asked us to create a Family Law Assistance class so they could develop the skills to help each other and other incarcerated mothers.

The Mothers' Alliance was formed by a group of incarcerated women who realized that they had a responsibility to advocate for themselves and their sisters in order to stem the tide of loss of parental rights as a result of incarceration.

The women overcame extraordinary obstacles to build this organization. It is extremely difficult to build community in prison. Prison policy bars the development of organizations that are not "sponsored" by a staff member. Without a sponsor, women are not allowed to congregate, which means that no more than three women can stand together at any time unless they are in their eight-woman cell. Budget constraints prohibit staff members from sponsoring new organizations. Fortunately, at VSPW the librarian eventually stepped up and allowed the Alliance to meet in the law library.

Cheauvon Brown, who is now released and in the process of reunifying with her young son, was one of the group's founders: "I was inspired to form the group because I saw other women suffering from not seeing their family. I wanted to get the women together for at least one hour a week to be able to talk about their kids because they get depressed from not seeing their kids. To attract members I made flyers and put them under people's cell doors. More people kept joining and the doors opened up. VSPW is its own community, like a little city, even though we are all locked up. Women learn about Mothers' Alliance by word of mouth, networking or through the California Coalition for Women Prisoners (CCWP) newsletter (Brown, Mellen, Cage and Negrete). I love to network and to push Mothers' Alliance.

"Incarcerated mothers support each other because we feel each other's hurt and help each other to get resources. If you know a person's background—like if there is a history of abuse—those women are unable to focus their attention on bettering themselves while in prison in ways they need to because they are so focused on their children. I may not have clicked with people in certain areas, but we always clicked when it came to reunification because we all had that pain of missing our children regardless of what was going on.

"Mothers' Alliance helped me to not get discouraged even when there are no breakthroughs. It kept me focused to keep going. Just to see other women reunify with their kids—it's just like, Oh my gosh! One woman was crying—so overwhelmed because her son was going to be put in the system, but she was taken to court and her son was able to be placed with his grandmother. This is what power looks like!" (Brown, personal communication).

At LSPC, we believe that those most impacted by a problem are the most able to forge a solution. For those of us on the outside, the Mothers' Alliance shows us the power of mothers working together to maintain a meaningful relationship with their children and of creating a mechanism for women to advocate for and support each other.

[1]In the United States, most people are held in county jails before their trials and, thus, have not been found guilty of any crime.

[2]Both "handcuffed" and "shackled" are terms used for being restrained. Many women draw a distinction between the two because of the physical danger and psychological humiliation of being chained around the legs or around the belly during pregnancy.

[3]While the stated reasons for their vetoes were different, we believe that each governor was influenced by the California County Sheriffs Association.

WORKS CITED

Brown, Cheauvon, Suzy Mellen, Lisa Cage, and E. Negrete. "Mothers to Mothers Alliance at VSPW." *The Fire Inside 41* (2009): 15. Print.

California Department of Corrections and Rehabilitation (CDCR). *Monthly Report of Population*. December 2008. Web. 29 December 2011.

Herndon, Debra, Associate Director, California Department of Corrections and Rehabilitation. Personal interview with Karen Shain, August 2011.

KPCC Radio. "More California women inmates serving time at home." n.d. Web. 29 December 2011.

Lieber, Sally. *Assembly Bill No. 478.* n.d. Web. 29 December 2011.

Liu, Senator Carol. *Senate Bill 1266.* 2010. Web. 29 December 2011.

Shain, Karen, Carol Strickman, Mia Kjaergaard and Courtney Smith. "Stop Shackling: A Report on the Written Policies of California's Counties on the Use of Restraints on Pregnant Prisoners in Labor." Prisonerswithchildren. org. 2010. Web. 29 December 2011.

Simmons, Charlene and Emily Danker-Feldman. "Parental Incarceration: Termination of Parental Rights and Adoption: A Case Study of the Intersection Between the Child Welfare and Criminal Justice Systems." *Justice Policy Journal* 2.10 (2010) Web. 13 February 2013.

Skinner, Nancy. *Assembly Bill 1900.* 2010. Web. 29 December 2011.

Skinner, Nancy. *Assembly Bill No. 568.* n.d. Web. 29 December 2011.

"Supreme Court stands firm on prison crowding." *USA Today* 24 May 2011. Web. 29 December 2011.

Incarcerating Mothers

The Effect on the Health and Social Well-Being of Infants and their Mothers

RUTH ELWOOD MARTIN, JOSHUA LAU AND AMY SALMON

IN THIS CHAPTER we will, firstly, review the evidence for the health and social benefits of prison mother-infant units; secondly, we will describe study findings related to a Canadian provincial women's correctional centre Infant and Mother Health Initiative, which attest to these benefits; thirdly, we will recommend future directions for prison mother-infant units in Canada.

THE BENEFITS OF PRISON MOTHER-INFANT UNITS

Throughout the world, incarcerated women tend to be younger than the general population; they tend to be of childbearing age and tend to be poorly educated. In addition, many women who are imprisoned have experienced physical and sexual abuse and traumatic childhoods (van den Bergh et al.). In addition to increased prevalence of all of these factors, Aboriginal women are disproportionately represented among incarcerated populations in Canada, when compared to the general population. For example, in British Columbia, studies indicate that 25 percent to 35 percent of provincially incarcerated women are Aboriginal (Elwood Martin et al.; Elwood Martin 1995, 2000), compared with three to five percent in the general population (Kong and AuCoin).

The World Health Organization KYIV declaration identifies women in prison and their children as a population with particular health needs that require gender sensitive approaches (WHO Europe 2009b), in particular as this relates to their children, as follows:

> Due to the small numbers of women in prison, countries generally only have a few prison facilities for women. Women are therefore often placed far from home, which further strains family ties. Many women in prison are mothers and usually the primary or sole carer for their children. It is estimated that, in Europe, around 10,000 ba-

bies and children younger than two years of age are affected by their mother's imprisonment. When considering all children younger than 18 years old, the number affected by their mother's imprisonment is much higher, counting hundreds of thousands. When women give birth or have care of an infant while in prison, it is important to have a regime that allows the mother to nurture and bond with her child. The age until which children can stay with their mothers in prison varies widely across Europe. Three years is the most common age limit.

Worldwide, an estimated nine percent of incarcerated women give birth while serving prison time (Knight and Plugge). Providing prison mother-infant units to women who have given birth to their infant while incarcerated is considered normal practice in most countries in the world. Published reports of prison "mother-infant units" exist for 22 countries including England, Wales, Australia, Brazil, Denmark, Finland, Germany, Greece, Italy, Netherlands, New Zealand, Russia, Spain, Sweden, Switzerland, some U.S. states (International Centre for Prison Studies), Kyrgyzstan, Ghana, Egypt, Mexico, India, Chile (Institute of Women & Criminal Justice; Bedi) and Thailand ("Inside Thailand").

International health experts, including the World Health Organization (WHO) and the American Academy of Paediatrics (AAP), strongly recommend that babies be exclusively breastfed until age six months, and that babies continue to breastfeed on demand until two years (WHO 2009a; Health Canada). In addition to the well-known health and nutritional benefits, breastfeeding is also important for psychosocial development; the associated physical contact, eye contact, and the quality of feeding promote attachment (Kope and Reebye).

The immediate postpartum period is known to be a critical time for the development of mother-infant relations, and a key time for concentrating services to promote parenting capacity. Maintaining close physical contact between mother and newborn is now considered best practice in a wide range of circumstances. A systematic review of 30 studies involving 1925 participants (mother-infant dyads) showed that babies interacted more with their mothers, stayed warmer, and cried less, were more likely to be breastfed, and to breastfeed for longer, if they had early skin-to-skin contact (Moore, Anderson and Bergman). International evidence confirms numerous health and social benefits to both mother and infant associated with the best practice of rooming-in, with mothers caring for newborns, both together in the same room, immediately from birth (Crenshaw; Murray, Ricketts and Dellaport; Prodromidis et al.; Lvoff, Lvoff and Klaus; WHO 2009a; Kennell and Klaus).

For substance dependent women, this practice (i.e., close physical contact, facilitated by 24-hour rooming-in, which is continuous contact and cohabitation immediately from birth) is also established as a safe and beneficial practice (Feldman et al.; Buranasin; Narayanan et al.; Norr, Roberts and Freese; Lvoff, Lvoff and Klaus). Outcome studies for mother-infant dyads at Fir Square Combined Care Unit, B.C. Women's Hospital, Canada, demonstrate that these benefits also extend to mothers and their newborns who have experienced a substance-exposed pregnancy (Abrahams et al.). Immediate and continuous rooming-in encourages mother-infant bonding and fosters infants' social, behavioural and language development (O'Connor et al.; Prodromidis et al.; Abrahams et al.). Moreover, rooming-in encourages maternal affection towards her infant, which in turn promotes a mother's capacity to parent effectively and lessen the risk of infant abuse, abandonment and neglect (O'Connor et al.; Prodromidis et al.; Abrahams et al.).

Studies have also confirmed that familial attachments are critical factors in mediating a woman's criminal behaviour. More so than with men, women who have children in their care and maintain family bonds are more likely to refrain from criminal activity (Alarid, Burton, and Cullen; Simons et al.; Benda, Harm and Toombs; Benda; Broidy and Cauffman). For incarcerated women, the relationship between a mother and her child is a positive predictor of a woman's successful transition into the community (Cauffman; Benda; Broidy and Cauffman). Approximately 66 percent of Canadian female inmates aged 19 to 34 years are mothers of children younger than five years (Poole, Urquhart and Talbot). In 2003, it was estimated that 20,000 Canadian children are impacted by their mothers' incarceration each year (Cunningham). The provision of supports to pregnant women and mothers with infants and young children is thus a key consideration for prison-, hospital-, and community-based services for incarcerated women.

Children need to maintain parental relationships with their incarcerated mothers (Cunningham). A 1990 Task Force for Federally Sentenced Women recommended an expansion of mother-infant programming in Canadian correctional facilities (CSC). Prison-based Mother-Infant Units in the United States have been more thoroughly studied than those in Canada; however reports of success in U.S.-based programs are consistent with the benefits described above. For example, in New York, children of incarcerated women were able to reside with their mother up to 18 months of age (Gabel and Girard). Participants reported benefits such as: increased self-respect, improved bonding with their infant, and developing of positive parenting skills (Gabel and Girard; Carlson). In an evaluation of a similar program in Nebraska, nearly 100 percent of incarcerated mothers reported that they developed a stronger bond with their infant as a result of the program (Carlson). A program in North Carolina demonstrated that mother-infant bonding was correlated with lower recidivism rates among incarcerated mothers (Brennan).

AN INFANT AND MOTHER HEALTH INITIATIVE, IN A CANADIAN PROVINCIAL WOMEN'S CORRECTIONAL CENTRE

An Infant and Mother Health Initiative at the major provincial correctional centre for women in B.C. began in 2005 as a partnership between British Columbia Corrections and the Ministry of Children and Family Development (MCFD); B.C. Women's Hospital's Fir Square Combined Care Unit (Fir Square) provided the peri-natal medical care (Abrahams et al.). The initiative allowed women who gave birth while incarcerated, and who were otherwise deemed by MCFD to be willing and able to provide appropriate parental care, the opportunity to return to the correctional centre with their infants in their care.

In this section, we explore the *benefit* of keeping babies and infants with their mothers during their incarceration—*benefits to the babies themselves* and the *benefits to the women* who are mothers—as reported previously (Granger-Brown et al.; Salmon, Thompson, Murphy and Fielding) from three studies involving mothers at the provincial correctional centre, that were conducted 2006 and 2008. Firstly, semi-structured interviews and questionnaires were conducted to examine the health and social outcomes of mother-infant dyads, with women who had delivered at Fir Square and then returned to the correctional centre with their babies. Secondly, two focus groups were held to discuss the concerns of incarcerated mothers regarding, and to explore the psychosocial impacts of, separation from their children. Thirdly, purposeful sampling was used to invite four formerly incarcerated women, with varied incarceration experiences, to participate in semi-structured in-depth interviews (Keogh). We will now describe a selection of Amy Salmon's study findings (Salmon et al.; Granger-Brown et al.; Keogh).

Thirteen babies were born to incarcerated mothers during the program's duration, nine of whom returned to the correctional centre with their mothers and stayed there until their mother's release. Fifteen months was the longest stay of any infant in the correctional centre. All nine babies who returned to the provincial correctional centre with their mothers stayed with them until their mothers were released. Three of the mothers were Aboriginal. Only two of the mothers who participated in the Infant and Mother Health Initiative have subsequently returned to prison at the time of this writing.

Mothers participating in the Infant and Mother Health Initiative described bonding with their babies as a turning point in their lives. Women participants of the Infant and Mother Health Initiative identified that prison health care staff themselves were a key source of mothering support. Mothers described ways that the environment of a prison-based program assisted them to access support, as one participant explained:

If I ever need anything I would just let one of them know. Health care was right next to me, so if I had a problem....The nurses would come in and when I was having complications, when I was pregnant, they would come in and check on me and stuff like that.

Women also identified the other incarcerated women as sources of mothering support, including practical assistance, encouragement, and emotional respite, which was particularly valued during the early mothering period:

We were all mentoring the young one who had never had a child before and she was scared. And didn't know what life was going to look like, what she would do with her life ... and so we worked as a team, all of us. Okay, if you need a shower, we'll watch your infant.

Seven of the eight babies, who returned to the provincial correctional centre with their mothers following delivery at Fir Square, were breastfed. All breast-fed for the entire duration of their incarceration (compared with 53.9 percent of mothers offering breast milk at six months, Canadian general population) (Chalmers et al.). Incarcerated mothers identified that the 'non stressful' environment, and regular access to supportive staff provided by the Infant and Mother Health Initiative, promoted breastfeeding on demand.

Interestingly, women who were separated from their children during incarceration also reported that they were positively impacted by the prison Infant and Mother Health Initiative. These women explained that they made connections, with the mothers and children, which were of similar therapeutic value to those experienced by the initiative's participants. In the words of one woman:

We were a family unit the four of us and the two kids...It was very cool, so therapeutic for me to sit, you have a lot of time to sit and talk with the moms and, like, all of us were very intimate. We all talked about our shame and our guilt, how we could have done things differently.

Some of us were at different ... areas of that resolution in our hearts and in our path in our journey and some of us did a lot of processing with each other. It was really therapeutic for the three of us, particularly the three of us who had lost children, to be with each other and to be able to support each other in the grief, in that joy.

In sharp contrast to the benefit of returning to prison with an infant following birth, the overwhelmingly negative impact of separation from children was the dominant finding among focus group participants. Women described feelings of "devastation," "helplessness," and "feeling useless." Separation from their children significantly undermined many women's sense of self:

> *As we are brought up, we are taught to be caregivers and mothers. So then they take your children away and now you are a bad mother, you're a bad wife, you're a bad person. You can't even take care of your children.*

Some women are separated from their children prior to their incarceration, because their children are apprehended by child welfare authorities, in most circumstances due to concerns about maternal substance use. Incarceration may prolong or intensify this previously-occurring separation. Many women reported that their problems with drug and alcohol use were exacerbated by their loss of contact with their children, as follows:

> *I cope with it by using. One issue gets on top of another and soon I don't know why I'm using. It seems so dumb. You feel like a failure.*

> *It's why I go back to being homeless, to doing crime, to living a life of chaos.*

Incarcerated women with children in the care of MCFD often felt as though no one was on their side when it came to regaining access to their children. Women reported difficulty in hiring lawyers with skill, values, or experience to represent their interests effectively in custody cases, such as this report:

> *I have been trying to get some information about a lawyer—availability, who to contact. The only thing they keep telling me is, "call Legal Aid," but they can only do so much. They can give you the names of lawyers. There is absolutely no way to pre-screen them, to know the history they have with the Ministry [MCFD], what their experience and success rate is. It is really hard to know anything just from a name.*

Many women reported that they had difficulty contacting legal help because they could not afford long distance calls; therefore, they were unable to obtain the help they need to resolve custody matters and have their children returned to their care. In addition, women described an often adversarial nature of their relationship with MCFD social workers. They often felt ill-prepared for meetings with social workers, and perceived that their actions and dialogue would fall under intense scrutiny.

Women also reported that they did not know who they can go to for "unbiased" support when negotiating for access to, or return of, their children, as one woman said:

It would be nice to have someone come with you as an advocate to meet with the social worker. They have been preparing for weeks, and I felt like a fool. I felt like anything I said was being held against me.

However, some women also recognized that a social worker could make a positive impact in their lives:

I had a social worker that I still remember to this day.... She helped me so much.... My social worker did everything she could to try to help me. She taught me a lot. What I know now, I wish I knew then.

In many cases, the incarceration itself precipitated the separation of mother and child. Women are incarcerated far from home because there is usually only one main provincial women's prison in each Canadian province. While most mothers expressed a strong desire to visit their children while they were incarcerated, they reported that contact with their children rarely happened during their incarceration. Poverty and limited social resources exacerbated the effects of geographic dislocation, as the high cost of travel and long distance telephones calls further separated incarcerated mothers from their children. The effect of these separations on the mother-child bond was readily apparent, as one woman explained:

I've only seen them once since I have been incarcerated. They brought them [her children] to see me here and they had no idea who I was. We had been separated so long.

Many women were concerned about the transition from prison to release, because whatever resources were available to them within the provincial correctional system were abruptly discontinued upon their release. They felt "set up to fail." One woman said: *"They just open the gates and say good luck. That's scary."*

Women reported that few resources were available to them to arrange for financial support and housing upon release; yet, they were expected to have these factors in place in order to have their children returned to their care. One woman explained her frustration: *"Often the girls aren't even approved for welfare when they get out. How are they supposed to make a start with nothing? What are you going to do?"*

Incarcerated women, who were serving a sentence without children in their care, wanted parenting programs available to them: programs related to mothering, including coping with the effects of separation and preparing women for the reunification process. In addition, women reported the need for addictions treatment facilities that will house women and their children *together.* As one woman noted, *"I don't think we're necessarily bad parents. We just need better skills."*

RECOMMENDED FUTURE DIRECTIONS FOR PRISON MOTHER-INFANT UNITS IN CANADA

Supports are needed to enable incarcerated mothers to maintain contact with their infants and young children. As penal populations in Canada rise, with the eventual introduction of Bill C-10 ("Parliament of Canada"), the number of incarcerated women who are mothers, and their children, will increase. During the year of 2002, approximately 85,000 of the admissions to the correctional system were women. That same year, incarceration resulted in approximately 20,000 children being separated from their mothers (Cunningham).

The relationship between a mother and her child should be strengthened, because the mother-child relationship is a positive predictor of a woman's successful transition into the community following incarceration. Women who experience traumatic separations from their children are significantly more likely to be re-incarcerated (Messina et al.), more so than with men (Benda; Broidy and Cauffman). These experiences were underscored by mothers at the provincial correctional centre, as evidenced by the low recidivism rates (2/9 [22 percent], at time of writing) among women who participated in the Infant and Mother Health Initiative.

Mothers and infants should be housed together with 24-hour contact, as essential for establishing and maintaining breastfeeding on demand. With regards to infant health, the high rate of breastfeeding observed among the women who participated in the prison Infant and Mother Health Initiative is noteworthy. Breastfeeding among incarcerated women should be encouraged, in order to promote optimal psychosocial development and reduce health inequities among their infants. As noted in our opening section, breastfeeding is important for infants' psychosocial development; and, babies who are not breastfed may also be at increased risk for diabetes, allergies, and gastrointestinal and respiratory infections.

Easy access to timely, appropriate information and services located outside of prison is needed, to facilitate reconnections between incarcerated mothers and their children, and to prepare women to resume parenting and mothering. Mothers who had been separated from their children described the myriad of ways that this separation had negative impacts on their physical and emotional well-being. Negative impacts identified in these three studies include devaluations of their sense of self, increased difficulties with substance use and ability to recover from addictions, and difficulties in making positive life changes following release from prison. In the absence of well-delineated structural supports to ensure that incarcerated mothers upon their release have ready access to one another, such supports were often found through the informal activities of prison staff and less often through community-based services.

The proven long-term negative effects of foster care placement on developing babies and young children must also be considered when removing children from incarcerated mothers who would otherwise serve as their primary caregivers. Specifically, experiences of multiple, temporary primary caregivers in early infancy have been shown to disrupt normal development processes by interfering with the infant's ability to form secure attachments (Kope and Reebye). Furthermore a recent report of the Office of the Provincial Health Officer and the Representative for Children and Youth (Representative for Children and Youth & Office of the Provincial Health Officer) indicates that very young children who have been in foster care are two to three times less likely to be adequately prepared for kindergarten than their peers.

Infant and Mother Health Initiatives should be opened in all female correctional centres in all provinces in Canada for incarcerated mothers and their infants. A 1990 Task Force for Federally Sentenced Women recommended an expansion of Infant and Mother Health Initiatives in Canadian correctional facilities (Correctional Service Canada). It is now internationally recognized that children need to maintain parental relationships with their incarcerated mothers (Fazel and Baillargeon). The British Columbia provincial correctional centre Infant and Mother Health Initiative was highly beneficial to both the mothers and infants who participated in it. In addition, the initiative had positive effects on other women incarcerated during its existence; also, women who had small children but who did not give birth while in custody overall found the presence of infants in prison a positive healing experience.

Addendum

In April 2008, the Infant and Mother Health Initiative in the provincial correctional centre was discontinued; subsequently, all infants born to mothers at provincial correctional facilities in B.C. were either placed with a relative or in foster care under the guardianship of MCFD. A B.C. Corrections spokesperson noted publicly that:

> *Our staff are not trained to supervise infants and they're not (trained) in infant first aid or anything ... if something went wrong and we didn't respond appropriately, we just couldn't risk putting an infant in that situation.* (Prison Justice)

Infant safety has not been reported as an issue in numerous countries where prison Infant and Mother Health Initiatives are well established. British

Columbia Corrections officials also expressed concern that providing the opportunity to women who gave birth while in prison to remain with their infants is potentially "unfair" to others who have small children but did not give birth while in custody.

On November 10, 2008, five women filed a claim with the B.C. Supreme Court maintaining that they have the constitutional right to keep their children with them while incarcerated in provincial correctional centres (File Number 087858). This court decision is pending.

WORKS CITED

Abrahams, Ronald R. et al. "Rooming-in Compared with Standard Care for Newborns of Mothers Using Methadone or Heroin." *Canadian Family Physician* 53.10 (2007): 1722-1730. Print.

Alarid, L. F., V. S. Burton, and F. T. Cullen. "Gender and Crime Among Felony Offenders: Assessing the Generality of Social Control and Differential Association Theories." *Journal of Research in Crime and Delinquency* 37.2 (2000): 171-199. Print.

Bedi, Kiran. *It's Always Possible: Transforming One of the Largest Prisons in the World.* New Delhi: Stirling Paperbacks, 2006. Print.

Benda, Brent B. "Gender Differences in Life-Course Theory of Recidivism: A Survival Analysis." *International Journal of Offender Therapy and Comparative Criminology* 49.3 (2005): 325-42. Print.

Benda, Brent B., Nancy J. Harm and Nancy J. Toombs. "Survival Analysis of Recidivism of Male and Female Boot Camp Graduates Using Life-Course Theory." *SO Source Journal of Offender Rehabilitation* 40.3,4 (2005): 87-113. Print.

Brennan, Pauline. "Intermediate Sanction That Fosters the Mother-Child Bond: A Process Evaluation of Summit House." *Women & Criminal Justice* 18.3 (2007): 47-80. Print.

Broidy, Lisa M. and Elizabeth E. Cauffman. *Understanding the Female Offender.* Unpublished report submitted to the U.S. Department of Justice. 2006. Web. Feb 20, 2013.

Buranasin, B. "The Effects of Rooming-in on the Success of Breastfeeding and the Decline in Abandonment of Children." *AsiaPacific Journal of Public Health* 5.3 (1991): 217-220. Print.

Carlson, Joseph R. "Prison Nursery 2000: A Five-Year Review of the Prison Nursery at the Nebraska Correctional Center for Women." *Review Literature and Arts of the Americas* 33.3 (2001): 75-97. Print.

Cauffman, Elizabeth. "Understanding the Female Offender." *The Future of*

Children 18.2 (2008): 119-142. Web. 9 Feb. 2012. Print.

Chalmers, Beverley et al. "Breastfeeding Rates and Hospital Breastfeeding Practices in Canada: A National Survey of Women." *Birth* 36.2 (2009): 122-132. Print.

Correctional Service Canada (CSC). "Women Offender Programs and Issues." *Creating Choices: The Report of the Task Force on Federally Sentenced Women.* Ottawa: CSC, 1990. Print.

Crenshaw, Jeannette. "Care Practice #6: No Separation of Mother and Baby, With Unlimited Opportunities for Breastfeeding." *The Journal of Perinatal Education* 16.3 (2007): 39-43. Print.

Cunningham, A. and L. Baker. *Waiting for Mommy: Giving a Voice to the Hidden Victims of Imprisonment.* London, ON: Centre for Children and Families in the Justice System, 2003. Print.

Elwood Martin, Ruth. "A Review of a Prison Cervical Cancer Screening Program in British Columbia." *Canadian Journal of Public Health/Revue canadienne de santé publique* 89.6 (1995): 382-6. Print.

Elwood Martin, Ruth. "Would Female Inmates Accept Papanicolaou Smear Screening if it Was Offered to them During their Incarceration?" *Canadian Journal of Public Health/Revue canadienne de sante publique* 162.5 (2000): 657-658. Print.

Elwood Martin, Ruth et al. "Drug Use and Risk of Blood-borne Infections: A Survey of Female Prisoners in British Columbia." *Canadian Journal of Public Health/Revue canadienne de santé publique* 96.2 (2005): 97-101. Web. 23 Jan. 2012.

Elwood Martin, Ruth et al. "The Development of Participatory Health Research Among Incarcerated Women in a Canadian Prison." *International Journal of Prisoner Health* 5.2 (2009): 95-107. Web. 15 Jan. 2012. Print.

Fazel, Seena and Jacques Baillargeon. "The Health of Prisoners." *The Lancet* 377.9769 (2011): 956-9651-10. Print.

Feldman, R. et al. "Comparison of Skin-to-Skin (Kangaroo) and Traditional Care: Parenting Outcomes and Preterm Infant Development." *Pediatrics* 110.1 (2002): 16-26. Print.

Gabel, Katherine and Kathryn Girard. "Long-Term Care Nurseries in Prisons: A Descriptive Study." *Children of Incarcerated Parents.* Ed. Kathryn Gabel and Denise Johnston. Lanham, MD: Lexington Books, 1995. 237-254. Print.

Granger-Brown, Alison, Jane A. Buxton, Lara-Lisa Condello, Dulce Feder, T. Greg Hislop, Ruth Elwood Martin, Amy Salmon, Megan Smith, and Jeannine Thompson. "Collaborative Community-Prison Programs for Incarcerated Women in BC." *British Columbia Medical Journal* 54.10 (2012): 509-513. Print.

Health Canada. "Duration of Exclusive Breastfeeding: Questions and Answers for Professionals – Infant Feeding." Ottawa: Health Canada, 25 Nov. 2004. Web. 7 Feb. 2012.

"Inside Thailand — 'Bangkok Rules' Adopted by the United Nations General Assembly." 2011. Web. 7 Feb. 2012.

Institute on Women and Criminal Justice. "Mothers, Infants and Imprisonment: A National Look at Prison Nurseries and Community-Based Alternatives." New York. Women's Prison Association, 2009. 1-39. Print.

International Centre for Prison Studies. *International Profile of Women's Prisons.* London: Author, 2008. Print.

Kennell, John H. and Marshall H. Klaus. "Bonding: Recent Observations That Alter Perinatal Care." *Pediatric Review* 19.1 (1998): 4-12. Print.

Keogh, Tara. "Mother Child Programs in Canadian Correctional Facilities: The Experiences and Views of Four Previously Incarcerated Women." Unpublished Master of Social Work thesis, Simon Fraser University, 2005.

Knight, Marian, and Emma Plugge. "Risk Factors for Adverse Perinatal Outcomes in Imprisoned Pregnant Women: A Systematic Review." *BMC Public Health* 5 (2005): 111. Print.

Kong, R. and K. AuCoin. "Les contrevenantes au Canada/Female offenders in Canada." *Juristat* 28.1 (2008): n. pag. Print.

Kope, Terry and Pratibha Reebye. "Attachment: Clinical Perspectives." *British Columbia Medical Journal* 4.49 (2007): 116-120. Print.

Lvoff, N. M., V. Lvoff, and M. H. Klaus. "Effect of the Baby-Friendly Initiative on Infant Abandonment in a Russian Hospital." *Archives of Pediatrics Adolescent Medicine* 154.5 (2000): 474-477. Print.

Messina, N. et al. "Childhood Adverse Events and Current Traumatic Distress: A Comparison of Men and Women Drug-Dependent Prisoners." *Criminal Justice and Behavior* 34.11 (2007): 1385-1401. Print.

Moore, E. R., G. C. Anderson, and N. Bergman. "Early Skin-to-Skin Contact for Mothers and their Healthy Newborn Infants (Review)." *Library* 1 (2009): n. pag. Print.

Murray, Erin K., Sue Ricketts and Jennifer Dellaport. "Hospital Practices that Increase Breastfeeding Duration: Results from a Population-Based Study." *Birth* 34.3 (2007): 202-211. Print.

Narayanan, I. et al. "Maternal Participation in the Care of the High Risk Infant: Follow-up Evaluation." *Indian Pediatrics* 28.2 (1991): 161-167. Print.

Norr, K. F., J. E. Roberts and U. Freese. "Early Postpartum Rooming-in and Maternal Attachment Behaviors in a Group of Medically Indigent Primiparas." *Journal of Nurse-Midwifery* 34.2 (1989): 85-91. Print.

O'Connor, S. et al. "Reduced Incidence of Parenting Inadequacy Following Rooming-In." *Pediatrics* 66.2 (1980): 176-182. Print.

"Parliament of Canada." *Publishing and Depository Services Public Works and Government Services Canada.* 2011. Web. 13 Feb. 2012.

Poole, N., C. Urquhart and C. Talbot. "Women-Centred Harm Reduction: Reducing Harms Across Social Determinants of Women's Health." *British Columbia Centre of Excellence for Women's Health* 4 (2009): n. pag. Print.

Prison Justice. "B.C. tries to quietly cancel mother and baby in prison program." Web. 14 Feb. 2012.

Prodromidis, Margarita et al. "Mothers Touching Newborns: A Comparison of Rooming-in versus Minimal Contact." *Birth* 22.4 (1995): 196-200. Print.

Representative for Children and Youth & British Columbia Office of the Provincial Health Officer. *Kids, Crime and Care. Health and Well-Being of Children in Care: Youth Justice Experiences and Outcomes.* Joint Special Report, Victoria, B.C., February 23, 2009. Web.

Salmon, Amy, Jeannine Thompson, Kelly Murphy, and Lisa Fielding. "Incarcerating Mothers: The Effect on Women's Health." *International Journal of Prisoner Health* (2013) (In review). Print.

Simons, R. L. et al. "A Test of Life-Course Explanations for Stability and Change in Antisocial Behavior from Adolescence to Young Adulthood." *Criminology* 40.2 (2002): 401–434. Web. 7 Feb. 2012.

van den Bergh, Brenda J. et al. "Imprisonment and Women's Health: Concerns About Gender Sensitivity, Human Rights and Public Health." *Bulletin of the World Health Organization* 89.9 (2011): 689-694. Print.

World Health Organization (WHO). *Nutrient Adequacy of Exclusive Breastfeeding for the Term Infant During the First Six Months of Life.* Geneva, 2002. Print.

World Health Organization (WHO). "Baby-friendly Hospital Initiative." 2009a. Web. 7 Feb. 2012.

World Health Organization (WHO) Europe. *Women's Health in Prison: Correcting Gender Inequality In Prisons.* Copenhagen, Denmark, 2009b. Print.

Mothering Against the Norms

Diane Wilson and Environmental Activism

DANIELLE POE

THE FIRST TIME I heard about Diane Wilson was through a colleague who recommended her book *An Unreasonable Woman: A True Story of Shrimpers, Politicos, Polluters, and the Fight for Seadrift, Texas*. Wilson's story of taking on a huge chemical company who was buying the favor of local people, local and national politicians, and even the Environmental Protection Agency both inspired and terrified me. She inspired me because she is fearless in her pursuit of justice and ultimately successful both on a personal level because she never wavers from her path even when success seems impossible and on a practical level because she gets two of these imposing chemical companies to agree to zero admission in their plants.

Her story terrified me because if she can take on these companies and be a force for justice, then what sacrifices should I endure? What sacrifices should my children endure for the sake of a just world? After all, Wilson is a mother of five, when she began her activism two of her children were young enough that she describes them as "babies," and one of those babies was autistic. I remain terrified of the prospect of being as fearless as Wilson who has been on many hunger fasts, been arrested numerous times, disrupted Senate hearings, and chained herself to a Dow Chemical oxide tower, but I tell her story as often as possible as an example of mothering at its best because her story reveals the interconnection of all children and the interconnection between all people and the environment.

Diane Wilson is a mother and an environmental activist, two roles that challenge common perceptions about what a mother is and what her obligations to her children are, and roles that challenge common stereotypes about environmental activists and the focus of their acts. Her story reveals the ways in which mothering is always practiced in a context and sometimes in order to work toward a society in which her children can thrive, a mother may have to challenge the context itself and take time away from her children. When

Wilson engages in questioning, challenging, and changing the world, she faces pressure from local and state politicians and international business leaders. Her refusal to cooperate with business interests at the expense of people and the environment leads her to acts of civil disobedience, which leads to jail time.

WILSON AS MOTHER

To think about Diane Wilson as a mother, I will start by analyzing her descriptions of mothering relationships. As with every mother, Wilson's story as a mother begins long before she has her children; it begins with Wilson the daughter and granddaughter. And, her story as a mother is broader than the human relationships she has, it includes the bay, which she describes as a grandmother.

While it is useful for explanatory purposes to consider Wilson as a mother and then Wilson as an environmental activist, I want to stress that the two are always intertwined in Wilson's descriptions of herself. Throughout her memoirs, Wilson describes her actions as though her path is destined. First, she seems destined to be a shrimper, and later she seems destined to be an environmental activist. In order to understand the connection between shrimping and environmental activism, we should notice that the genealogical descriptions that appear in Wilson's memoirs are about her literal genealogy—her blood relatives both maternal and paternal—and her metaphorical genealogy when she describes Lavaca Bay as a grandmother.

As a shrimper, Wilson traces her relationship to the bay back to her paternal lineage. Although fishing is primarily practiced by men—who consider a woman on the bay at best unusual and at worst courting disaster—Wilson inherits the tradition and takes it up in spite of any pressure for her to stay on the shore. She describes how inevitable it is that she is an exception to the rule that only men fish, "everybody knew I was on the bay 'cause *my* daddy was on the bay, and my daddy was on the bay 'cause *his* daddy was on the bay, and *his* daddy was on the bay 'cause *his* daddy had pitched him over the side of a homemade fishing skiff and said, 'Sink or swim. Swim or drown. Make up your mind, boy!'" (*Unreasonable* 2005: 49). While she acknowledges that it's unusual for women to fish, her descriptions remind us that she feels only a continuity between herself, her family, and the bay.

Her descriptions of fishing and the bay teem with the relationship between generations, both the ways in which fishing is passed on from one generation to the next (*Unreasonable* 48-54), but also the way in which there's a familial relationship between the water and those who fish. In his foreword, Kenny Ausbel captures the rich sense of relationship that Wilson has to Lavaca Bay,

"Growing up, Diane said the bay was like her grandmother; she spent endless hours in private conversation with her. She took the destruction of the bay very personally. Call it family values" (*Unreasonable* 11). Wilson says, "I could see the bay as an old grandmother with long gray hair and a dress made of matted foaming seaweed flowing out with the tide" (*Diary* 9). The description of the bay as a grandmother is not simply a nostalgic description of the environment, it calls to mind the reality that human life depends on forces beyond us that create the conditions for our lives. In her family, their existence relied on the presence of the bay and the health of the bay. For all of us, our physical being is only possible because of our human grandmothers and our mothers. But, beyond that our physical being depends on the environment in which we live. Our particular lives are shaped by the histories and the stories of those who come before us. For Wilson, her love of the bay, of fishing, and of silence are all shaped by her ancestors, some were immigrants, others were Native American (her father's father is Cherokee), and all of whom are shaped by the environment.

Of course to think about Wilson as a mother, we have to turn to her descriptions of her children and her descriptions of herself as a mother. Wilson's children are a constant presence in her life and her journey to becoming an environmental activist. They come with her as she works at the fish house playing in piles of ice, the older girls come with her to protest against a politician who refuses to take Wilson's calls or acknowledge the petitions that she has sent him, they move with her from home to home after she and her husband divorce, and throughout her memoirs Wilson describes her autistic son Crockett's particular ways of moving through the world (*Unreasonable* 53, 114, 176; *Diary* 25, 27). She writes about her turn from "reclusive fisherwoman with five kids to controversial hell-raiser with five kids" (*Diary* 14). I will return to this quote and the turn from recluse to activist in the following section, but for now I want to point out that her identity as a mother with five kids remains constant and shapes every aspect of her story.

Wilson does not detail her children's reaction to her as a woman who refuses to conform to social norms, first as a shrimper and later as an activist, but the pull between social norms for mothers and her actions as an activist are evident in several anecdotes that she describes in *Diary of an Eco-Outlaw: An Unreasonable Woman Breaks the Law for Mother Earth*. Wilson relates several incidents when her family intervenes and tries to get her to give up her activism. In one anecdote, Wilson's mother wants her to stop her activism because she's worried about what will happen to Wilson's children if she dies. Even when her girls are grown and have moved away, and Crockett is sixteen, Wilson's mom tells her that "Kids never grow up" (*Diary* 43), implying that Wilson is a negligent mother for jeopardizing her health. Later, Wilson describes her aunt's attempt to get her to give up a hunger fast and threatening to bring Crockett to witness the fast. Because Crockett would be upset to see his mother fasting, the aunt hopes that Wilson will stop in order to spare Crockett. Wilson's observation is that, "If anyone ever thought that corporations brought in the heaviest gunfire on a hunger strike, they were sadly mistaken. Family and friends beat corporations by a landslide" (*Diary* 55). Of course, neither her aunt nor her mother is successful in getting Wilson to stop her activism, and I will argue that this makes her the best kind of mother.

The expectation that she will stop her activism if she sees that it is harming or could potentially harm her children comes from an understanding of obligations to one's particular children as distinct from obligations to prevent harms that happen to the environment or to other people's children. We have already seen, though, that Wilson does not see herself or her children as isolated from the environment and from other children. Hence, to be a mother to her children, she defends the environment and other children. This connection will be especially clear in the next section when she begins her fight for justice for the people of Bhopal, India.

WILSON AS ACTIVIST

The connection between Wilson, her children, the environment, other people, and places both near and far becomes explicit when she's invited to Bhopal, India to take part in testimonies against Union Carbide whose mismanagement and business practices led to explosions in Seadrift, Texas and Bhopal. The Bhopal disaster killed more than 3000 people and sickened many thousands (Zhang). While she is there, her experiences as a mother become part of her response to the suffering of other mothers and their losses. In *Diary of an Eco-Outlaw*, Wilson describes being on a bus in India as she prepares to give testimony about Union Carbide and the dangers that chemical plants pose to people and the environment. While on the bus, a man throws in a handkerchief that contains photos of ten dead babies, laid out on white sheets covered with blood. She comes to find out that, as a result of the deadly poisons released in the explosion, those babies were spontaneously aborted by their mothers as they ran from the Union Carbide plant in Bhopal. She writes that after seeing these pictures and entering them into evidence against Union Carbide the connection between those babies and her own children haunted her, "All I knew was that those dead babies with their frail arms flung across the white sheets seemed a whole lot like my own sleeping babies in their cribs at night and when I got back to Texas, those tiny fists pounded me in my dreams and railed against me forgetting" (23). The memory of her own children as vulnerable babies reverberates in her response to seeing the babies who were never born, not because they were unwanted but because of the toxic effects of the chemicals of the Union Carbide plant. Rather than ignoring the connection between those babies and her own, Wilson directs her considerable energies toward getting other people to remember as well calling for the people of Seadrift, Texas to think about Bhopal and to see connections between Union Carbide's practices in India and Texas, which calls attention to the way that human and environmental needs are connected everywhere.[1]

Derrick Jensen describes Wilson's activities as directed toward delegitimizing corruption and dismantling injustice (*Diary* ix-xii). By planning disruption, organizing protests, and encouraging others to stop cooperating with injustice, governments and corporations are unable to sustain corrupt practices. But, convincing people to stop cooperating with unjust practices is an incredibly difficult proposition. One of the first things that Wilson's actions reveal is that corporations that pollute the environment spend much time and money in convincing people that they are good for communities because they bring jobs, provide tax revenue, and give charitable contributions (*Diary* 81). The corporations that Wilson faces, such as Union Carbide, Formosa Plastics, and Dow Chemical, are multi-national companies with enormous power and long histories of acting as though laws do not apply to them. For example, when Warren Anderson, CEO of Union Carbide and the person ultimately responsible for the Bhopal disaster, is wanted on a warrant for murder by the Indian government, he is able to flee India and live in the U.S. because the U.S. government refuses to pursue extradition. Frequently, people ask Wilson what she could possibly hope to accomplish against this kind of power. In the face of these obstacles, most of us cannot imagine risking embarrassment, harassment, and imprisonment in order to challenge business as usual. For Wilson, though, every action disrupts the illusion that these companies are all-powerful, cannot be challenged, and their actions are inevitable.

Wilson's story of becoming an activist provides a model for how others might also move past being intimidated by these enormous corporations. One reason Wilson is such an inspiration as a mother and environmental activist is that she initially comes to this life reluctantly; she is not born into a life of outspoken activism. The descriptions of her early life depict her love of silence and solitude. She shaped the rhythms of her life with the rhythms of the bay, and when these rhythms were disrupted she finds her love of silence and solitude transformed and begins to walk a new path.

As someone who inherited the life of fishing, Wilson is keenly aware of changes to the conditions for fishing. Even before she knew about the pollution happening in Calhoun County, she knew that the shrimping in Lavaca Bay had changed. She describes a time before the pollution when shrimpers could find places that hadn't been searched and netted, and she contrasts that with the signs of pollution she's observed: red tide, brown tide, green tide, dead dolphins, empty nets (*Unreasonable* 18-19). As I stressed in the previous section, for Wilson not only is the bay a source of livelihood, but it is also a source of life. Even when fishing becomes almost impossible from the pollution Wilson describes the need to keep fishing that characterizes the people who fish, "They couldn't quit. But if one did, he never fully recovered. He was a dead man walking" (*Unreasonable* 19). When Wilson calls a fisherman who quits fishing "a dead man walking," she reminds us of the devastation inflicted on the whole community. The destruction of the bay destroys the way of life that had been passed on between generations and destroys the conditions for nurturing life from one generation to the next, which is precisely the work of mothering.

Wilson inadvertently discovers the cause of the changes in the bay while working at her brother's fish house, when a fisherman comes in with a newspaper article, which states that Calhoun County has more land toxins than anywhere else in the U.S. This statistic became available because industries in the U.S. were now required to report all of their emissions (*Unreasonable* 36). Initially, Wilson responds in the way that most of us respond to news that seems too awful for any individual to address, "So I did the only thing you can do after winning something like that. I pretended I never saw the newspaper. It could lie down alongside the rest of the bad news that lined up so well in a dying town" (*Unreasonable* 27). Unlike most of us, Wilson does not stay in a state of denial, she responds to this bad news by taking one step after another to find information, to pass on that information, and to act in response to the information. She describes the day that turned her into an activist, "That day is good as any at explaining why my life turned 360 degrees from reclusive fisherwoman with five kids to controversial hell-raiser with five kids" (*Diary* 14). This description calls us back to the point that I want to make about Wilson's work, which is that even though her activism will sometimes take her away from the daily tasks of mothering, it is a life-giving part of her work as a mother. The conditions of her community have undermined her children's possibility of becoming the next generation of fisherwomen and the conditions of the world are undermining the possibility of the next generation to live healthy lives and to find meaningful work.

In order to understand why her actions pose such a challenge to her context, and qualify Wilson as a "controversial hell-raiser," I turn to analysis from Vincent J. Miller in *Consuming Religion: Christian Faith and Practice in Consumer Culture*. As part of his analysis of the difficulties of critiquing and changing unjust social structures, Miller analyzes how people's desires are shaped by consumer culture, particularly the way in which the media's portrayals of suffering become a spectacle that conditions us to respond passively. The media uses suffering to incite emotion, but the lack of analysis of causes and context encourages viewers to accept suffering as inevitable, an opportunity to feel shock rather than an opportunity for action (130-137). Miller emphasizes that our response to suffering that we observe on the news, read about in newspapers, and even see around us is not a selfish, unsympathetic response. Instead, the response may be quite sympathetic, and we are frequently moved to do something. Miller draws the conclusion that even when we sympathize with others, the structure of consumer culture tends to paralyze our ability to respond because we remain ignorant of the causes of the suffering. If we cannot understand the history, then the inequity and suffering seems inevitable. This inevitability paralyzes our ability to imagine different circumstances, which would lead us to act. Consider how different Wilson's actions are as compared to how most people would act upon hearing about the disaster at Bhopal. Most of us, upon seeing pictures of the spontaneously aborted fetuses of women exposed to chemicals would feel heartsick and wish that the explosion had never happened. But, Wilson links those children and their well-being to the well-being of her own children and she continues to find ways to draw attention to their plight and the fact that the man responsible for the disaster is being protected by the U.S. government.

When we further apply Miller's analysis to the impact of Wilson's activism, we can see why her actions challenge the status quo. When she reads the newspaper article about the pollution in Lavaca Bay, she asks questions, looks for the context, and looks for causes. At every step she continues to ask questions and to seek out answers in spite of being told that she won't understand the answers, that she's jeopardizing investment in the area, and that she needs to go back home. She discovers that the difficulties that shrimpers have finding shrimp is not some mysterious, uncontrollable, and unlucky twist of fate, but that the change in shrimping conditions is directly related to pollution in the bay. Even when she discovers the link between fishing conditions and pollution, politicians, business owners, and lawyers for industry pressure her to consider the pollution an unfortunate consequence of "development" and "jobs," suggesting that fishing is outdated and fishers need to find jobs in the chemical plants. Rather than accepting these perspectives, Wilson continues to investigate until she traces the pollution back to its source, Formosa, an international corporation that systematically violates environmental protection laws around the world. She researches their plans to build a plant in Seadrift, Texas, researches the relevant laws for permits that Formosa needs to build its plant and the laws that could be used to challenge their plans, and she calls meetings to educate people who would be effected by the plant. Ultimately, her persistence leads her to press for zero-emissions, and they agree to this demand, even though they first try to claim that no such technology exists.

Another helpful perspective comes from Judith Butler's book, *Frames of War: When Is Life Grievable*. Butler analyzes the frames through which people, especially U.S. citizens, view the world. She reveals the perspectives that allow people to grieve some deaths and to overlook other deaths. Butler uses this analysis to critique American militarism and to provide the means to look beyond the frames that we take for granted in order to live more justly. Her methodology is applicable in many situations where the frames that we take for granted perpetuate injustice. I will use Butler's methodology to reveal how Wilson's activism disrupts unjust frames and provides a means to construct just ways to live. The point that Butler makes is that we have to consider the ways in which narratives are framed such that questions about justice cannot be asked. For Wilson, we have to consider how corporations, such as Formosa and Dow Chemical, present themselves and how Wilson disrupts that narrative.

Wilson describes the opposition from corporations when she asks questions about their destructive practices. The opposition reveals that these corporations frame their business practices using the language of investment. By highlighting jobs provided by the plant, these companies portray themselves as good for the community because the workers would otherwise be unemployed and without healthcare. They also portray themselves as responsive to the concerns and needs of the community by giving one town a water purifying plant, hosting town picnics, and giving college scholarships. Finally, they control their public image through campaign contributions. The effectiveness of the companies' framing is evident when friends, family, politicians and business leaders beg her to stop her petitions, her meetings, and her protests because they are afraid that she will scare away the supposed investment in the community.

The willingness of politicians, workers, and of course the owners and managers of these chemical companies to accept this framing makes sense: they have a financial interest in building a plant that produces PVC (*Unreasonable* 156-157); further, they can continue their work most easily by remaining ignorant of the effects of that production on the environment, the health of the workers, and the health of the community. One of the most striking and disheartening aspects of Wilson's memoirs is that in spite of an abundance of evidence of corporate wrongdoing (deliberate dumping of toxic chemicals, hiding the quantity and kind of chemicals released in the ground and in the air, hiding information about the toxicity of chemicals to which workers are exposed), officials with the EPA, OSHA, and the courts refuse to enforce the laws which have clearly been broken.

Undaunted, Wilson continues to collect evidence and testimony from inspectors, managers, and workers. And, in spite of enormous pressure to be silent, she finds ways to speak out and to get information from governments and corporations who are not accustomed to being questioned, much less defied.

Just as a central task of mothering is allowing children to develop their own talents and voices, Wilson finds ways to give voice to those around her. Her methods of breaking the frames depend on the relationships that she builds. First, her relationship with the bay itself leads her to investigate the pollution and the effects of the chemicals going into the bay. Second, her relationship to the other fishermen allows her to break the frame that these chemical plants are good for workers and jobs. The economic development does not apply to the fishermen; they are the ones who can no longer make a living from the bay. Instead of economic development, fishermen notice that the once plentiful fish are now scarce, once healthy fish and dolphins are now floating on the surface and washing up on shores dead, and they have to sell their boats and go to work for the chemical companies.

Yet, rather than listening to the testimony that they might offer, politicians blame the problems in the gulf on the fishermen themselves (*Unreasonable* 160), and Wilson must also draw attention to the frames which prevent the politicians from taking seriously the harm to the bay and to the fishermen. One way that she does this is to point out how much these companies' investments are costing communities. Formosa Plastics, for instance, wants to build an polyvinyl chemical plant in Calhoun county, but in exchange they want millions of dollars in tax subsidies and abatements (*Unreasonable* 143-148, 157) and no outside interference such as EPA studies of the impact of the proposed plant (165).

Finally, Wilson dismantles the idea that these chemical companies are good for workers by talking to the workers themselves. The workers seek out Wilson to provide her with documentation about forged reports, illegally hidden toxins, willful misrepresentation of leaks and spills, and effects of these chemicals on their health. She delivers this information to officials who are reluctant to act on it; nevertheless, she reveals the systematic choices that companies make to maximize profits at the expense of workers, communities, and the environment.

FIDELITY AND THE POSSIBILITY OF SUCCESS

Throughout this paper, I have presented Wilson as a woman whose activism is directly related to her work as a mother and experiences of mothering. As a woman whose children participated in demonstrations with her, witnessed her suffering during hunger fasts, and suffered ill-treatment when they visited their mother in jail, many people might declare her a failure as a mother. These same people might also declare her a failure as an activist by looking at the targets of her activism who have escaped prosecution and enforcement for their parts in killing workers, ruining the health of workers and their families, and destroying the environment. Further, one could note that while people such as

Tony Hayward, the CEO of BP Oil responsible for the 2010 spill in the Gulf of Mexico, and Warren Anderson, the CEO of Dow Chemical—current owner of Union Carbide—responsible for the Bhopal tragedy in 1984 and wanted by the Indian government continue to avoid prison, Wilson has been arrested many times and spent time in jail again and again for drawing attention to their illegal actions. In response to those critics, the analysis that I have provided demonstrates her success as a mother and activist, and her fidelity to justice.

A common theme in the narratives of great activists—from Socrates to Wilson, from Dan Berrigan to Dorothy Day, from Cesar Chavez to Molly Rush—is that they work out of fidelity to peace, not by calculating probabilities for success. For some, the inspiration to act comes from religious commitment. For others, the inspiration is that the only possibility for creating peace is to be peaceful regardless of the outcome. These activists acknowledge that they can never guarantee that their actions will produce justice, but they can guarantee that doing nothing will perpetuate injustice.

Rather than choosing a path that she knows will be successful, Wilson stands in solidarity with oppressed people. She never knows as she protests, files lawsuits, and goes on hunger strikes, if her actions will lead to justice for workers, communities, and the environment. But, if she stays silent, then the companies and politicians will certainly continue to put profit above justice. While she has no guarantee that her actions will change these corporations' practices, the only possibility for change is breaking through the silence and frames that industries have created and bought for themselves.

Because Wilson acts when she could be silent, listens to those who have been silenced by politicians and corporations, and refuses to let the threat of prison stop her, she is a successful mother. Her example encourages us to make sure that our children understand the interconnection between all people and between people and the environment. She demonstrates that we are capable of much more than we ever knew, when we are part of communities and systems larger than ourselves. Truly acknowledging this interconnection allows us to create conditions in which all children can thrive. She encourages us to take risks and to become better. She rejects a calculus in which the only things worth doing are things that are guaranteed to work, instead she teaches us that what is just is worth doing, regardless of the consequences.

Because Wilson makes CEOs, companies, and politicians accountable for their actions, she is a successful activist. She is successful in her faithfulness to those who suffer from injustice. She will not settle for what seems to be the best offer simply to say that she accomplished something, instead she pushes companies to do more for workers and the environment. In some instances, her persistence causes companies to change as when Formosa and Alcoa chemical companies agreed to use zero-emissions at their plants. But, she is successful because she breaks the frames that prevent others from seeing the harms that are being done to them and the harms with which we are complicit when we remain unquestioning and silent.

[1]The hunger strike referenced in the previous section was done in support of Bhopal victims.

WORKS CITED

BaoBao, Zhang. "Five Things You Need to Know about the Bhopal Disaster." *PBS.org* June 8, 2010. Web.

Butler, Judith. *Frames of War: When is Life Grievable?* London: Verso, 2009. Print.

Miller, Vincent Jude. *Consuming Religion: Christian Faith and Practice in a Consumer Culture*. New York: Continuum, 2004. Print.

Wilson, Diane. *Diary of an Eco-Outlaw: An Unreasonable Woman Breaks the Law for Mother Earth*. White River Junction, VT: Chelsea Green Pub., 2011. Print.

Wilson, Diane. *An Unreasonable Woman: A True Story of Shrimpers, Politicos, Polluters, and the Fight for Seadrift, Texas*. White River Junction, VT: Chelsea Green Pub., 2005. Print.

Sorry I left you

JULIE HERRNKIND

For Missy, Diane, Sylena, Alexia, Jose and Ryan

Sorry I left you
Alone and scared
Sorry I left you
After promises of I'll forever be there
Sorry I left you
Screaming my name as the tears rolled down your face,
into an endless flood at the emergency room gate
Sorry I left you
To fend for yourself
Sorry I left you
To keep the family together
Sorry I left you
To grow up way too soon
Sorry I left you
To hear years and years of lies and distortions
about a mother you once worshipped
Sorry I left you
And they made you change your name
even though you were already 3 and 9 years old
Sorry I left you
Oh how I wish things could change
Sorry I left you
And you may never know, the truth of what really happened
And all the love I will always hold for you all and it is forever deep in my soul
Sorry so, so, sorry I left you all
Tears of sorrow and regret for not being the person I am today

flood my prison cell floor and still
I'm sorry I left you
To never know how you made me happy
Sorry I left you
To never realize that you saved my life on more than just one night
Sorry I left you
So young that you probably don't remember who I am
or the love I gave to you all
Sorry I left you all
But I hope to get to tell you one day, it was really all out of my control,
Sorry I left you
To be separated into 3 separate homes and to not visit each other very often
Sorry I left you
And I had to write this poem
Sorry I left you
and you never received my mail
Sorry I left you
And you were left to question whether your mother still loved you
Sorry I left you
To learn from the streets or the TV
Sorry I left you
I desperately pray you never follow the cycle
and have more self worth than I ever did anyway
Sorry I left you
To a world so unkind
But please remember
I'll always be your mommy
And you'll always be a baby of mine
Sorry I left you all
But my love remains the same
I only hope one day you'll be here to accept it openly
Sorry I left you
And I hope you know had I had a choice
I would never have ever let you go
I say sorry I left you
Because my choices brought me here and got us all separated
and your sisters gone with no more years
Sorry I left you
Whether I had control or not at the time is really irrelevant
when your whole life is gone and you're sitting in a prison cell for 25 years
So, so, sorry I left you all

Is just not enough
Sorry I left you
Can you ever forgive me for not being the mother you needed me to be
Sorry I left you
Can you forgive me for being so lost, empty, scared
and stuck in the darkness that the only light I had was all of you
and I just couldn't see past my hands to see anything different, any other way
Sorry I left you
I wanted you all to know
That even though we're not together
I think about you every waking minute of every day
Sorry I left you
Though it's not enough and I would've never done it on my own
I'm sorry I left you all so, so alone

Contributor Notes

CO-EDITORS

Gordana Eljdupovic, Ph.D., C. Psych., is a clinical and forensic psychologist whose doctoral research focussed on incarcerated women's experiences of mothering. Upon completion of her doctoral degree, she worked with incarcerated women in a Canadian prison for a number of years. She feels immensely privileged, honoured and humbled by their trust. Dr. Eljdupovic has presented her work at a number of different local, regional, and international settings. She is currently an Associate Researcher with the Center for Community Research, Learning and Action (CCRLA) at Wilfrid Laurier University, and she continues to work in areas where gender, policy, the justice system, and mental health concerns intersect. She is mother to two wonderful children: a daughter and a son.

Rebecca Jaremko Bromwich is a Part-Time Professor at the University of Ottawa Faculty of Law and Ph.D. Candidate at Carleton University. A lawyer in private practice for seven years before returning to the academic world, she has been a member of the Bar of Ontario since 2003 and has an Ll.M. and Ll.B. from from Queen's University. Rebecca also has a graduate certificate from the University of Cincinnati, where she taught as an adjunct professor in the Department of Women's, Gender and Sexuality Studies. She has also been an adjunct at the University of Western Ontario Faculty of Law. Rebecca balances her professional work and scholarship with her role as mother to four amazing children.

CONTRIBUTORS

Courtney Arseneau received her Bachelor of Science in 2011 while she coordinated a recreational rehabilitation program working closely with Aboriginal inmates in the psychiatric healing centre of a federal penitentiary. Currently completing her Master's degree, she is a student member of the International Investigative Interviewing Research Group (IIRG) and works closely with the Indigenous Health and Social Justice Research Group at Wilfrid Laurier University in her research on forensic interviewing in Aboriginal communities.

Eileen Baldry, Ph.D., is Professor of Criminology, School of Social Sciences at the University of New South Wales and is an Australian citizen. She has taught social policy, social development and criminology over the past two decades. She focuses on social justice matters including mental health and cognitive disability in the criminal justice system; homelessness and transition from prison; Indigenous social work; community development and social housing; and disability services.

Lori Curtis holds a Ph.D. in Economics from McMaster University, she is currently a Professor in the Department of Economics and the Director of the South Western Ontario Research Data Centre at the University of Waterloo. Her research interests revolve around examining the relationship between social policy and the health and well-being of marginalized populations. Dr. Curtis's work in the health care field, as a registered nurse, in government, as a specialist in economic evaluation, and academia provide her a unique set of experiences which she brings to health and policy research.

Meredith Crough is an undergraduate student at the University of Calgary in the Bachelor of Arts in Development Studies program. She has also worked on the project "Breaking the Cycle of Homelessness and Incarceration Using Community Based Research," a study addressing women's experiences and support needs in relation to homelessness and incarceration.

Manuela P. da Cunha is an anthropologist teaching at the University of Minho and a researcher at the Centre for Research in Anthropology, (CRIA-UM) and at the Institut d'Ethnologie Méditerranéenne et Comparative IDEMEC-CNRS (France). She is Portuguese. She has focused on issues of power, knowledge, identity, and did extensive fieldwork in total institutions. Publications include "Race, Crime and Criminal Justice in Portugal," in *Race, Crime and Criminal Justice: International Perspectives* (2010), and "Closed Circuits: Kinship, Neighborhood and Imprisonment in Urban Portugal" (*Ethnography*, 2008).

Dena Derkzen is a Canadian citizen and a doctoral candidate at Carleton University in the Department of Psychology. She is the acting Director, Women

Offender Research Division, Research Branch, Correctional Service of Canada. Her research interests include impulsivity and aggression, assessment and treatment of violent offenders, women offender issues, and program evaluation.

Sarah DeWath worked on a project, "Working Together," using photographs to strengthen the ties between incarcerated women and their children while an undergraduate at Carnegie Mellon University. She is now a second-year law student at Golden Gate University. Ms. DeWath served as a summer intern at Legal Services for Prisoners with Children in 2011.

Brooke Fry completed her undergraduate thesis on Indigenous and non-Indigenous perspectives on land under the supervision of Dr. Mitchell, which was published in the *Native Studies Review* journal. She is a member of the Indigenous Health and Social Justice Research Group at Wilfrid Laurier University and continues to work in the area of Indigenous rights and governance.

Amber Gazso is an Associate Professor of Sociology at York University. Her research interests and areas of publication include: citizenship; gender and family relations; the feminization and racialization of poverty; social policy and the welfare state.

Alison Granger-Brown has worked with federally and provincially sentenced women for thirteen years in a therapeutic capacity. Her educational career began with Nursing in England, becoming a Recreation Therapist in 1999 and gaining an MA in Training and Leadership in 2007. She is currently completing an MA in Human and Organizational Systems and a Ph.D. in Human Development. The combination of this education and experience is the basis of her knowledge about issues relating to women in prison as well as organizational culture, wellness, and leadership through an appreciative, solutions focused approach. Her particular area of interest is the learning styles and needs of women offenders within the setting of a prison.

Rafaela Granja is a sociologist at Centro de Investigação em Ciências sociais at the University of Minho (CICS-UM). She is Portuguese. She is currently working on research by undertaking ethnographic observation and interviews with social actors inside and outside prison walls, focusing on identity and family relationships during incarceration.

Martine Herzog-Evans, Professor, teaches law and criminology at Reims University, Law faculty, France. She also teaches at the Universities of Nantes and Bordeaux IV/National Penitentiary Academy. She has published extensively (see http://herzog-evans.com). Her latest book is *Droit de l'exécution des peines*, 4th ed. (Dalloz, 2011). She also published, inter alia, *Transnational Criminology Manual* (three volumes) (Wolf Legal Publishers, 2010); *L'évasion* (L'Harmattan, 2009); *L'intimité du détenu et de ses proches en droit comparé* (L'Harmattan, 2000); and *Droit pénitentiaire*, 2nd ed. (Dalloz, 2012). She has also published on legal aspects of mothering (*Les droits des mères*, two volumes, with Sophie Gamelin) and *Allaitement maternel et droit*. She is currently conducting research on prison guards' job satisfaction.

Deseriee Kennedy is a Professor of Law at Touro Law Center. Kennedy teaches Family Law, Domestic Violence, and Civil Procedure. She has written a number of legal and interdisciplinary articles including, "The Good Mother: Mothering, Feminism, and Incarceration" 18:2 *William & Mary Journal of Women & the Law* 161 (2012); "Children, Parents, and the State: The Construction of a New Family Ideology" 26.1 *Berkeley Journal of Gender, Law, & Justice* 78 (2011); "Transversal Feminism and Transcendence" 15.1 *U.S.C. Law and Women's Studies* 65 (2005); "The Feminist Pervasion: How Gender-Based Scholarship Informs Law and Law Teaching" (an edited panel discussion with: Ann Bartow, F. Carolyn Graglia, and Joan Heminway), 15.1 *U.S.C. Law and Women's Studies* 3 (2005); "Intertwining of Poverty, Gender, and Race: A Critical Analysis of Welfare News Coverage from 1993-2000" (co-authored with Drs. Catherine Luther and Terri Combs-Orme) 12.2 *Journal Of Race, Gender, & Class* 9 (2005).

Upneet Lalli holds a Ph.D. in Psychology and a law degree from Panjab University, Chandigarh, India. She has taught Psychology at Punjabi University, Patiala. Presently is Deputy Director of the Institute of Correctional Administration, Chandigarh. She has authored various research papers and articles and co-authored a book on 'Problems of Women Victims of Crime', (in Hindi) which was awarded the Gobind Vallabh Pant Award (2008-09) by the government of India.

Joshua Lau, BSc, MPH Candidate 2012, graduated from University of Toronto's Human Biology program with a Bachelor of Science in 2010. He is now completing a Masters of Public Health at University of British Columbia with an academic interest in prison health, addictions, drug policy and knowledge translation. Having worked at a prominent spinal cord injury research group in Vancouver, B.C., he understands the need for researchers to effectively communicate their findings so their work is correctly translated into policy and practice. During his practicum at the Collaborating Centre for Prison Health and Education, he facilitated the development of a policy statement regarding the health implications of mandatory minimum sentencing for incarcerated individuals, as outlined in Bill C-10.

Lauren Liu is a progressive Asian American womyn who is a recent alumna of the University of California, Berkeley, where she earned a BA in Ethnic Studies and Asian American Studies. Ms. Liu was a summer intern at Legal Services for Prisoners with Children in 2010 and 2011.

Ruth Elwood Martin, MD, FCFP, MPH, is a Clinical Professor at the University of British Columbia, where she is also Lead Faculty for Research in the family medicine residency program and Director of the Collaborating Centre for Prison Health and Education. From 1994-2011, she worked part-time as a family physician in medical clinics of correctional centres in British Columbia. She has been a member of the College of Family Physicians of Canada since 1981, and was made a Fellow of the College in 2003. Her academic interests include participatory research, primary care research, cervical cancer screening, women's health and narrative medicine. From 2005-2007, she engaged with women inside prison in a participatory health research project, which continues today in the outside community as "Women In2 Healing."

Ruth McCausland is a Ph.D. candidate in the School of Social Sciences at the University of New South Wales and she is an Australian citizen. She has a background in human rights research and policy, with a particular focus on the rights of Aboriginal and Torres Strait Islander peoples and women, and a Masters in International Social Development. Her Ph.D. is on alternative policy responses to the disadvantage and discrimination experienced by Aboriginal women leaving prison.

Terry Mitchell, Ph.D., C. Psych., is an associate professor in the Department of Psychology at Wilfrid Laurier University. Her doctoral dissertation, *Old Wounds New Beginnings: Challenging the Missionary Paradigm in Native White Relations* was based on her work with Aboriginal communities in the Yukon. Mitchell is the director of the Laurier Indigenous rights and social justice research group and is working on a project on the Internationalization of Indigenous rights and governance with the Centre for International Governance Innovation. Her current work focuses on the impacts of colonial trauma, Aboriginal rights and governance issues, and political pathways to healing.

Danielle Poe, Ph.D., is an associate professor of philosophy at the University of Dayton. Her research interests are in contemporary issues of peace and the work of Luce Irigary. Her recent work includes, "Woman, Mother, and Nonviolent Activism" in *Positive Peace: Reflections on Peace Education* (2010); "Donut Shops and World Peace: Subsidiarity and the Bias for the Local" in *Journal of Globalization Studies* (2010); and "Mothers and Civil Disobedience" in *Peace and Justice Studies* (Summer 2009). She is the editor of *Communities of Peace: Confronting Injustice and Creating Justice* (Rodopi Press, 2011).

Amy Salmon, Ph.D., is the Coordinator for Sheway, a community-based program providing health care and social services to pregnant women and mothers with substance use problems in Vancouver's Downtown Eastside. She is also a Clinical Assistant Professor at the University of British Columbia's School of Population and Public Health, and a Collaborating Scientist at the Centre for Addictions Research of B.C. at the University of Victoria. Her research examining the primary health care and health education needs of substance-using women and mothers, and developing intervention strategies for FASD prevention, has been funded by the Canadian Institutes of Health Research, the Michael Smith Foundation for Health Research, the Social Sciences and Humanities Research Council, the Victoria Foundation, and Health Canada's First Nations and Inuit Health Branch. She is the co-editor *Alcohol, Tobacco, and Obesity: Morality, Mortality, and the New Public Health* (Routledge Press, 2011) and *Prevention of Fetal Alcohol Spectrum Disorder: Who is Responsible?* (Wiley-Blackwell, 2011), and her publications appear in journals such as *Critical Public Health, Social Science and Medicine, Nursing Inquiry,* and *The International Journal of Drug Policy.*

Olivia Scobie is a policy analyst at Centennial College and freelance journalist. She completed her M.A. in Sociology at York University and the presented chapter is based on the findings from her thesis. Her research interests include the criminalization of mothers, gendered experiences of education and the effects of neoliberal policies on Canadian families.

Karen Shain is policy director of Legal Services for Prisoners with Children in San Francisco. She is co-author of "Stop Shackling: A Report on the Written Policies of California's Counties on the Use of Restraints on Pregnant Prisoners in Labor" (2010), and "California's Mother-Infant Prison Program: An Investigation" (2010). Her chapter, "Incarcerated Mothers: Mothers First and Foremost," appears in Demeter Press's new book *The 21st Century Motherhood Movement: Mothers Speak Out on Why We Need to Change the World and How to Do It.*

Kelly Taylor is Canadian and holds a doctorate in psychology from the University of Ottawa. She has spent the better part of the last decade researching issues regarding women offenders and is the Senior Director of Correctional Research, Correctional Services Canada. Research interests include mental health, therapeutic alliance, and sexual offending.

Christine Walsh is an Associate Professor, Faculty of Social Work, University of Calgary. She has a program of community-based research aimed at developing solutions for marginalized populations including women experiencing poverty, homelessness and incarceration.